THE LAW

OF

BUSINESS

CONTRACTS

by

ANDREW J. COPPOLA

Professor of Law

Bernard M. Baruch School of Business

and Public Administration

The City University of New York

A HELIX BOOK

ROWMAN & ALLANHELD
Totowa, New Jersey

Reprinted in 1984 as A HELIX BOOK, published by
Rowman & Allanheld, Publishers (a division of
Littlefield, Adams & Company) 81 Adams Drive,
Totowa, New Jersey, 07512

PREFACE

This book is intended for use in a one-semester undergraduate course in Business Contracts of two or three classroom hours per week.

The material presented is current and significant to those engaged in the area of business and to business students, and is designed to instill an awareness of the consequences of business transactions and the need for legal counsel and advice. A training in contract law is indispensable to a better understanding of the relationships resulting from daily business contact, and it lays a foundation for further rhetorical knowledge in the field of business law generally. It should prove of value to the accountant who traditionally is reliant on a thorough understanding of legal relationships, and also to credit, finance, marketing, and management students who must gain experience in reasoning and decision-making.

The text is supplemented with a set of problems drawn to test the student's knowledge and comprehension of the rules of contract law.

The material herein revised is an excerpt from the book, Business Law: a CPA Review, by Coppola and Katz, copyright John Wiley & Sons, 1963, and is reproduced here with the permission of the copyright holder.

ANDREW J. COPPOLA

New York City

CONTENTS

Preface iii
1. Introduction 1
2. Definitions 8
3. Manifestation of Assent 11
    A. The Offer 11
    B. The Acceptance 17
4. Reality of Assent 28
    A. Fraud and Misrepresèntation 28
    B. Mistake of Fact 33
    C. Duress and Undue Influence 39
5. Capacity of Parties 41
6. Statute of Frauds 49
7. Consideration 61
8. Illegal Bargains 78
9. Interpretation and Parol Evidence Rule 88
10. Conditions 93
11. Breach of Contract 102
12. Rights of Third Parties 106
    A. Third-Party Beneficiaries 106
    B. Assignees 110
13. Discharge of Contracts 115
    A. Discharge by Performance of Contract 115
    B. Discharge by Breach of Contract 117
    C. Discharge by Agreement 119
    D. Discharge by Operation of Law 121
14. Remedies for Breach of Contract 129
Problems 138
Index 187

1. INTRODUCTION

Law and Society. To the layman, the law is a body of rules, hard and fast, arbitrary and inflexible, momentarily designed and passed by a law-making body to shape, regulate, and control life in the community. He does not understand that all law is not written, that is, enacted; that, although a part of the law is codified, there is a large body of law—the common law —which is unwritten; that the rules and standards of conduct, whether or not they have been codified, were not conceived on the spur of the moment as desirable means of shaping and regulating society; and that these regulations and standards of behavior were born out of long and fine experience and are regarded by society as the accepted standards of conduct in community life. The law grew and developed out of the process of evolution. As the conditions of the social order and community life changed, the rules of law governing one person's relationship to another also changed.

Some knowledge and understanding of the law is necessary to all persons. In our complex economic life, each member of society must deal with others according to the recognized rules of law. Indeed, each day the individual must take steps to satisfy his needs and wants as well as the needs and wants of others. The manufacturer or producer must satisfy the wants of others as well as his own. He may produce such commodities as clothing, food, shelter, or tools for others, and each day he enters into relationships with others for the marketing and distribution of such items, but he must also enter into relationships with others with respect to business needs such as raw materials, tools, machinery, labor, and space, and with respect to his personal needs and the needs of his family. Each day, then, every member of society enters into legal relationships with others. One may contract for the transportation or sale of his goods, for the purchase of goods, for the hiring of labor, for the leasing of space, for insurance on his life or property, for the purchase or sale of real estate, for the lending or borrowing of money, for recreation, or for the services of another to represent him in any of these transactions. In the formation of these relationships, and in the performance of the duties incidental to them, he must conform to the established principles of law. Some knowledge of the rules involved in these relationships can be helpful, not in the sense that with such knowledge one can then adequately represent himself in a given situation, but rather in the sense that he will appreciate that the particular transaction confronting him is of sufficient gravity and importance to require the advice of one trained in the law.

The Common Law. The system of law whose development commenced in England in the thirteenth century is known as the common law. In the early stages of its development, when the English society was still maintained as a feudal system, the courts were concerned chiefly with problems affecting land. But the jurisdiction of the courts slowly expanded to include contracts and, eventually, mercantile transactions. The colonists brought the English system of law to this country, and it was adopted by the original states and by others as they entered the Union. The single exception was Louisiana, which when ceded by France had adopted the system of law known as civil law, which originated in Rome and spread throughout the continent of Europe and to what is today Latin America.

The Law Merchant. In the early stages of the development of the common law, as trade and commerce were being established in England, it was found that the law based on the feudal system was not adaptable to the problems arising among merchants. Thus, the traders themselves commenced to develop a body of rules and standards to govern their transactions. These rules were based mainly on the customs and usages of the traders from different nations who traveled from country to country, and they came to be known as the law merchant. Special courts were then created in England to administer these rules in disputes between traders and merchants, but gradually these controversies were brought before the common law courts. In the course of time, these courts developed out of the customs and usages of the merchants a set of distinguishable rules governing mercantile transactions. Thus, the law merchant was absorbed into the common law system.

Equity. During the development of the common law system in England, there was established in London a Court of Chancery. The powers of this court developed over the years until, in the eighteenth century, it had powers to grant remedies unknown to the law courts. The Court of Chancery would exercise its extraordinary powers, however, only when the law courts were powerless to grant suitable relief either because the application of an established rule of law would result in a hardship, or because the relief the law court could grant would be inadequate in the circumstances.

The powers of the Lord Chancellor who presided over the Court of Chancery were not limited, as were those of the common law judges, by a body of rigid rules. The Lord Chancellor had the power to note any extenuating or mitigating circumstances and fit the remedy to the particular case. The rules and procedures established by this Court over the years came to be known as rules of equity, and the remedies it granted as equitable remedies, and today they form part of the general law. However, the basis of equity jurisdiction, the inadequacy of a remedy at law, prevails today even in jurisdictions where law and equity have been amalgamated by statute. Equity jurisdiction is now complementary to and not competitive with the jurisdiction of the law courts. The more important equitable remedies granted today are *specific performance*, a decree directing one to perform his contractual obligation on pain of being incarcerated until he does; *rescission*, a decree declaring that no contract exists and restoring the parties to the status quo; and the *injunction*, a decree ordering one to perform an act or prohibiting or restraining one from performing an act.

Stare Decisis. Although many of the rules which our courts apply exist in the form of statutes enacted by law-making bodies, there are a vast number of rules which have been adopted by the courts. These are judge-made or court-made rules; they result from judicial legislation. Decisions of the courts add to and on occasion alter the established law. A perusal of the law reports will readily indicate that judges make rules and apply them. It has been argued, however, that the rules pre-existed the courts, and that they are merely discovered by the courts as a scientist or an explorer makes discoveries; that a judge does not invent rules any more than an explorer invents his discovery, and that if a rule applied by a court in a previous case is rejected by the court in a later case, the court does not make a new rule—it merely says that the old rule never existed.

In the various state governments and in the federal government there are trial courts, intermediate courts of appeal, and a highest court of appeal, and rules announced by the higher courts are followed by the lower courts. Thus, the highest court must make the rules. Where the highest court has made and applied a rule of law in a given case, it and the lower courts will regard its decision as authoritative in later similar cases. The prior decision establishes a precedent, which by the doctrine of *stare decisis*, "let the decision stand," is to be followed in such later cases. Accordingly, we may know at any time what the law is, and we may govern our relationships with others pursuant to the law. But, if the highest court in the later case is convinced that the rule it applied in the previous case is manifestly erroneous, it would seem that the court should discard it. The common law is not a stagnant system; it is one which constantly and steadily may be improved by judicial action with the innovations of time and the progress of society. It is true that stare decisis makes for certainty, but certainty must yield to progress to avoid injustice.

However, most courts have indicated strong support of stability and certainty in the law. Many have said that it is more important that rules be settled and fixed than just, and that the hardship that sometimes will result is unavoidable. They have announced that justice means equality of treatment; that it is fair and just that the rule applied in the case of *A* against *B* should be applied in the subsequent similar case between *C* and *D*, especially if *C* and *D* based their transaction on the rule announced in the case of *A* against *B*. These courts leave the question of modification or change in the law to the law-making bodies.

Res Judicata. Once the highest court has made a decision determining the rights and liabilities of the litigants, the dispute is settled. The decision on the issues presented is regarded as *res judicata*, "the thing is judicially settled," and the parties to the suit, or other parties claiming through them, cannot later raise the same issues. In the interests of society, there must be an end to litigation. A party should not again be made a defendant for the same cause.

Uniform Laws. In the field of commercial law, diversity from state to state in the rules of the common law are obviously disadvantageous. Many commercial transactions overstep state lines, and the participants are often required to know the law of another state, or to know whether their business dealings will be regulated by the law of one state or another. This has led to an increasing effort to codify the common law in this field. The Commissioners on Uniform State Laws, with members from each of the states, prepared drafts of uniform laws in several branches of commercial law for enactment in the various states. The most successful of these drafts are the Uniform Negotiable Instruments Law, adopted in all of the states, the Uniform Sales Act, the Uniform Bill of Lading Act, and the Uniform Warehouse Receipts Act, each adopted in most states. The acceptance of the Uniform Partnerships Act has not been so widespread. The Uniform Commercial Code (UCC), drafted and approved by the American Law Institute and the National Conference of Commissioners on Uniform State Laws, replaces the prior uniform acts on Negotiable Instruments, Sales, Warehouse Receipts, Bills of Lading, Trust Receipts, Stock Transfers and Conditional Sales, as well as legislation regulating Bulk Sales, Chattel

Mortgages, Factor's Liens, and Bank Collections. It also codifies rules relating to letters of credit and the financing of accounts receivable. The UCC has been well received, and at this writing has been adopted by all of the states except Louisiana.

Restatements. In certain branches of commercial law, such as Contracts, Agency, and Trusts, where the Commissioners on Uniform Laws made no recommendations to the several states, effort was made to bring about in systematic form a statement of the rules at common law. The American Law Institute, a group of scholars and judges, was organized in 1923 for that purpose. The result of the efforts of that group were restatements of the law in the branches mentioned. Though they are not binding on the courts, the restatements are of great value as exhaustive treatments of the several subjects.

Arbitration. Not infrequently, the parties to a contract who are involved in a dispute may voluntarily agree to submit the dispute to arbitration by a third person, or by a board of three persons, one chosen by each of the disputants and the third selected by the two so chosen, and to abide by the award made. Should one of the parties refuse to proceed with the arbitration or to honor the award, the courts of some states, pursuant to statute, will entertain an application by the aggrieved party to direct that the arbitration proceed as agreed. If the recalcitrant party has failed to select an arbitrator, the court will do so. Of course, the refusal of one party to proceed to arbitration constitutes a breach of the agreement, and if he commences legal action on the dispute the courts will, in a proper case, stay the action or even dismiss it.

When, however, the parties to a contract agree to submit to arbitration a future dispute, under the common law the agreement is violative of public policy as an agreement binding the parties not to resort to the courts. In some states, statutes now provide that such agreements are valid and enforceable.

Generally, no requirement exists, and the parties themselves do not often provide that the arbitrator shall award some specific type of redress. Thus, in shaping the form of redress, the arbitrator is not bound by the common law and statutory restrictions which ordinarily bind the courts. If one party refuses to comply with the arbitration award, the courts will on proper application grant judgment compelling such compliance. However, they will not do so if it appears that the award was procured by fraud, corruption, or some other unlawful or unfair means, that the arbitrator showed evident partiality, that he refused to hear material evidence, or that the award itself was contrary to law or to public policy.

System of Courts. The ownership of legal rights would be valueless without the existence of some ordered method or procedure for their enforcement. For this purpose, the system of courts was evolved, as a medium to which an individual or the general public, with legal rights denied or violated by others, may go for redress.

Under the federal form of government, in which the national government and the states exercise dual sovereignty, separate federal and state court systems have been established for the recognition and enforcement of legal rights in their respective jurisdictions.

Federal Courts. The United States Constitution provides that the federal judicial power is vested in the Supreme Court and in such inferior courts as Congress may from time to time ordain and establish. Pursuant to the power so conferred upon it, Congress has created courts subordinate to the Supreme Court. In the federal court system, general original jurisdiction is placed in district courts. Appeals from district court decisions are normally taken to courts of appeal, and from there to the Supreme Court.

District courts sit in each state, and the number of such courts in a given state depends on the volume of judicial business in the area. The courts of appeal, on the other hand, exercise jurisdiction over so-called circuits, each of which includes a number of states; at present there are ten circuits covering the states, and a separate circuit for the District of Columbia.

In addition to the courts described, which possess general jurisdiction, Congress has established other judicial tribunals with specialized jurisdiction. For example, the Court of Claims is concerned with claims against the federal government, the Court of Customs and Patent Appeals deals with custom and patent matters, and from time to time other such courts have been established to handle controversies falling within special federal powers.

If a case before the federal courts involves the statutory or unwritten law of a state, such courts will apply the law that prevails in the state where the right of action arose.

State Courts. In each state there are courts of original jurisdiction, and intermediate and higher appellate courts to review the decisions of lower courts on appeal. State courts apply their own statutory and judge-made law, unless the question is within the federal sphere. For example, in a case involving the interpretation of the Federal Constitution, the decisions of the Supreme Court must be followed.

Administrative Law. Because of the growing complexity of our civilization, a procedure has recently evolved by which legal rights are enforced as an adjunct to the judicial procedure. Under this method, jurisdiction over matters of a specialized nature is often committed to an administrative body. One such administrative agency is the Federal Trade Commission which, among other things, holds hearings and makes determinations on matters of unfair business practices and price discrimination. Under the law, provision is made for appeals to the courts from adverse decisions by administrative agencies.

2. DEFINITIONS

1. Value of Definitions. We set forth here a few definitions and expressions, but not with the idea that they will be helpful in determining the basic principles or concepts of contract law. Principles of law were not formulated to fit existing definitions, but rather to reach just and equitable results in the great variety of disputes which have come before the courts. For the most part, definitions which have been proposed are based on principles and concepts developed by the courts. Thus, to thoroughly understand a definition, one must be completely familiar with these basic principles and concepts.

2. Contract. There have been many definitions of the term contract, and perhaps no one of them is any more authoritative than any other. The most popular is the definition offered by the American Law Institute, Restatement, Contracts—"a contract is a promise or set of promises for the breach of which the law gives a remedy, or for the performance of which the law in some way recognizes a duty." Corpus Juris states that "a contract is an agreement between competent parties, supported by a legal consideration and in the form, if any, prescribed by law, creating an obligation on the part of one or both to do or refrain from doing some legal thing." The Uniform Commercial Code (hereinafter referred to as the UCC), in Sec. 1-201(11), states that "contract" means the "total legal obligation which results from the parties' agreement as affected by the Code and any other applicable rules of law," and it defines an "agreement" in Sec. 1-201(3) as the "bargain of the parties in fact as found in their language or by implication from other circumstances including course of dealing or usage of trade or course of performance. . . ."

3. Requisites of Contracts. The requisites of a contract, each of them a fundamental concept, are:

(*a*) *A real mutual assent* of two or more *offer and acceptance*

8

(b) *competent parties*, in a ~~two or more~~
(c) *form required by law*, supported by ~~legal form must be in writing~~
(d) *a valid consideration*, and having a ~~supported~~
(e) *valid purpose* and a *valid subject matter*.

4. Quasi-Contract. A quasi-contract is not a contract. It is an obligation imposed by law which rests on the equitable principle that one should not be unjustly enriched at the expense of another. It is entirely lacking in the elements of a contract. Where one comes into possession of money or property belonging to another, which he should not in good conscience retain, the law places on him the quasi-contractual duty to return it. When a physician renders services to a person who suffers such injury that he is not in a condition to assent to medical aid, the physician may recover the reasonable value of his necessary services.

5. Express Contract. An express contract is one in which the terms are agreed upon orally or in writing.

6. Implied Contract. An implied contract is one in which the parties thereto evidence their agreement by acts and conduct rather than by words oral or written. A physician who treats a patient with his consent but without any express agreement as to compensation is entitled to recover the reasonable value of his services. The patient accepts the services with knowledge of the expectation of pay, and his promise to compensate the physician is implied. The rendering of the services is the offer, and the patient's taking the services is the acceptance.

7. Executory Contract. An executory contract is one which has not been fully performed by either or all of the parties thereto.

8. Executed Contract. An executed contract is one which has been fully performed by either or all of the parties thereto.

9. Voidable Contract. A voidable contract is a contract which may be avoided (rescinded or disaffirmed) at the election of a party thereto. Where one is induced by fraud to enter into a contractual relationship for the sale of goods, he may avoid the contract by rescinding it and returning or offering to return the price received. He thereupon becomes entitled to a return of the goods. If, however, the buyer has resold the goods to an innocent third person for value without notice of the facts before the seller avoids the contract, such third person acquires a valid title and may keep the goods [UCC Sec. 2-403(1)].

10. Void Contract. A void contract is not a contract at all. It has no legal effect. In some states there are statutes declaring wagering contracts and usurious contracts void.

11. Unenforceable Contract. An unenforceable contract is a valid contract which cannot be proved as required by law. Oral contracts required to be evidenced by a writing under one of the various provisions of the Statute of Frauds, and contracts which, if breached, can be remedied only by violating the Statute of Limitations, are unenforceable should the defendant interpose the appropriate defense.

12. Bilateral Contract. Where an offeror makes an offer containing his promise and requiring the offeree to accept by communicating his promise, and the offeree so accepts, the parties have made a bilateral contract. Each promise was made in exchange for the other, and both parties are under obligation.

13. Unilateral Contract. Where an offeror calls on an offeree to perform an act or to refrain from performing an act in exchange for a promise by the offeror, and the offeree complies with the request, a unilateral contract results. There is a promise given in exchange for a performance or a forbearance. The offeree is in no way obliged to conform or comply with the offer. but if he does he is under no further obligation. The contract comes into existence when the offeree performs or forbears in accordance with the offer, and once in existence only the offeror who made the promise is under an obligation.

14. Entire Contract. A contract is entire when full and complete performance on one side is intended to be given in exchange for full and complete performance on the other. A contract to purchase six refrigerators and six gas ranges for $2,500 is an entire contract. The items to be tendered by the seller cannot be apportioned to the price.

15. Severable Contract. A severable contract is one in which, by its nature, the items of performance on one side may be apportioned to the consideration. The failure to perform one item does not necessarily entitle the other to refuse further performance, or to rescind the entire contract, or to pay for items already performed. Further, the fact that one of the items to be performed is illegal will not affect the obligations of the parties in respect of the remainder of the contract. A contract to paint a house, barn, and windmill for $750 is an entire contract. But a contract to build a house, barn, and windmill, with payment of $7,500 for the house, $2,700 for the barn, and $3,000 for the windmill, is severable. The builder is to perform separate items, and the price to be paid is apportioned to each item.

3. Manifestation of Assent

A. THE OFFER

16. In General. Usually, contracts are concluded through the process of offer and acceptance. One party proposes a transaction and the other, willing to assume an obligation in respect thereto, accepts the proposal. The proposal, oral or in writing, shows the assent of one to be bound on the terms of the proposal, and the acceptance shows the assent of the other to assume an obligation according to the terms of the proposal. Thus, each party has manifested his assent to assume a binding obligation. They have manifested a mutual assent.

It must be understood, however, that the court has no concern with what either party actually has in mind when he offers a proposal or when he accepts it. It is concerned only with intent as manifested by the words or the conduct of a party. The question is: Did the person, whatever his actual intent, use such language or act in such a way as to indicate to a reasonable person an intent to enter into a contractual relationship? Courts look not to subjective intent but to objective intent, not to secret intent but to manifested intent.

17. The Offer. An offer is a communication, oral or in writing, by one person to another, which shows his assent to enter into a contractual relationship with the other. It may manifest that the offeror agrees or is willing to do something if the other, the offeree, will do or promise to do something or refrain from doing something. Whatever its terms, it must indicate the apparent assent of the offeror to enter into a contractual relationship.

18. The Offer; Necessity of Communication. An offer, to be effective, must be communicated to the offeree. An offeree cannot accept an offer of which he has no knowledge.

EXAMPLES

1. If S writes to B offering to sell S's white horse, Domino, for $100, and B, at the same time, writes S offering to buy S's white horse, Domino, for $100, these communications, crossing each other in the mail, are offers, and neither writer will be deemed to have accepted the offer of the other, of which he had no knowledge.

2. If B, noticing that A's stable is afire, rescues A's horse, Domino, intending to be paid for his efforts, A is not liable to B *on a contract*. There was no offer communicated to B, and without an offer there can be no acceptance.

19. The Offer: Necessity of Assent. The offer must manifest the intent and assent of the offeror to enter into a contractual relationship according to the terms of the offer. Thus, an offer obviously made in jest, or made in such circumstances that a reasonable man would not understand it to manifest an intention to contract, cannot be accepted.

EXAMPLES

1. S's horse, Domino, has just won an important race. B, who witnessed the race, approaches S and says, "You have a beautiful and valuable horse in Domino." S laughingly replies, "I'll sell her to you for $5." B, as a reasonable man, would understand in the circumstances that S had no intent to sell the animal and that the offer was made in jest. The offer cannot be accepted. But where, although the offer is made in jest, the offeree is justified in believing that the offer was seriously made, he may accept it.

2. A discovers that a thief has broken into his hen house and made off with two chickens. A, greatly excited about his loss, shouts in the presence of B, "I will give a thousand dollars to anyone who catches the thief!" B apprehends the thief. Whether B can collect the $1,000 depends on whether he as a reasonable man, considering A's excitement, stress, and emotion, was justified in believing that A intended his statement to be an offer.

20. The Offer: Delivery of a Writing. No serious problem is encountered where an offeror incorporates his offer in a writing and delivers it to the offeree for his acceptance. The offeree after receipt of the offer may determine whether he will accept. If he is to accept by sending a communication to the offeror he may, of course, determine whether he will do so. If it is contemplated that the acceptance shall be manifested by his signing the writing, he will be deemed to accept only if he signs.

There is a class of cases in which the question arises whether the mere receipt of a writing delivered in connection with a transaction engaged in by the parties constitutes an acceptance of its terms. These cases involve the purchase of railroad tickets, steamship tickets, and the like, check-room tickets, luggage checks, or parking-lot tickets. Not infrequently, such tickets set forth language affecting the rights and obligations of the parties particularly with reference to personal injury or loss or damage to property. Where the person to whom such ticket is delivered reads the language printed thereon he is, of course, bound thereby. If his attention is called to the language at the time of delivery to him of the ticket, it seems that he is bound thereby whether or not he reads the language. But is he bound when he is not aware that it contains a writing? The reported cases are in conflict on the question. One line of cases, followed in New York, takes the position that if a reasonable man would understand, from the nature of the transaction and the particular circumstances, that the ticket embodies the terms and conditions of the transaction, he is bound by his acceptance of the ticket. But where as a reasonable man he regarded the ticket as merely a token or means of identification, his receipt of the ticket does not evidence assent to its terms. According to this reasoning, the delivery of a steamship ticket is an offer, and its receipt is as much an acceptance of its terms as is the receipt of a bill of lading or policy of insurance; but the receipt of a check-room ticket or an automobile parking-lot ticket is not an acceptance of its terms.

21. Invitations to Offers. *general goods* Merchants or other persons who issue price lists, quotations of prices, or circulars and catalogs listing goods for sale at certain prices, who advertise for bids, or who advertise their wares at indicated prices do not make offers to sell. Such publications are merely invitations to the readers to make offers to buy at the prices indicated, which the merchant may or may not accept. This is not to say, however, that one may not make an offer in a circular or newspaper advertisement. An advertiser may couch his advertisement in such language as to make it reasonable to conclude that he intended to make an offer to sell a specific article at a definite price.

An auctioneer who conducts an auction sale of goods does not make an offer to sell; he merely requests that offers be made to buy. The auction sale is complete when the auctioneer so announces by the fall of the hammer or in any other customary manner. Where one makes a bid while the hammer is falling in acceptance of a prior bid, the auctioneer may declare the goods sold under the prior bid or he may reopen the bidding, at his discretion. The auction is with reserve unless the goods are expressly put up for sale without reserve. Where the goods are put up for sale with reserve, the auctioneer may withdraw the goods at any time before completion of the sale. Where the auction is without reserve, the goods cannot be withdrawn from sale unless no bid is made within a reasonable time. However, whether the auction is with or without reserve, a bidder may

Bids at an auction

terms of aal with .

retract his bid before completion of the sale. Such retraction does not revive any previous bid [UCC Sec. 2-328(2)(3)].

22. Termination of Offer. An offer, before it has been accepted, may be terminated by (*a*) revocation by the offeror, (*b*) rejection by the offeree, (*c*) death or insanity of the offeror, (*d*) lapse of time, (*e*) destruction of an essential thing, or (*f*) supervening legal prohibition of the proposed contract.

23. Revocation of Offer. At any time before an offer is accepted it may be withdrawn by the offeror, but withdrawal is not effective until received by the offeree. The offer remains in existence and may be accepted by the offeree at any time before he receives notice of withdrawal or revocation. Any language which fairly indicates to the offeree that the offer has been withdrawn is a sufficient revocation.

Usually, notice of revocation is given by the offeror to the offeree orally or in writing. Some cases indicate, however, that a notice of the offeror's revocation given to the offeree by a third party is sufficient if, in the circumstances, the notice is reliable.

EXAMPLES

1. S, by mail, offers to sell his white horse, Domino, to B for $100. S then mails to B a revocation of the offer. Before receipt of the revocation, B mails an acceptance of the offer. There is a contract. S's revocation is not effective until received. Hence, S's offer was still in existence at the time of B's acceptance.

2. S, by mail, offers to sell his white horse, Domino, to B for $100. Immediately thereafter, S enters into an agreement to sell the same horse to C. C advises B that he has purchased Domino from S. B then accepts S's offer. There is no contract. S, by his sale to C, revoked his offer to B. B received notice of the revocation from C before he accepted the offer.

There are cases in which it is held that an offer is effectively revoked although the offeree receives no actual notice of revocation. An offeror may make offers to sell the same property to several persons "subject to prior sale." Prior sale itself is a revocation without notice to the offerees. Also, where the offeror has made an offer to the public at large by publication in a newspaper, or in handbills or circulars generally distributed, he may revoke the offer by similar publication of his withdrawal of the offer.

EXAMPLE

A publishes in a newspaper an offer of reward for the apprehension of a criminal. *B* reads the offer and takes steps to accept. *A* then publishes a revocation of the offer. *B*, not having read the notice of the revocation, apprehends the criminal and demands the reward. There is no acceptance of the offer by *B*. It was effectively revoked before his acceptance.

24. Revocation of Offer: Option Contract. Where the offer states that it will be kept open for a specified time, it may nevertheless be revoked by the offeror within that time. The offeror is not bound to keep the offer open unless there is a consideration given by the offeree to support it. Where a consideration is given for such offer, the offer is called an option contract. An option contract cannot be terminated by revocation or by death or insanity of the offeror. Local law should be consulted to determine whether statutory provision exists, as it does in New York, which dispenses with the requirement of consideration if the option is in writing and signed by the offeror. The New York statute provides: "Except as otherwise provided in Sec. 2-205 of the Uniform Commercial Code with respect to an offer by a merchant to buy or sell goods, when an offer to enter into a contract is made in a writing signed by the offeror, or by his agent, which states that the offer is irrevocable during a period set forth or until a time fixed, the offer shall not be revocable during such period or until such time because of the absence of consideration for the assurance of irrevocability. When such writing states that the offer is irrevocable but does not state any period of time of irrevocability, it shall be construed to state that the offer is irrevocable for a reasonable time."

Sec. 2-205 of the UCC states that where a merchant makes an offer to buy or sell goods in a writing signed by him and the offer contains an assurance that it will be held open, the offer is not revocable, for lack of consideration, for the time stated or if no time is stated for a reasonable time, but the period of irrevocability shall not exceed three months. Where a consideration is given to support such assurance, it is irrevocable for the period stated even if such period exceeds three months. *case # 5*

Can revoke offer before the specific time mentioned because it does not state so specifically

EXAMPLES

1. *A*, owner of a plot of land, writes a letter signed by him to *B* in which he describes his land and offers to sell it to *B* for $15,000. The offer states that it "shall remain open for four months." *A* is bound to keep the offer open for 4 months even though *B* gave no consideration for *A*'s undertaking. UCC Sec. 2-205 has no application as neither goods nor merchant are involved.

2. *A* makes an offer to sell his used car to *B* in a signed writing which states that the offer shall be irrevocable for 4 months. *B* gives no consideration for *A*'s undertaking. *A* may not revoke the offer within the 4-month period. UCC Sec. 2-205 does not apply since *A* is not a merchant.

UCC is more specific than NY General law

3. *A*, a dealer in produce, makes an offer in a writing signed by him to sell to *B* 1,000 bushels of beans at $2.00 per bushel. The offer states that *B* shall have 4 months to accept. *B* gives *A* no consideration for *A's* undertaking to keep the offer open. *A* is bound to keep the offer open for 3 months. If *B* gave *A* consideration for *A's* assurance, *A* would be bound to keep the offer open for 4 months. UCC Sec. 2-205 applies.

A merchant is defined in the UCC, Sec. 2-104, as a person who deals in the goods involved or who by his occupation holds himself as having the knowledge and skill peculiar to the practices or goods involved in the transaction, or who employs an agent or broker who by his occupation holds himself out as having such knowledge and skill.

25. Rejection of Offer. An offer, even if in the form of an option contract, terminates upon rejection by the offeree. A rejection need not take any particular form; any communication to the offeror indicating that the offeree rejects or intends not to accept the offer is sufficient.

A counteroffer is a communication by the offeree to the offeror which sets forth terms or conditions at variance with those in the offer, and it constitutes a rejection. Thus, the original offer cannot be accepted after a counteroffer is made and there can be no contract unless the counteroffer is accepted by the original offeror. A counteroffer will not be deemed a rejection, however, if the offeree indicates that he is still considering or keeping the offer under advisement, or if the offeror has invited the counteroffer.

Each of the following examples assumes that the offeree has a specified time within which to accept and that the time has not expired.

EXAMPLES

1. *S* offers to sell *B* a painting for $500. *B* replies, "I will pay you four hundred fifty dollars." *S* refuses $450. *B* then accepts *S's* offer to sell for $500. There is no contract. *S's* offer was terminated by *B's* counteroffer and could not thereafter be accepted.
2. *S* offers to sell *B* a painting for $500. *B* replies, "Will you take four hundred dollars?" *B* receives no response. *B* then accepts *S's* offer. There is a contract. *B's* reply is deemed an inquiry and not a counteroffer.
3. *S* offers to sell *B* his motor cruiser, *Penguin*, for $5,000. *B* replies, "I am considering your offer but if you want to make a quick sale I will pay you forty-two houndred dollars." *S* replies, "I will not accept forty-two hundred dollars." *B* then accepts *S's* offer. There is a contract since *B* did not intend by his communication to reject *S's* offer.
4. *S* offers to sell *B* his motor cruiser, *Penguin*, for $5,000, payable in 10 monthly instalments, but advises *B* that if he is interested in making a

purchase for cash S will be glad to consider his proposal. B replies, "I will pay you forty-five hundred dollars spot cash." S declines the proposal. B then accepts S's offer. There is a contract. B's proposal, having been invited by S, is not deemed a rejection of S's offer.

26. Death or Insanity. Where the offeror or offeree dies or becomes insane, the offer terminates. It should be noted, however, that if the offeror dies the rule applies only to offers that were revocable by him. Thus, if the offer is a binding option, it cannot be revoked by the offeror, and consequently does not terminate by his death or insanity within the time specified. (See § 24 above.)

27. Lapse of Time. An offer terminates with the lapse of time provided in the offer for its acceptance. Where it does not state that it shall remain open for a designated time it expires upon the lapse of a reasonable time. What constitutes a reasonable time depends on the nature of the offer, the subject matter, usages of trade, and the particular circumstances of the case. An offer to sell a commodity whose value fluctuates momentarily must be accepted immediately. Such an offer received during business hours on one day cannot be accepted the next day. An offer to sell perishable goods must be accepted sooner than an offer to sell staple goods.

28. Death or Destruction of Person or Thing. The death or destruction of a person or thing essential to the performance of the contemplated contract terminates the offer. Thus, an offer to sell a specific motor cruiser terminates if the cruiser is destroyed by fire prior to acceptance. An offer which contemplates the hiring of the offeree to render personal services terminates upon the death of the offeror or offeree.

29. Supervening Legal Prohibition of the Proposed Contract. Where the contract contemplated by the offeror is prohibited by an act of a law-making body or a judicial decision after the offer is made and before acceptance, the offer terminates. Thus, if the offer is to lease certain premises for dance-hall purposes, and before acceptance a zoning ordinance is passed prohibiting dance halls in that locality, the offer terminates.

B. THE ACCEPTANCE

30. The Acceptance. The acceptance of an offer is the manifestation by the offeree of his assent to enter into a contractual relationship upon the terms and conditions of the offer. Upon acceptance of an offer, there is a manifestation of the mutual assent of the parties, the offeror's assent being shown by his offer and the offeree's by his acceptance, and a contract comes into being.

To determine, however, whether the offeree's communication constitutes an acceptance, we must see that the terms of the offer have been complied with. Was it made in the proper manner, at the proper place, at the proper time, and by the proper person?

31. Who May Accept. Where an offer is directed to a particular person, only that person may accept. If *C* learns of an offer by *A* to *B*, *C* cannot accept it. His attempted acceptance will constitute no more than an offer to *A*, which *A* may or may not accept. If the offer is made to the public generally, it may be accepted by any person who has knowledge of it. If made to a particular class of persons, it may be accepted by any person within the class who knows of it.

32. Manner of Acceptance. An acceptance may consist of (*a*) the making of a promise, (*b*) the performance of an act, (*c*) a forbearance, or (*d*) silence.

33. Acceptance by Promise. If the offer indicates that the offeror intends that acceptance shall consist of a promise to perform by the offeree, the offeree's making of the promise, as directed by the offer, is an acceptance. Performance alone will not constitute an acceptance.

EXAMPLES

1. *A* writes to *B*, "I will repair your motor cruiser if you promise to pay me $200." *B* writes to *A*, "I promise to pay you $200 for the repair of my cruiser." There is a contract.

2. *A* writes to *B*, "I will pay you $200 if you repair my cruiser." *B* replies, "I promise to repair your cruiser." There is no contract. *A*'s offer called for the performance of an act and not a promise. Thus, *B*'s promise is not an acceptance.

Where the contract consists of a promise in exchange for a promise, the contract is said to be bilateral. Both parties are then obligated to perform the contract.

34. Acceptance by Performance of Act. Most offers made by business men contemplate the formation of bilateral contracts; the offers call for a promise by the offeree to perform in accordance with the terms of the offer. Some offers do, however, require the performance of an act as an acceptance, and, as a general rule, the courts have held that the acceptance consists of the complete performance of the act requested, and that if the offer is revoked before the act is completely performed, no contract results. But in some cases the application of this rule is unjust and works a hardship on the offeree. Assume an offer calls for the performance of an act over a period of time:

EXAMPLE

A writes to B, "I find that I am now physically unable to operate and maintain my farm. If you and your family will come to live with me, care for me, and operate and maintain my farm until I die, I will, upon my death, leave to you my farm and everything on it." B moves his family to the farm and enters upon the performance of the act requested. After 10 years A revokes his offer.

To hold that the offer is effectively revoked, and that A is accordingly free from liability is manifestly unjust. One view is that the revocation is effective but B may recover from A the reasonable value of the benefits conferred upon A by B's part performance. A second view concludes that from the offeree's part performance we may imply a promise by him to perform the act requested and a bilateral contract results. This result is extreme. The parties never intended a bilateral contract. If the offeree fails to perform in full the act requested, is he liable for breach? A third view is that proposed by the Restatement, Contracts. If the offeree enters upon performance of the act requested, the offeror is denied the right to revoke the offer, and a contract comes into existence when the act is completely performed in accordance with the terms of the offer.

It should be noted that the first view does not reach a fair result in a case where the performance of the act involves no benefit to the offeror but does involve serious expense to the offeree. Revocation of the offer subjects the offeree to loss and leaves the offeror without liability. Under the third view, revocation is ineffective. Cases involving offers of the kind set forth in the example above are relatively few in number, and the opinions of the courts are in conflict.

As a general rule, where an offer calls for the performance of an act, a promise by the offeree to perform the act will not result in a contract. This rule is subject to one statutory exception. In Sec. 2-206(1)(b), the UCC provides that an offer to buy goods for prompt or current shipment shall be construed as inviting acceptance by the seller by prompt or current shipment or by a prompt promise to ship. If it is accepted by prompt or current shipment, there is a contract even if the goods shipped do not conform to the offer to buy. The shipment in such case constitutes a breach of contract by the seller unless he seasonably notifies the buyer that the shipment is offered the buyer only as an accommodation to him. To avoid this rule, the buyer must make it clear in his offer that only prompt or current shipment of conforming goods will constitute a contract.

EXAMPLE

B writes to S, "If you make prompt shipment of 50 barrels of apples, I will pay you $200." By return mail, S promises to make prompt shipment of 50 barrels of apples. There is a contract [UCC Sec. 2-206(1)(b)].

Occasionally, an offer is made which calls for the performance of an act which the offeree cannot perform without the cooperation of the offeror. If the offeror refuses to cooperate, it is impossible for the offeree to accept and there will be no contract.

EXAMPLE

S writes to B, "If you pay me $500 I will sell you my automobile." B appears and offers $500 to S. S revokes his offer. There is no contract. The act requested was not completely performed at the time of revocation. There was no payment. The act of payment could not be performed by B unless S accepted the money.

In its application to one class of offer, this rule has been modified by special statute in New York. It provides that, where an offer by a creditor or obligee calls for the performance of an act by the debtor or obligor in satisfaction or discharge of the debt or obligation, a tender of performance by the debtor or obligor before revocation of the offer will constitute an acceptance if the offer is in writing and signed by the creditor or obligor.

EXAMPLE

C, a creditor, makes an offer in a writing signed by him to D, his debtor, proposing that if D delivers to C 500 bales of cotton, C will accept the same in full satisfaction of the $5,000 debt owing by D. D makes a tender of delivery of the cotton pursuant to the offer, but C rejects the tender and revokes his offer. In the absence of statute, there is no contract. D could not deliver the cotton unless C accepted it. Under the New York statute, D accepted the offer by the tender of delivery prior to revocation and C is bound by contract.

Where an offer calls for the performance of an act as an acceptance, it is not necessary that the offeree give notice that the act has been performed. However, some states make one exception to this rule. They hold that, where an offer provides that if the offeree extends credit to a third person the offeror will guarantee payment by the third person, the offer is not accepted until credit is extended and notice thereof is given the offeror. The requirement of notice in such case is not in harmony with the principle that complete performance of the act is alone an acceptance. The better rule, followed in New York, is that notice is not necessary unless required by the terms of the offer.

Often a continuing offer is made which contemplates that the offeree shall perform a series of acts, each act constituting an acceptance of the offer and hence a contract. Such an offer may be revoked by the offeror before the performance of any particular act, but acts performed prior to the revocation result in contracts.

EXAMPLE

A makes an offer to B in which he states that if B will discount notes for X, he, A, will pay any note which X fails to pay. A's offer is a continuing one which contemplates that B make a series of discounts. When B discounts a note for X, he accepts the offer and A becomes bound on his guaranty. However, before B discounts any particular note, A may revoke his offer, and any discounts made by B subsequent to A's revocation will not constitute acceptances. It should be noted that A's offer is one of guaranty, and a discount by B amounts to an extension of credit to X.

35. Acceptance by Forbearance. The offer may require that the offeree accept by forbearing or refraining to perform an act for a fixed period of time or for a reasonable time. Thus, where an offer requests that the offeree refrain from the use of tobacco, of liquor, from playing cards, the offeree may accept only by conforming absolutely to the terms of the offer. The offeree must refrain from doing the various things mentioned for the time specified, or, if no time is fixed, for a reasonable time. Where the offer calls for the performance of an act or a forbearance by the offeree, and the requested act is completely performed or the offeree forbears as required by the offer, the offer is accepted. The resulting contract is said to be unilateral. Once the offeree has performed and the contract comes into existence, there is nothing more for the offeree to do. The only obligation then existing is that of the offeror.

36. Acceptance by Silence. Ordinarily, an offeror may not regard silence on the part of an offeree as an acceptance, nor may he couch his offer in language which will make silence an acceptance. An offeree is not bound to speak in respect of an offer he chooses not to accept. An offeror who makes a proposal and states that if he does not hear from the offeree he will deem the proposal accepted, does not thereby place a burden on the offeree to communicate with the offeror.

However, there are cases in which the courts have readily held that an offeree by his silence impliedly accepted an offer. These cases were decided on the theory that the offeree was required to speak in the particular circumstances, or that he availed himself of the benefits of the transaction, or that he exercised dominion over the subject of the offer.

EXAMPLES

1. S, without an order from B, ships goods to B and writes B that, if B does not return the goods by a certain date, they will be considered sold. B refuses to take delivery from the carrier and fails to communicate with S. It appears that on several occasions in the past S did the same thing and B accepted the goods. B by implication accepted S's offer and is liable for the price. In the circumstances, B has led S to believe that his silence was a manifestation of assent. The prior course of dealing between the parties having placed upon B a duty to speak, his silence is misleading and inconsistent with honest dealings.

2. A, a publisher, continues to send magazines to B although B's subscription has expired. B accepts the magazines, believing that A expects to be paid, and reads them. B has accepted. He has accepted the benefit of the magazines with the knowledge that A expected to be paid.

3. S sends goods to B advising B that, unless he hears from B to the contrary, he will deem B to have accepted the goods. B does not communicate with S, but resells the goods to X. S may treat the resale as an acceptance. B's exercise of dominion over the goods is an acceptance.

37. Communication of Acceptance. We have seen that the acceptance may consist of a promise, performance of an act, or a forbearance by the offeree, depending on the terms of the offer. Where acceptance is by performance of an act or a forbearance, generally no notice thereof need be communicated to the offeror. The forbearance or the act is in itself the manifestation of the offeree's assent to enter into the contractual relationship. But where the offeree is to accept by a promise, his promise is not considered an acceptance until it is communicated to the offeror in the manner, at the time, and at the place required by the offer. Where the offeror and offeree stand face to face, and a proposal orally made is orally accepted, the acceptance is, of course, communicated to the offeror.

38. Communication by Authorized Means. Where the parties are at a distance, the acceptance is effective and a contract is formed when acceptance is sent by the offeree by any means the offeror has authorized the offeree to use. The authorized means of transmission is the means specified in the offer or, if none is specified, the means used by the offeror for the communication of his offer, or the means customarily used in similar transactions at the time and at the place where the offer is received. When the acceptance is so dispatched, a contract comes into existence as soon as the acceptance is out of the possession of the offeree, whether or not it is received by the offeror. Where the authorized means is the mail, the acceptance, to be effective when sent, must be properly addressed and postpaid.

NB

EXAMPLES

1. A sends an offer to B by mail specifying that B send his acceptance by telegraph. B delivers his acceptance to a telegraph office for transmission to A. There is a contract. The fact that transmission is delayed or that the acceptance is never received has no effect. The offeror having authorized the means of communication takes the risk of delay or non-receipt.

2. A sends an offer to B by mail. B writes a letter of acceptance, places it in an envelope properly addressed and postpaid, and deposits it in a postoffice mail box or mail chute in his office building. There is a contract as soon as the acceptance is deposited. Note that in these illustrations a revocation by the offeror is not effective unless received by the offeree prior to such dispatch of his acceptance.

NB

The UCC provides in Sec. 2-206(1)(a) that an offer to make a contract for the sale of goods may be accepted in any manner and by any medium reasonable in the circumstances. This section rejects the rule that acceptance be by the authorized means of communication. If the offeror wishes to avoid the application of this rule, he should make clear in his offer that there will be no contract unless a particular manner or medium of acceptance is used.

39. Communication by Unauthorized Means. Where the acceptance is sent by a means of communication the offeree was not authorized to use, a contract comes into being when the acceptance is received, if received within the time that an acceptance by the authorized means would have been received. It is received when it comes into the possession of the offeror or someone authorized by him to receive it for him, or when it is placed in his mail box or letter slot in his door. Upon such receipt, there is a contract whether or not the acceptance is read and whether or not the offeror was there to receive it.

NB

An offeror sends an offer from Atlanta to Denver by mail and requests a reply by return mail. The offeree replies by telegraph. The acceptance is effective upon receipt by the offeror if it is received within the time that the return mail would have been received. The offeror intends not that the mail should be used to the exclusion of other means of communication, but that the acceptance is to be received by him by a certain time. He knows how long it will take for the mail to reach him and desires to receive the acceptance by that time.

40. Use of Unauthorized Means Excluded. This is not to say, however, that the offeror may not require that a particular means of communication shall be used to the exclusion of all others. An offeror may include in his offer a statement that "there will be no contract unless you accept by return mail." It seems that the offeror regards as the matter of importance not the time element, but the means of communication, and acceptance sent other than by return mail should not constitute an acceptance whenever received.

41. Acceptance Must Accord to Offer. In order for a contract to come into existence, the acceptance must in every way conform to the terms of the offer. If the offeree's communication or act or forbearance does not correspond with the offeror's terms, it is a counteroffer which may in turn be accepted by the offeror.

This rule is affected by UCC Sec. 2-207. Subsection (1) provides that "A definite and seasonable expression of acceptance or a written confirmation which is sent within a reasonable time operates as an acceptance even though it states terms additional to or different from those offered or agreed upon, unless acceptance is expressly made conditional on assent to the additional or different terms." This subsection deals with the situation where (a) an agreement has been reached either orally or by correspondence and one party sends to the other a confirmation embodying the terms agreed upon and an additional or different term, and (b) a communication which states that it is an acceptance of an offer but which includes an additional or different term. It provides that in both cases there is a contract embodying the terms agreed upon but not including the additional or different term. But if the confirmation or acceptance expressly requires assent to the additional or different term, and no assent is given, there is no contract. If there is assent given, the additional or different term becomes part of the contract.

Subsection (2) provides that the additional term is to be construed as a proposal for addition to the contract. There is some difficulty with this subsection since it makes no express reference to "different" terms. The Official Comment to the section states, "Whether or not additional or different terms will become part of the agreement depends upon the provisions of subsection (2)." Hence, there may be an intention that "additional" include "different" in that subsection. The balance of subsection (2) provides that where the parties involved are merchants, such terms become part of the contract unless "(*a*) the offer expressly limits acceptance to the terms of the offer; (*b*) they materially alter it; or (*c*) notification of objection to them has already been given or is given within a reasonable time after notice of them is received." The Official Comment indicates that terms which materially alter the contract are those which would result in surprise or hardship if incorporated into the contract. Examples given are a term disclaiming standard warranties in circumstances in which they would normally attach; a term requiring 100% delivery where a usage in the trade allows some leeway; and a term requiring complaint to be made within a materially shorter time than is customary or reasonable.

Failure to object to a different or additional term within a reasonable time after notice of it amounts to assent to such term and it becomes part of the contract if it does not materially alter the contract and if the offer does not limit acceptance to its terms.

Where each party sends to the other a confirmation of their bargain and terms in each are conflicting, each party will be deemed to have objected to such terms and they do not become part of the contract. In such case, the terms agreed upon constitute the agreement.

UCC Sec. 2-207 alters the common law rules of offer and acceptance, but it must be noted that it has no application except to a transaction involving the sale of goods.

EXAMPLES

1. A writes to B, "If you will agree to repair my motor cruiser, *Penguin*, I will pay you $500 upon completion of your work." B promptly replies, "I agree to repair *Penguin* for $500 payable in advance." There is no contract. B's reply is a counteroffer since its terms do not accord to the offer. UCC Sec. 2-207 does not apply.

2. A mails a letter to B offering to sell a painting, Dawn, for $5,000, "delivery to be made on June 1st next." B promptly replies, "I accept your offer. Deliver Dawn on May 20th." Under the Code, there is a contract. B's reply is a definite and seasonable expression of acceptance, even though it states a term different from that offered. The different term, " deliver Dawn on May 20th" is a proposal for addition to the contract (UCC Sec. 2-207).

3. Assume the offer in (2) above. B replies promptly, "I will buy Dawn if you will deliver on May 20th. Please advise." Under the Code, there is no contract. B's reply does not appear to be a definite expression of acceptance. Further, it requires assent to the different term.

4. Assume that A and B are art dealers and A, by mail, offers to sell his painting, Dawn, to B for $5,000 C.O.D. B promptly replies, "I accept your offer to sell Dawn for five thousand dollars. Payment to be made sixty

days after delivery." Under the Code the different term is not part of the contract. Between merchants different or additional terms become part of the contract unless they matérially alter the offer. The credit term in *B*'s acceptance is a material alteration of the offer.

42. Acceptance Must Accord to Offer: Delay or Non-receipt. The offeror may, by suitable provisions and stipulations in his offer, protect himself from the operation of the basic principles of offer and acceptance. We have seen that an acceptance by a means of communication authorized by the offeror gives rise to a contract when dispatched, whether or not received by the offeror. In the event of non-receipt, the offeror may, in the belief that the offeree is not interested in his proposal, deal with another in respect of the same subject matter, and find himself liable on two contracts. He may protect himself against such possibility by inserting in his offer a provision that the acceptance, however sent, shall not be effective until received. To protect himself against possible delay in transmission, he may further provide that it shall be received by a certain time. He may include in his offer any conditions he sees fit, provided that they are not illegal or against public policy.

43. Mistake in Transmission of Offer. Where the offeror uses the services of a telegraph company to transmit his offer, the company is generally deemed his agent, and as between the offeror and offeree the offeror bears the loss resulting from errors committed by the company in transmitting the offer. Thus, where an offer to sell a quantity of goods at eleven cents per unit is delivered to a telegraph company for transmission to the offeree, and the offer as received by the offeree states the price as ten cents per unit, and the offeree accepts, there is a contract. It would seem, however, that where the offer as received states a price so grossly at variance with the current market that the offeree knows or should know that a mistake has been made, it would be unconscionable to allow him to accept.

A few cases have concluded that the telegraph agency is not an agent of the offeror but an independent contractor, and that the offeror cannot be held bound by the acceptance of an offer which he did not make. But these are not considered the better reasoned cases.

44. Agreement Followed by Formal Writing. Often parties reach an agreement orally or by informal writings with the understanding that their bargain shall thereafter be incorporated into a formal contract in writing. The question arises whether the parties intended that their agreement should become binding when the formal contract was executed by them, or whether they intended their informal agreement to be binding and the formal writing to be merely a memorial of their agreement. To rule in all such cases that there can be no agreement until the formal writing is executed would on occasion permit one who has decided that he has made an unadvantageous bargain to escape its consequences. Accordingly, the courts have said that the intention of the parties must control. In determining their intention, the informal agreement will be examined to determine whether it contains all the terms deemed essential to that type of contract. If it is found that it omits provisions ordinarily included, it is held that the informal agreement is but a preliminary negotiation and there is no contract until the formal agreement is signed.

45. Agreement Must Be Definite and Certain. The contract formed must be sufficiently definite and certain in its terms to enable a court to determine its meaning and the rights and duties of the parties thereto. For example, the X Railroad agreed with A that, if A would erect at a certain station on the line a first-class eating house and maintain it in a first-class style, the X Railroad would support same by stopping trains at the station. A erected what he deemed to be a first-class eating house, and maintained it in what he considered to be a first-class style, and alleged that the railroad failed to support it by stopping trains. The agreement is too indefinite and uncertain to be capable of enforcement. What is a "first-class" eating house? What is maintenance in a "first-class style"? Must the railroad stop every train? If not, how many trains must stop? Does the fact that A considered the eating house to be "first-class" and his maintenance to be in "first-class style" make the provisions definite and certain? The courts will not make contracts for the parties and, therefore, cannot determine the obligations and rights of the parties.

46. Agreement to Agree on Essential Term. Where parties make a bargain but provide that one of its essential terms is to be left for future agreement, and they fail to so agree, the contract is unenforceable. Thus, an agreement to sell real property which provides that "the amount to be paid on the signing of the contract to be agreed upon," and an agreement of lease which provides that the lessee may extinguish the lease and become owner of the property by payment of $10,000 "at a time to be agreed upon," were held to be unenforceable where the parties failed to reach agreement on the matters left open.

In respect of a contract for the sale of goods, UCC Sec. 2-204(3) states that, even though one or more terms are left open, the contract does not fail for indefiniteness if the parties have intended to make a contract and there is a reasonably certain basis for giving an appropriate remedy.

4. Reality of Assent

One who induces another to enter into a contract as a result of an intentionally or recklessly false statement of a material fact is guilty of fraud. Contract become voidable

A. FRAUD AND MISREPRESENTATION

47. In General. Under the topics of Offer and Acceptance, we discussed the requirement of mutual assent. The law, in determining whether an offer was made and whether it was accepted, concerns itself not only with the *apparent assent* of the parties, as has been indicated, but also with the *reality* of that assent. Not only must the parties manifest an apparent mutual assent, but also the assent of each must be real—that is, it must have been given under circumstances that indicate it is the real and true assent of each and was in no way brought about by fraud, misrepresentation, mistake, duress, or undue influence.

48. Essentials of Fraud. To establish fraud as an actionable wrong, it is necessary to establish all of the following:

(*a*) Representation of a material fact
(*b*) Falsity of the representation
(*c*) Representation made with knowledge of its falsity
(*d*) Representation made to induce contract
(*e*) Reliance of representation, and injury.

If proof of any of these elements is lacking, no fraud has been committed. *The injured party may rescind contract or sue for damages*

49. Representation of Material Fact. The representation is material if it appears that the contract would not have been made if the representation was not made. It must be one of fact, and not a statement of opinion or belief, or a prediction or a promise. Statements that a buyer will make a profit, or that land will produce a certain quantity of corn, statements of the value of property, or statements by a seller which amount to seller's talk or seller's puff, do not constitute statements of facts. Statements which have a bearing on the value, such as statements about the cost of property

28

or statements that a third person has made a certain offer for the property, are statements of facts, and if the other elements of fraud are present they constitute frauds.

Promissory statements about what one will do in the future or predictions of what will take place in the future generally are not actionable. It has been held, however, that a statement of what one intends to do is a statement of fact in that it refers to his present state of mind, and that if at the time the statement was made there was actually no such intention, the statement is actionable. It should be noted that, if a statement of one's intention is true when made, it does not become false if he later changes his mind. To make a statement of intention actionable, there must be clear proof that the statement was false when made, and that there was not merely a change of mind.

50. Representation Must Be False. Where a statement of fact is made to induce one to contract, there is a right to rely on the statement. The law does not require one to make an investigation to determine whether the statement made to him is false. This does not mean, however, that he may close his eyes and his mind to the situation confronting him. If, in the circumstances, the falsity of the statement would be obvious to one who uses ordinary intelligence or who keeps his eyes open, it cannot be asserted that he believed the statement to be true. Further, where the knowledge he has or the facts with which he is confronted should cause him to doubt the truth of the statement, he is not entitled to rely on its truth.

51. With Knowledge of Falsity. To establish fraud it is necessary to prove that the person who made the representation knew that it was false. When one, not knowing whether it is true or false, affirms that a statement is true, and it is later proved to be false, he is charged with knowledge of falsity. An affirmation that a statement is true seems to imply a knowledge that it is true, and if there is no such knowledge the statement is false.

Where one authorizes a statement to be issued in the honest belief that it is true, but is negligent by failing to examine it to determine the truth of the statement before its issue, it is usually held that there is no actionable fraud. Negligence is not the equivalent of knowledge of the falsity of the statement. Want of care does not include an intent to do a wrongful act. Fraud presupposes an intent to deceive; want of care merely indicates a failure to exercise a duty.

52. False Representation to Induce Contract. The person who makes the false representation of fact must intend to deceive and induce the formation of a contract. Where one is actually deceived by the statement and enters into a contract, the fact that he was deceived is proof of an intent to deceive since the person who made the statement is presumed to have intended the natural and proximate consequences of his own misrepresentation.

It is not necessary that there be an intent to deceive a particular person. One who applies for credit and submits to a commercial agency false information in writing about his financial status, intending that the statement be displayed by the agency to anyone willing to extend credit, is liable for fraud to anyone who extends credit relying on the truth of the statement.

53. Reliance on Representation and Injury. Unless one is induced to enter into a contractual relationship relying on the false representation and suffers loss, there is no actionable fraud. Where the facts indicate that he would have entered into the contract even if the representation was not made, reliance is absent.

Where the victim of a fraud wishes to recover damages, he must prove the fraud and pecuniary injury resulting therefrom, but where he seeks rescission and a return of the consideration parted with, proof of further injury is not necessary.

An examination of the essentials of a fraud as set forth above seems to indicate that there can be no fraud unless a false statement has been made. It is possible, however, that a fraud can be committed by conduct or by silence.

54. Fraud by Conduct. The commission of an act with intent to induce one to contract may constitute a fraud. One can be as eloquent in the performance of an act as he can by the use of words, and if his purpose is to deceive he is guilty of a fraud. One who is negotiating the sale of a motor cruiser "as is," and causes the cruiser to be placed in the water so that a defect in the hull will not be detected, commits a fraud on the purchaser. It has been held that one who conceals a defect in a piece of machinery by concealing it with putty and paint so that it cannot be detected on inspection is liable to a purchaser for fraud.

55. Fraud by Silence. Ordinarily, silence does not constitute fraud. One's silence is not deemed wrongful unless he is under a duty to speak in the circumstances. Such duty exists, the early cases hold, where an inquiry is made or where there is a relation of trust and confidence between the parties. However, the more recent cases indicate a relaxing of this rule, and impose a duty to speak even where no inquiry is made and no such relationship exists. It has been said that if one conceals a fact with knowledge that the other assumes no such fact exists, it is as much a fraud as if the existence of the fact were denied. Thus, if one sells commercial paper knowing that the maker or drawer is insolvent, or having knowledge of other facts making the paper substantially valueless, he is under a duty to reveal the facts to the purchaser, and his failure to do so constitutes a fraudulent concealment. The same result is reached where one sells property knowing that it is dangerous because defective. He is under a duty to reveal the fact to the buyer.

56. Remedies for Fraud. A contract procured by fraud is voidable at the election of the victim of the fraud. Should he elect to avoid, his remedy proceeds in disaffirmance of the contract. Where he elects not to avoid, he may sue for damages resulting from the fraud. In such event, he proceeds in affirmance of the contract.

57. Rescission. Where the injured party elects to avoid, he may do so by rescinding the contract and returning or offering to return whatever he has received thereunder. The parties will be restored to the position they occupied before the contract was made. Of course, if he is sued upon the contract he may defend by setting forth the fraud and rescission, or he may counterclaim his damages for fraud.

The remedy of rescission proceeds on the theory that his assent to contract was induced by the fraud perpetrated and is not a real and genuine assent since it is vitiated by the fraud. When he rescinds, he takes the position that no contract ever existed; his rescission relates back to the date of the contract and vitiates it as of that time.

58. Limitations on the Right to Rescind. The right to rescind is not, however, an unlimited right. It has been held in many cases that the fraud may be condoned or the contract ratified. A buyer of goods who pays the price for them after discovery of fraud by the seller, or the buyer of shares of stock who, having determined to rescind for fraud committed by the seller, accepts dividends from the corporation, will be deemed to have condoned or waived the fraud and ratified his purchase.

The right to rescind for fraud is an equitable right which must be promptly asserted. Unreasonable delay (laches) after discovery of the fraud will destroy the right. Further, there must be restoration or a tender of restoration of the consideration received. However, where this is impossible by reason of destruction without fault, or where the consideration is of no value, or where the consideration has deteriorated due to natural causes or reasonable use, the right of rescission is not affected.

Lastly, where a buyer by fraud induces the seller to sell goods to him, and before the seller rescinds the buyer resells the goods for value to a purchaser who has no knowledge of the fraud, the seller may no longer rescind. The buyer, whose title is voidable for fraud, passes a complete and indefeasible title to such purchaser (UCC Sec. 2-403).

59. Action for Damages. At common law, the remedies of rescission and damages for fraud were inconsistent, the former proceeding on the theory that there was no contract and the latter on the theory that there was, and therefore they were mutually exclusive. Unless local statute modifies the common law rule, the victim of the fraud may elect one remedy or the other; he may not have both. In New York, it is provided that a claim for damages sustained as a result of fraud or misrepresentation in the inducement of a contract or other transaction shall not be deemed inconsistent with a claim for rescission or based on rescission. In an action for rescission or based on rescission, the aggrieved party shall be allowed to obtain complete relief in one action, including rescission, restitution of the benefits, if any, conferred by him as a result of the transaction, and damages to which he is entitled because of such fraud or misrepresentation, but such complete relief shall not include duplication of items of recovery.

The UCC in Sec. 2-721 provides that neither rescission of a contract for the sale of goods nor a rejection or return of the goods shall bar or be deemed inconsistent with a claim for damages.

In England and in many states, including New York, the purpose of an action for damages for fraud is indemnity. Damages are measured by the amount necessary to indemnify the victim for his actual pecuniary loss sustained as a direct result of the wrong. Thus, where one is fraudulently induced to purchase shares of stock for $300 upon representations of fact indicating a value of $500, and the shares have an actual value of only $100, the measure of damages is the difference between the price paid and the actual value of the shares received, or $200, plus interest. However, a majority of the states fix the measure of damages as the difference between the actual value of the shares received and the value they would have had if the false statements were true, and they allow, on the facts stated, damages in the amount of $400. Since these states allow the injured party to reap the benefit of his bargain, they do not proceed on the theory of indemnity.

60. Misrepresentation. The difference between misrepresentation and fraud is that in misrepresentation the person who makes the false statement has no knowledge of its falsity. A misrepresentation is a false statement made in good faith to induce one to enter into a contractual relationship.

61. Remedy for Misrepresentation. In equity, the remedy of rescission will be granted although the person who makes the false statement honestly believes it to be true. This right to rescind for a misrepresentation is limited in the same respect as is the right to rescind for fraud. (See § 58 above.) At common law, misrepresentation did not give rise to an action for damages. However, where statutes exist, such as that enacted in New York (See § 59 above), the remedies of damages and rescission are allowed.

B. MISTAKE OF FACT

62. Nature of Mistake. A mistake is an erroneous belief that a present or past fact exists. It is a state of mind not in accord with the facts. Often such erroneous belief or state of mind induces one or both of the parties to express agreement or assent. The effect of the mistake on the legal relationship of the parties in a given case depends on the facts. The erroneous belief may go to the essence of the contract or it may be immaterial. One of the parties may know or have reason to know that the other is mistaken. The mistaken party may act under an erroneous belief because of his own negligence. One party may be in some way responsible for the other's mistake. Both parties may have entered into a transaction in the erroneous belief of the existence of the same material fact, or only one party may have been so mistaken. Further, it may be impossible in the circumstances to restore the parties to the status quo. It is possible that any one or more of these facts may exist in a given case, and the conclusion must be determined accordingly. Hence, in determining the various cases presented to them, the courts must consider the particular facts and circumstances, and cannot limit their statements to the particular type of mistake involved. The same mistake may involve different facts in different cases and differing results will necessarily be reached.

63. Mutual Mistake. Many courts have broadly stated that relief will not be granted for mistake unless both parties were mistaken as to the same fact—that is, unless the mistake is mutual. Often, however, relief has been granted where the mistake was unilateral because of a consideration of the particular facts involved. Where no relief was granted, it was usually because the facts and circumstances involved precluded relief. For example, where A enters into a contract with B believing him to be C, and B does not induce and is in no way responsible for A's erroneous belief, it is usually said that the mistake is not mutual and relief must, therefore, be denied. But if B induced the mistake, or knew or had reason to know that A acted under mistake, relief is usually granted though the mistake is unilateral.

64. Mistakes Classified. The erroneous belief that induces one to express assent may be:

(*a*) a mistake as to the identity of a contracting party,

(*b*) a mistake as to the nature of a document, or

(*c*) a mistake as to the subject matter. This may consist of a mistake as to the existence, nature, quantity, price, identity, and ownership.

As indicated above, the rules to be applied are not determined by the nature of the mistake alone. The facts involved in the particular case must also be considered.

65. Mistake as to Identity of Contracting Party. Mistakes about the identity of a contracting party are always unilateral mistakes. One is mistaken as to the identity of the other, but the other has no mistaken belief as to his own identity.

EXAMPLES

1. During the bargaining process, *A* is led to believe by *B* that he, *A*, is dealing with the B Company, a partnership. The contract made by *A* is void if in fact he dealt with the B Corporation. The mistake is unilateral, but it was induced by the representative of the B Corporation and *A* may repudiate the bargain.

2. *B*, falsely stating that he is agent for *C*, induces *A* to enter into a contract. The contract is void. *A* alone is mistaken, but his erroneous belief was induced by *B*.

3. *A*, an agent of *P*, enters into a contract with *X*, without disclosing his agency. The contract is valid. *X* made no mistake. He intended to contract with *A* and did contract with *A*. An agent who contracts for an undisclosed principal is also a party to the contract.

4. *A* and *B* enter into a contract, *A* believing that he is contracting with *C*. *B* does not induce *A*'s erroneous belief, and *B* does not know and has no reason to know of it. The contract is valid. It is usually held that the mistake is unilateral, and no relief will be granted. Actually, the reason is that there are no facts involved which compel a contrary result.

66. Mistake as to Nature of Document. This mistake occurs where a person signs a writing in the erroneous belief that its nature is something other than what it is. The courts have generally held that where a literate person signs a document without reading it, his negligence will preclude him from asserting that the document is void because of mistake. This result is reached, however, only because he was not induced to sign by any false statement as to the nature of the document made by the party with whom he contracts. Where he is fraudulently induced to sign, his negligence in failing to read the document will not result in an estoppel, and the contract will be deemed void.

67. Mistake as to Existence of Subject Matter. Where the parties contract to buy and sell a specific thing, and unknown to either that thing has ceased to exist at the time the contract is made, the contract is void, and the buyer may recover any payment made. There is a mutual mistake as to the continued existence of the thing which caused them to contract. *no contract*

EXAMPLE

A enters into a contract to sell to B for $100 A's white horse, Domino, "now in X's stable." Unknown to the parties, the horse died before the contract was made. There is no contract. The parties were mutually mistaken as to the continued existence of the horse.

68. Mistake as to Nature of Subject Matter. Where there is a mistake as to the nature of the subject matter which goes to the very essence of the contract, so that the subject is of an essentially different nature than supposed, and the mistake is mutual, or unilateral but induced by fraud, there is no contract.

EXAMPLES

1. A found a small stone and sold it to B for one dollar. Actually, the stone was a diamond worth $500. B had no greater knowledge in the matter than A had. The contract is valid. Since neither party had attributed to the stone any particular nature or quality, there was no mistake in that respect. They were merely mistaken as to the value of the stone.

2. A, the holder of a promissory note, sells it to B. Neither A nor B has any knowledge of the fact that prior to the sale the maker of the note had become insolvent. The sale was held valid, the court saying that there was no mistake as to the nature of the note, that the parties did not have in mind a subject matter other than the one their contract identified, and that if there was a mutual mistake it was only in respect of the value of the note.

Generally, no relief is granted for mistake as to the value of the subject matter of a contract. Value is a variable thing. It varies from time to time, from place to place, and with different buyers and sellers. The parties when they contract are aware of this, and ordinarily they assume the risk of error as to value.

Often, however, one's judgment as to value depends on some fact, such as nature or quality, which either or both parties assume has been definitely established. While risk is assumed on the question of value, is it not necessarily assumed in respect of the nature or character of the subject matter.

3. *A* contracts to sell *B* a specific bar of silver. Both parties suppose that the bar is pure silver. It has, however, a much larger admixture of base metal. The American Law Institute's Restatement, Contracts, states that the contract is void. The mutual mistake goes to the nature and character of the subject matter and not merely to the value. The value that may have been attributed to it was the result of mistake as to its nature.

4. If both parties to a contract for the sale of a stone assume it to be a diamond, and the contract price is fixed at $500, no relief will be granted if they are mutually mistaken as to its value. They take the risk about the value of the stone as a diamond, but not about its nature and character. Thus, if the stone is actually a topaz, relief should be granted.

5. *A* and *B* enter into a contract for the sale of a blooded cow, which both parties believe is barren, for $80. Before delivery it is discovered that the cow is with calf and worth a large sum as a breeder. In a well-known case it was held that the contract was voidable by the seller, the court holding that the mistake of both went to the essence and root of the contract, and, although the cow is the same animal the parties thought her to be, a barren cow is a different creature from a breeding cow. The cow was understood to be barren and the parties assumed the risk of the value of such a cow, but they were mutually mistaken as to the nature and character of the cow. They did not make their agreement with the understanding that they were taking a risk that the cow was not barren.

However, there are many cases holding that the parties assume the risk as to value and the risk as to existence of any fact upon which the opinion as to value depends. Other cases have recognized, as indicated above, that where the parties have contracted in the belief that a certain material fact exists, it is not equitable to deny relief to the injured party merely because it affects judgment as to value.

69. Mistake as to Quantity. Frequently in transactions involving the purchase and sale of land mistakes are made about quantity or area. Where the agreement fixes the price per acre, the usual remedy is an abatement of the price or an additional payment as the case may be. Where the contract fixes a price for an entire tract rather than by acre, but the parties assume that the area contains a certain acreage, the courts will again grant an abatement of the price in the event of a deficiency or compel an additional payment for an excess. If in such cases the difference in the number of acres is so great as to frustrate the purpose of the purchase, the purchaser is allowed to rescind. Where, however, the price is fixed for a tract without reference to or understanding of the number of acres involved, the quantity is immaterial.

EXAMPLES

1. *A* desires to purchase a farm. He examines *B*'s farm and determines that it contains about 50 acres. *A* and *B* contract for the purchase and sale of the farm by metes and bounds. *A* later discovers the farm is a 40-acre tract. The contract is valid. The subject matter was a farm, not a farm of a certain number of acres. *A* was mistaken, but *B* did not induce the mistake and had no knowledge of it.

2. *A* and *B* enter into a contract to purchase and sell 50 acres of land for $5,000. *B* learns there are only 48 acres in the tract. There is a mutual mistake as to quantity. The buyer is entitled to an abatement of the price of 2 acres. If there are only 25 acres in the tract and such discrepancy frustrates the buyer's purpose in purchasing, he is entitled to rescission of the contract.

70. Mistake as to Price. If an offeror makes a mistake in the price and the offeree accepts knowing or having reason to know of the offeror's mistake it would be unconscionable to allow the offeree to enforce the contract. However, many courts have held that an acceptance in good faith by the offeree results in an enforceable contract. Avoidance is not permitted merely because of the offeror's mistake. He must bear the consequences of his own negligence. However, there are some decisions to the effect that, if the error is substantial, and notice of the mistake is given after acceptance but before the acceptor has changed his position relying on an enforceable contract, the contract is voidable by the mistaken party.

EXAMPLES

1. *A*, in response to a request by *B*, submits an itemized bid for the supply of various kinds of goods. Mathematical computations of the various prices are erroneously made and they appear on the face of the bid. *B* accepts. The contract is voidable by *A*. *B* knew or should have known of the mistake.

2. Assume in the example above that *A*'s errors appear on his work sheets, and not made part of his bid. A lump sum price is submitted to *B*. Acceptance by *B* results in a valid contract, unless *B* knew of the mistake or should have known of it. Note that *B*'s errors were made before he made his bid, and that the amount of his bid was the amount he intended to bid. There is a mutual assent.

3. *A* makes an offer to sell at $200. *B*, understanding *A* to have offered at $100, accepts the offer. Both parties act honestly. There is no contract. The parties did not mutually agree on the price.

71. Mistake in Identity of Subject Matter. Not infrequently, cases arise in which each party misunderstands the expressions of the other. The mistake is mutual since each party is mistaken as to the meaning of the other. The case most frequently cited as an example is one in which an agreement is made to buy and sell cotton to arrive by the ship *Peerless* from Bombay. At the time of the contract there are two ships named *Peerless* at Bombay, and each is to arrive at a different time. The seller knows of one of them and the buyer knows of the other. The buyer refuses to receive and pay for the cotton on arrival. It was held that no contract existed.

In contracts for the sale of land, mistakes may be made as to the identity of the particular tract. Where the contract describes clearly and accurately the land the seller intends to sell, there is no mistake on his part, but the purchaser, who before contract examined a different plot, intends to buy a different plot. If the purchaser fails to read the seller's description, or having read it, fails to observe that the seller has described a plot other than what the purchaser has in mind, his negligence precludes rescission. Where the purchaser's mistake cannot be determined by a reading of the description, it is generally held, though the mistake is unilateral, that the purchaser may rescind.

72. Reformation. Where the parties reduce their contract to writing and, because of error, the writing does not express their intent, a court of equity, if the evidence is clear and compelling, may order the writing changed to conform with their intentions. The court will grant the remedy of reformation to reach the actual intention of the parties. The parol evidence rule has no application. The proof is not offered to change the contract but rather to have the writing conform to the contract they intended to make.

73. Mistake of Law. There are many cases in which the courts have denied relief on the ground that the mistake was a mistake of law and not one of fact. A mistake of law is made when one, although he knows the facts, is not aware of the legal consequences of those facts; he does not know how the rules of law are applied to those facts. However, the more recent cases indicate that, where the mistaken party is induced to contract by the fraudulent statement of the other as to the law, or even by the innocent misrepresentation of the other, and the mistaken party is entitled to rely on the statement due to the relation in which the parties stand, relief will be granted. In a few states, statutes have been enacted putting a mistake of domestic law on the same footing as a mistake of fact; in some others, the same result has been achieved by judicial decision. But, while one is generally presumed to know the domestic law, he is not presumed to know the law of another state or country. Accordingly, a mistake of foreign law is a mistake of fact in most states. In New York it is provided by statute that, when relief against a mistake is sought, it shall not be denied merely because the mistake is one of law rather than fact.

C. DURESS AND UNDUE INFLUENCE

74. Nature of Duress. In the early common law, duress did not exist unless the victim was put in fear of illegal imprisonment or great bodily harm. Gradually, the courts broadened the rule, and recent cases indicate that to constitute duress there must be some actual or threatened power over the *person* or *property* of another so as to compel him to contract. Where duress is exercised, it must overcome the free will of the victim. When the victim is in fact prevented from exercising his free will, the severity of the threat or act performed is not important. In determining whether a person was coerced by threat or by violence, the state of his health, his experience, age, and intelligence are considered.

Ordinarily, violence or a threat of violence against a person's parent, child, wife, or husband constitutes duress. There are, however, cases that extend the relationship to include a brother, a grandparent, and even a son-in-law.

If the person threatening bodily harm, imprisonment, or injury to property does not apparently have the power or the ability to carry out his threat, there is no duress. A threat to carry out or enforce one's legal right, as a threat to sue for breach of contract, is not sufficient coercion.

75. Effect of Duress on Assent. Since duress compels a manifestation of assent to contract without volition, the assent is not genuine or real. The victim may, however, elect to ratify his contract and regard it as enforceable against him, or he may avoid the contract and have it rescinded in equity or defend on the ground of duress in any action against him at law. Of course, if he elects to treat the contract as binding on him, he may enforce it. His contract is ordinarily voidable, not void.

76. Nature of Undue Influence. Undue influence in the procurement of a contract is a species of mental coercion which induces one to enter into a contract against his will. The real difference btween duress and undue influence lies in the means employed, not in the result reached. The result is the same—the will of the victim is overcome. Thus, undue influence exists when the will of the victim is overcome by means which do not amount to duress.

Where the relationship between the parties is a family or fiduciary relationship, or where one of the parties is mentally weaker, or destitute, or in extreme distress, and the contract made is palpably unfair, it is presumed that undue influence was exercised. Obviously, such presumption is made because in such cases it is comparatively easier to unduly influence the victim. To rebut the presumption, the dominant person must show positively that he did not take unfair advantage. A fiduciary relationship would include that between a principal and his agent, an attorney and his client, a guardian and his ward, a trustee and a beneficiary, and a financial or business adviser and his client. A family relationship is not generally a fiduciary one, but it may be in a given case. A father and son are in a fiduciary relationship if the father entrusts his business affairs to his son.

77. Effect of Undue Influence on Assent. Undue influence renders the contract voidable. The victim may avoid it by rescission in equity, or by an action at law to recover the consideration parted with. Where action is brought against him, he may plead the undue influence as a defense.

5. Capacity of Parties

78. In General. Under the law, certain parties lack sufficient judgment and perception and are deemed incapable of entering into agreements. Assent is necessary to the formation of a contract, and one who lacks the legal capacity to assent receives the protection of the law. Where, however, a liability is imposed by law and is not based on assent, as in the case of a quasi-contractual obligation or a tort liability, capacity to contract is not essential.

Those parties generally deemed to lack capacity to contract are infants, insane persons, drunken persons, corporations, married women, spendthrifts, aliens, and convicts.

79. The Infant. At common law, an infant is a person, male or female, who has not attained the age of 21 years. While most state statutes fixing the age of maturity are merely declarations of the common law, a few have altered the rule. For example, some provide that a female becomes of age when she attains the age of 18.

Since the law, in this respect, does not take notice of parts of a day, it is firmly held in this country that the infant reaches the age of consent at the beginning of the day before the eighteenth or twenty-first anniversary of birth, as the case may be.

80. Infant's Contract Voidable. Generally, an infant's contract is voidable at the election of the infant, and not void. The infant may repudiate or disaffirm the contract; the adult who contracted with him may not. However, until the infant elects to disaffirm, his contract is deemed binding on him.

81. Disaffirmance by Infant. The privilege of disaffirmance may be exercised by the infant at any time during his infancy or within a reasonable

41

time after he reaches majority. But he may disaffirm a conveyance of real estate made by him only after he has attained the age of majority.

Disaffirmance may consist of any acts or words which fairly signify the intention of the infant to repudiate. His disaffirmance may be express, as where he gives definite notice in words of his election to disaffirm, or implied, as where, being under contract to sell goods to X, he sells them to Y. An action by an infant to recover the consideration he parted with under the contract is a disaffirmance. His defense of infancy to an action brought against him has been held a disaffirmance. Disaffirmance by the infant renders the contract void as of the date of its making.

Where the infant sells goods to X and before the infant disaffirms X resells them to Y who pays value for them without knowledge that an infant was formerly the owner, Y acquires an indefeasible title. The infant may not recover the goods from Y [UCC Sec. 2-403(1)].

82. Disaffirmance by Infant: Duty to Restore Consideration. At the time of disaffirmance, the contract may be executory or executed. Where it has not been performed by either party, it is wholly executory; where it has been performed in full by both, it is executed. A contract which has been performed on one side and remains to be performed on the other is executed on one side and executory on the other.

Where any contract is fully executory and the infant disaffirms, neither party is liable to the other. If it is executed on the part of the infant and executory on the part of the adult, the infant may disaffirm and recover the consideration he parted with.

Where the contract is fully executed, it is generally held that the infant may disaffirm if he returns to the adult the consideration received. Where, however, he no longer has the consideration received, as where he has used or squandered it, is is quite uniformly held that he may nevertheless disaffirm and recover the consideration he parted with. Less agreement exists where the adult has fully performed and the infant has partially performed, as where under a contract for the purchase of personal property the infant has received and used the property, but has paid only part of the price. May the infant disaffirm, return the property, and recover the portion of the price paid without accounting for the deterioration of the property through use? Some jurisdictions hold that the infant may recover the price paid; others, including New York, hold that there may be a deduction made from the price paid for deterioration.

EXAMPLES

1. A, an infant, contracts with B to buy a bicycle from B for $45. A

has not yet paid any part of the price, and *B* has not yet delivered the bicycle. Upon disaffirmance by the infant, neither party is liable to the other.

2. Assume in (1) above that the infant has made part or full payment and has not yet received delivery of the bicycle. The infant may disaffirm and recover the payment made.

3. *A*, the infant, has received the bicycle but has not yet paid any part of the price. He may disaffirm and return the bicycle without accounting for deterioration through use.

4. *A*, the infant, has paid the price in full and has received the bicycle. He may disaffirm upon returning or offering to return the bicycle. By the weight of authority, if the bicycle has been destroyed or completely worn out, he may nevertheless recover the price paid.

5. *A*, the infant, made a part payment of $20 and received the bicycle. Having used the bicycle for a time, he now seeks to disaffirm. He returns the bicycle and sues to recover the $20. By the majority view he may recover the $20 in full. By the minority view, the New York rule, the infant is chargeable for deterioration through use of the bicycle up to the amount of the payment made.

There is a growing tendency to limit the right of the infant in cases where he has squandered or used the consideration received by him. A few states (New York not included) have passed statutes providing that an infant over 18 years of age must return the consideration received or an equivalent amount in money in order to disaffirm. These states recognize that the rule permitting an infant to disaffirm without a return of the consideration received or its equivalent in money often works injustice, and that while the infant must be protected against his own imprudence and folly, the law should not allow the privilege of disaffirmance to be exercised to overreach the other party.

In New York, by statute, a contract made by an infant between the ages of 18 and 21 in connection with a business conducted by the infant is binding if it was reasonable and provident when made. New York also provides that a husband and wife who occupy real property, or affirm that they are about to occupy real property as a home, shall each have the power, regardless of the minority of either or both, to enter into a contract for a loan or loans with a lending institution whose home office is in New York, or with an insurance company authorized to do business within the state, with respect to such real property. Each is also empowered to receive, hold, and dispose of such real property, and to make contracts, notes, deeds, mortgages, and other instruments necessary and appropriate to acquire such property, and to dispose of such real property. No such husband or wife shall have the power to disaffirm, because of such minority, any such act or transaction he is empowered to perform, nor shall any defense based on minority be interposed in any action arising out of such act or transaction.

83. Infant's Liability for Necessaries. A wholly executory contract for necessaries may be disaffirmed by an infant without liability. However, the infant must pay the reasonable value of necessaries supplied him. His liability is not on the contract, but is imposed by law on the theory of quasi-contract. If the reasonable value of necessaries furnished him is less than the contract price, he is liable only for that value. If it exceeds the contract price, he is liable for no more than the contract price.

84. What are Necessaries? What constitutes a necessary depends on the facts and circumstances of the particular case. Items such as food, shelter, clothing, and medical services are generally listed as necessaries since they are generally regarded as essential to life, but the term is not limited to such things. It includes all things indispensable to or suitable to the particular station in life of the infant. What is a necessary to one infant is not a necessary to another. It is generally held that an elementary school education is a necessary but that college or professional education is not. Some recent cases hold that a high school education is a necessary. The purchase of a bicycle, an automobile, or a horse, a correspondence course, theater tickets, and flying lessons have been held not to be necessaries. Medical services, dental services, and legal services rendered for the protection of the infant's person are necessaries.

In any event, where the infant resides with his parents and is properly maintained by them, he is not liable for even the necessaries of life. Further the infant cannot be held liable for necessaries unless there is a real need for them. Thus, ordinary clothing is a necessary, but an infant who has contracted for and has been supplied with twenty suits of clothing will be held liable for the reasonable value of only the number deemed necessary. Quantity is as important as the nature of the commodity in determining what is a necessary.

85. Misrepresentation as to Age. Most states, including New York, hold that an infant is not denied the right to disaffirm a contract merely because he fraudulently induced the adult to contract with him by false statements as to his age. It is usually said that to estop the infant from showing his infancy would be to deprive him of the protection the law affords, and to indirectly hold him liable on his contract. Indeed, even where action is brought against the infant for such fraud, most courts say that to permit the recovery would be to indirectly hold the infant liable on his contract, and this though an infant is generally liable for his torts. It should be noted, however, that the infant's fraud gives the other contracting party the right of rescission.

86. Ratification by Infant. One cannot ratify a contract while an infant. It is only as an adult that he may ratify any contract he made as an infant. In general, any words or conduct indicating his intent to affirm or recognize the contract as binding will constitute a ratification. The acceptance of the benefits of the contract, in whole or in part, or a resale of property received while he was an infant, or a failure to plead infancy when sued on the contract, constitutes a ratification.

Failure to disaffirm within a reasonable time after attaining the age of consent also constitutes a ratification. What constitutes a reasonable time is a question of fact to be determined according to the facts and circumstances of the particular case.

Ratification, like disaffirmance, must be of the entire contract. One cannot ratify that part of a contract which is advantageous to him and disaffirm the balance.

87. Emancipation of Infant. Emancipation of the infant results from the relinquishment of parental control and authority over the infant. Emancipation by reason of marriage, or the parents' failure to support him, or the parents' desertion does not affect the infant's liability on contracts made by him. In spite of emancipation, the infant's contracts remain voidable at his election. The effect of emancipation is the surrender by the parent of his right to the infant's income and services.

88. Insane Persons. It is quite well settled that a person is not insane unless his will and judgment are so affected that he cannot appreciate or understand the nature and effect of the particular contract or transaction. The mental impairment must be more than mere weakness of mind or lack of astuteness. A person must be unable to exercise his judgment and will with understanding.

It is, of course, true that a person may be insane in one respect but not in others. One may suffer a particular delusion or mania, yet fully appreciate the nature and effect of his contract. He is then not an insane person in respect of his contract. Further, a person who is insane may at times enjoy completely lucid intervals. His contracts made during such periods are valid and may not be avoided by him.

89. Insane Person's Contract Voidable. An insane person's contract is generally held voidable and not void, unless at the time he made the contract he was judicially declared insane, in which case his contract is void. Where voidable, the insane person may avoid on the ground that his assent was not a true or real assent. The fact that the contract was manifestly a fair one or that lunacy was not suspected does not affect his right. The person who has contracted with the lunatic has no right of avoidance.

It is usually held that a lunatic may disaffirm while insane, or within a reasonable time after regaining his reason. His personal representative, or his estate in the event of his death, may disaffirm for him.

Where his contract has been fully executed, or partially executed in that the lunatic has received performance from the other party, he is required, as a condition to disaffirmance, to restore to the other party the consideration received. Where, however, it was known that he was insane and the contract is manifestly an unfair one, the lunatic may disaffirm without returning what he received.

90. Insane Person's Liability for Necessaries. The lunatic's liability for necessaries furnished him, like that of the infant, is measured by the reasonable value of the goods. It is a quasi-contractual liability and not one based on the lunatic's contract. In general, it seems that whatever is a necessary in the case of an infant is a necessary in the case of the lunatic.

91. Ratification by Insane Person. A lunatic may ratify a contract during a lucid interval or by failing to disaffirm within a reasonable time after regaining his reason. As an infant may not be held to ratify during his infancy, so an insane person may not be held to ratify while he is insane. The rules for ratification by a lunatic are similar to those for an infant.

92. Drunken Persons. A contract made by a person who is in such a state of intoxication that he does not understand the nature of his undertaking or its consequences is voidable and not void.

The drunken person, like the infant and the lunatic, is liable for the reasonable value of necessaries furnished him. He has a reasonable time after becoming sober to determine whether he will disaffirm a contract made while drunk. If he fails to do so, he will be deemed to have ratified.

If he is judicially declared incompetent by reason of habitual drunkenness, his contracts made thereafter are void, not voidable.

In the event of disaffirmance of his contract for drunkenness at the time of its making, he is obligated to return the consideration received. If he has used, wasted, or spent the consideration received, he is denied the right to disaffirm unless it appears that the person who contracted with him took undue advantage.

93. Married Women. At common law, the married woman, or *femme covert*, lacked the capacity to contract or to acquire or dispose of property.

Property owned by her while single passed to her husband upon her marriage; debts owing to her before marriage passed to her husband, and he acquired the right to collect and keep the money paid him. Debts owed by her while she was single became the legal obligations of the husband upon marriage. In general, her contracts were absolutely void whether or not she and her husband were legally separated. However, a dissolution of the marriage or the husband's conviction of a felony, or his abandonment of his wife, terminated her disability to contract and she became a single woman, *femme sole*, with full contractual capacity.

Generally, by statutes in the various states, married women now have the same right to contract and hold and convey property that the husband has. The enactments differ, however, and some retain restrictions and qualifications on her capacity. For example, some provide that a married woman cannot contract with her husband or become surety for him.

94. Corporations. A corporation is a legal person which is created and exists by the law of the state. It is a legal entity separate and distinct from its officers, directors, and stockholders. It may contract debts, acquire rights or property, convey property, and sue or be sued in its own name.

Generally, the powers of a corporation are those listed in the certificate and all others incidental thereto, and those conferred upon it by statute. Where the corporation makes a contract falling outside its powers, the contract is deemed *ultra vires*, or beyond the power of the corporation. The Business Corporation Law of New York provides that "No act of a corporation and no transfer of real or personal property to or by a corporation, otherwise lawful, shall be invalid by reason of the fact that the corporation was without capacity or power to do such act or to make or receive such transfer . . ." [BCL Sec. 203(a)].

95. Spendthrifts. At common law, the spendthrift suffered no incapacity or disability to contract. This rule exists in most states today. However, where under statute a guardian is appointed for the spendthrift, he loses his capacity to contract.

96. Convicts. At common law, a person who was convicted of a felony was deemed civilly dead and was denied access to the courts to enforce any contracts made by him. However, he could be sued. Generally, this rule is not followed today. Many states now provide by statute that the rights of one convicted of a felony are suspended while he is confined in prison. He may make contracts, and while they are enforceable against him they are not enforceable by him while he is serving his term. His rights

are suspended but his creditors' rights are not. Some states, following a
New York statute, provide that he is deemed civilly dead if sentenced to
life imprisonment.

enemy alien

✓   **97. Aliens.** An alien is a person who resides in this country, but who
was born in another country and has not been naturalized under our law.
He is a subject of a foreign government and owes allegiance to it. If that
government is at war with the United States, the alien is an enemy alien;
if not, he is an alien friend. Generally, the capacity of aliens to contract
is regulated by statutes and treaties. The alien friend usually has the same
rights as a citizen, but some states provide that an alien may not acquire
real estate. The enemy alien may be sued on a contract, but he may not
enforce it during hostilities.

6. Statute of Frauds

98. In General. In 1677, the English Parliament passed a statute for the "Prevention of Frauds and Perjuries." In two sections of this act it was provided that certain oral promises were not enforceable unless evidenced by a signed writing. Thus, it constituted a limitation on the power to make enforceable contracts. The mutual assent necessary to create a binding contract, in the cases covered by the enactment, was required to appear in the form prescribed. Statutes patterned after the English Act are in force in virtually all of the states. Most of those in effect in New York require a subscription rather than a signature.

One of the purposes of the statute was to prevent the commission of perjury by testimony that an oral contract was made when in fact no promise was made at all. The requirement that certain types of contracts be evidenced by a signed writing undoubtedly achieves its purpose, but only to a limited extent. It does not prevent oral proof that the signed evidence of the contract was lost or destroyed, and does not prevent one from committing a fraud by forgery of the signature of another. Moreover, the provision enables one to repudiate his oral promise where in fact a contract exists, since a strict application of the statute requires the conclusion that mutual oral promises are within its scope and are not enforceable. The courts have recognized this, and many have attempted to interpret the statute to enforce oral contracts honestly made. However, this effort has to some extent resulted in a lack of uniformity in interpretation of the various provisions of the statute.

99. Oral Promise of Executor or Administrator. It is generally provided by statute that no action shall be brought to charge an administrator or executor upon a special promise to answer damages out of his own estate. The promises included within this provision are those that answer for the debt or default of the decedent or of his estate arising at his death.

49

Such promise by an executor or administrator to pay out of his own assets is within the statute and, if oral, is unenforceable. If the oral promise is one to pay a debt which was not owing by the decedent or his estate, it is not within the statute, and it is enforceable unless it be within some other statutory provision requiring a writing.

The oral promise by the executor or administrator to pay the debt of the decedent or his estate is generally regarded to be a promise to answer for the debt or default of another, and in determining whether the promise is within the provision above the same rules are applied as in the case of a surety or guarantor. (See § 103.) Thus, if the promise is made to serve the interest of the executor or administrator, the promise may be valid though oral.

100. Promises to Answer for Debt or Default of Another. A special promise to answer for the debt, default, or miscarriage of another person is unenforceable unless it or some note or memorandum thereof be in writing and signed by the party to be charged therewith or his lawfully authorized agent. By "special" promise is meant an express promise resulting from words or acts, and not a promise implied by law where no actual assent appears. The words "debt, default, or miscarriage" apply to the legal obligation to pay or to perform, whether it be contractual or non-contractual. They include promises to pay debts as yet unmatured and to pay damages that may be caused by a future breach of contract. The duty to pay or perform may come into existence before the promise is made, at the time it is made, or after it is made. In any event, the promise must be made to a person who is a creditor at the time of the promise or who becomes a creditor after the promise is made. If the promise is made to a debtor to pay his debt to a creditor, it is not within the statute, and it is enforceable, though oral, by the debtor, or by the creditor as a creditor beneficiary. Thus, an oral promise by A to B that A will pay B's debt to C is not within the statute. A's promise is enforceable at the suit of B or C as an absolute undertaking and not a secondary promise.

The form of the promise made does not in itself determine whether the statute applies. The true test is whether the debtor is or becomes indebted to the creditor and whether the promisor has, for the benefit of the debtor, promised the creditor to pay that debt. Accordingly, if X requests C to sell goods to D on the credit of D, and promises C that "I will pay if D does not pay," or that "I will pay the bill," or that "I will see you paid," X's promise, if oral, is within the statute and is unenforceable.

101. Debts of Another: Performance of Promise Must Discharge Debt. A promise to answer for the debt of another is a promise the performance of which will discharge in whole or in part the debt of another. A promise to pay a creditor $10 if he will forbear suit for $100 against the debtor for 30 days is valid though oral. Payment of $10 does not reduce the $100 claim. Further, an oral promise by X that he will pay to C the debt of D if C releases or discharges D's debt, is enforceable. If C accepts X's offer by discharging D, there is a substitution of debtors with the consent of the creditor. Performance by X of his promise does not discharge D's debt since it has already been discharged by C. This transaction is called a novation, and it does not come within the statute.

102. Debts of Another: Promise to Indemnify. The statute is aimed at promises made to a creditor to answer for the debt or default of a debtor. Where X orally promises C that if C will sell goods to B on credit X will indemnify C against loss, X's promise is unenforceable. X's promise is one to pay B's debt to C. But where X orally promises that if B purchases ten shares of stock of the Y Corporation X will indemnify him against loss, X's promise is enforceable. B is not a creditor; there is no person who owes him a legal duty or obligation. Thus, contracts of indemnity are within or not within the statute according to whether the promise to indemnify or "save harmless" is made to a creditor.

103. Debts of Another: Main-Purpose Rule. We have seen that an oral promise made to a creditor for the benefit of a debtor to answer for his debt is unenforceable. It has been held that where the oral promise is made to serve the promisor's own interest rather than to benefit the debtor, it is enforceable. Where the promise is made for the benefit of the debtor, it is within the statute and the promise is called collateral. Where it is made to benefit the promisor it is valid though oral, not within the statute, and it is called original.

Of course, the mere fact that there is a consideration moving to the promisor in exchange for his promise is not enough to say that the promise was made to serve his own interest or for his own benefit. His promise, whatever its nature, needs a consideration to support it or it will be deemed unenforceable in spite of the statute. The question is whether the consideration is such that the promisor's main purpose was to benefit himself rather than to answer for the debt of another. The main purpose of the promise is not found in the promise itself or in its performance. It must be found in the consideration for the promise. Where one purchases real estate subject to a mortgage which he does not assume to pay, but later orally promises the holder of the mortgage to pay the mortgage debt if the holder will forbear foreclosure proceedings, does he make his promise to benefit the mortgagor or to protect his own equity of redemption? While the promise itself appears to be one to answer for the debt of the mortgagor, and while the performance of the promise will undoubtedly benefit the mortgagor, it would appear that the main purpose of the promise is to protect his equity of redemption and not to answer for the mortgagor's debt. The consideration for his promise, forbearance by the promisee, benefits the promisor. Accordingly, his oral promise is deemed original, not within the statute, and not collateral.

The main-purpose rule has had frequent application in building contract cases. For example, *D*, a contractor, is under contract to erect a dwelling for *X*. *D* enters into a contract with *C* to purchase from *C* all the lumber needed for the project. The lumber is to be delivered in installments, each installment to be separately paid for. Several installments are delivered but *D* has not paid for them and *C* withholds further deliveries. *X* orally promises that if *C* will make further deliveries to *D*, *X* will pay if *D* does not. *C* makes further deliveries and *D* does not pay. *X*'s promise is enforceable though oral. His promise is made to get the building completed. That is his main purpose.

104. Debts of Another: Del Credere Agent, Assignor. A *del credere* agent, usually a broker, is an agent who guarantees to his principal for an additional consideration that third persons will perform their obligations to the principal. If the agent is selling goods on behalf of the principal, the undertaking is a guaranty of payment by a third party. The oral promise of such agent is not within the statute. It is said that he makes the promise for his own benefit, such promise enabling him to get more business and make larger profits. Further, he is a stranger to the purchasers with whom he may deal and has no right to be reimbursed by them for any amount he may be required to pay his principal. He is in effect an insurer against loss. He does not make his oral promise for the benefit of the third persons, but for his own benefit, and it is enforceable against him.

Where one who holds a claim assigns the same and orally guarantees to the assignee that the claim will be paid, it is held that the assignor, like the *del credere* agent, is an insurer, and his guaranty is not a promise to answer for the debt of another, though it appears to be. This result is reached on the theory that he makes such guaranty to get a larger price for the assignment, to serve his own interest, and not to benefit the debtor. Accordingly, the oral guaranty is enforceable.

105. Contracts for the Sale of Real Property. State statutes patterned after the English statute generally provide that a contract for the leasing for a period longer than one year, or for the sale of any real property, or an interest therein, is void unless the contract, or some note or memorandum thereof expressing the consideration, is in writing *subscribed* by the party to be charged or by his lawfully authorized agent. At least half the states have included a provision, similar to that in New York, that where an agent is to execute the contract, note, or memorandum, his authority must be evidenced by a subscribed writing.

An agreement to execute and deliver a mortgage on real estate is an agreement to convey an interest in land and is within the statute. If oral, it is unenforceable. An easement so affects the use and enjoyment of land that it is held to constitute an interest in land. Thus, a contract to create an easement is within the statute and must be evidenced by a writing. On the other hand, a license, which is a revocable permission to use land, has been held to be such a slight interest that it does not come within the statute.

106. Sale of Real Property: Part Performance. An oral contract for the sale of land or an interest therein may become enforceable if there is part performance by one party. It is clear that, if the seller has performed and conveyed the land or an interest therein, the purchaser should be required to pay the price in equity by a decree of specific performance.

There are many cases where the purchaser makes part performance before any notice of repudiation by the seller and is granted specific performance. But it is required that the part performance be made pursuant to the contract and in reliance on it, and that it evidence the existence of a contract. Performance which can be explained on some ground other than the existence of a contract is not sufficient. It must be shown that the performance would not have taken place if there were no contract. However, this is not to say that the part performance must have been pursuant to the duty of him who seeks to enforce the contract. One who takes possession of the property and makes substantial improvements thereon is entitled to specific performance not because he was under a duty to do so but because he has shown reliance on the contract.

The rule of part performance is a flexible device to prevent the statute from working an injustice. Many courts have said that where there has been a sufficient part performance by one party, to allow the other to plead the statute and escape his duties would be to permit him to commit a fraud. However, the courts of a few southern states have consistently refused to recognize the rule, and they have flatly denied specific performance of such oral contracts.

107. Payment of Price by Purchaser as Part Performance. Payment of the price or a part thereof is performance or part performance by the purchaser of his contract, but it is not sufficient to entitle the purchaser to a decree of specific performance. Generally, the courts will not disregard the provisions of the statute if it appears that the purchaser can be restored to his original position by restitution of the price paid.

108. Possession and Improvements as Part Performance. In almost every state, specific performance of an oral contract to sell real property will be decreed if the purchaser takes possession relying on the contract and makes substantial permanent improvements to the property. In most cases of this kind, the making of the improvements is the court's basic reason for relief.

In the case of the oral promise to make a gift of real estate, there is a lack of consideration as well as a failure to comply with the requirements of a writing. But if the promisee takes possession of the real estate and makes thereon permanent and substantial improvements in reliance on the promise, the promise becomes enforceable. The promisee's substantial change of position in reliance on the promise, while not a technical consideration because not bargained for, renders the promise enforceable. Specific performance of the promise will be decreed because of the possession taken and improvements made.

109. Leases of Real Property. Statutes in the various states provide that a lease of real estate must be evidenced by a writing signed by the party to be charged therewith if the term of the lease exceeds a certain period. Most states, including New York, fix the period at one year, but others prescribe a period of three years. The rule of part performance described above applies also to oral leases of real estate.

110. Contracts Not to Be Performed Within One Year. A contract that is not to be fully performed within one year from the making thereof is unenforceable unless there be some note or memorandum of the contract in writing and signed by the party sought to be charged thereon. This provision has been adopted in almost all of the states.

It seems under the interpretation generally given the language of this statute that if there is any possibility that a contract can be fully performed within one year of its making, it is enforceable though oral. It does not matter how long performance actually takes, or how long the parties expect performance will take. Thus, if a contract provides that performance must be completed *within* three years, it is not within the statute; it is possible that complete performance can be rendered within one year. The fact that performance of such contract actually takes two years or more does not bring it within the statute. A promise to perform when a certain ship sails, or when it returns to port, or to pay when certain goods are sold, is not within the statute since the event upon which performance is conditioned may take place within one year. A promise to perform for the life of a specified person, or to support a person for his life, contemplates a continued performance for an uncertain period of time, but it is not within this statute since death may occur within one year. The fact that performance has continued for more than one year does not render the contract unenforceable. It should be noted, however, that where provision exists, as it does in New York, requiring contracts not fully performable before the end of a lifetime to be evidenced by a writing, an oral agreement to hire one for life is rendered unenforceable.

A promise to employ a person for two years is within the statute even though either employer or employee may die within one year. Upon the death of either party the duty to further perform is discharged by operation of law but the letter of the contract has not been fully performed. In this respect it differs from a promise to employ one for his life.

A contract to employ a person for one year, the employment to begin at a future date, is within the statute. Full performance cannot be rendered within one year from the date the contract is made. But if employment is to begin on the day following that on which the contract is made, it is generally held that the statute does not apply since employment will terminate one year after the contract is made.

111. Performance Within Year: Bilateral and Unilateral Contracts. Not infrequently, a contract will provide for a performance by one party within one year and a counter-performance extending beyond one year. If neither performance has been rendered, the contract is within the statute and must be evidenced by a writing. The Restatement, Contracts, provides that where in a bilateral contract a promise has been fully performed on one side, the contract is withdrawn from the statute and is enforceable though oral. It also provides that where the contract is unilateral and the act is performed in full in exchange for a promise to perform for more than one year, the promise is enforceable though oral. The majority of the reported cases are in accord with the Restatement in both classes of cases.

112. Contracts in Consideration of Marriage. The statute provides that no action shall be brought to charge any person upon any agreement made upon consideration of marriage unless a note or memorandum of the agreement is signed by the party to be charged. This provision applies to bilateral and unilateral agreements the consideration for which is marriage or a promise to marry, but it does not apply to mutual promises to marry. Many states which have enacted this provision expressly exclude from its coverage mutual promises to marry. It is generally held that the statute covers contracts for a settlement in consideration of marriage or of a promise to marry. It applies to B's promise to marry A if A will pay B $1,000 or if A will promise to pay B $1,000; to a promise by A to settle certain property upon B upon B's marriage to A; to a promise by C to pay an annuity to B in consideration of B's marriage to A; and to a promise by B to release a debt owing by A upon A's marriage to B or upon A's promise to marry B.

It is generally held under this statute that the promise given in exchange for the marriage or for the promise to marry remains within the statute even if the marriage is performed.

113. Contracts for the Sale of Goods. The UCC in Sec. 2-201(1) provides that a contract for the sale of goods for a price of $500 or more is not enforceable unless there is some writing which sufficiently indicates that the parties have made such contract and the writing is signed by the party against whom enforcement is sought, or his agent or broker.

Under this subdivision, a writing may be deemed sufficient to indicate a contract has been made even though it omits or incorrectly states a term agreed upon. The writing must name the parties but need not state which is the seller and which is the buyer. It may omit the price, the time and place of delivery, and the time and place of payment. If the writing otherwise indicates a contract for sale has been made, these items may be shown by oral evidence of the contract. The writing must, however, state a quantity of goods, and the contract is not enforceable beyond the quantity stated even if inaccurately stated. Thus, the requirements of the writing are that it must (a) indicate that contract has been made, (b) name the parties to the contract, (c) be signed, and (d) state a quantity of goods.

In the case of a sale at auction, the memorandum made by the auctioneer, usually in his sales book, of the nature of the goods sold, the identity of the seller and the buyer, the price, and the terms of the sale is held sufficient, the auctioneer acting for this purpose as agent of both parties.

114. Contracts for the Sale of Goods; The Signature. A signature may consist of any symbol executed or adopted by a party with intention to authenticate the writing. A printed, stamped or written name, initials, a thumbprint, etc., is a signature if it is affixed or adopted with intention to authenticate the writing.

115. Contracts for the Sale of Goods: Between Merchants. UCC Sec. 2-201(2) provides that where the seller and the buyer are merchants and one of them sends to the other a confirmation of the oral contract sufficient to bind the sender, the other who receives it and has reason to know its contents is bound by it unless he gives written notice of objection to its contents within ten days after it is received.

The confirmation is sufficient against the sender if he has signed it, if it names the parties to the oral contract, if it sufficiently indicates that a contract has been made, and if it states a quantity of goods. Note that the receiver of the confirmation may be bound by it although he has not signed it.

116. Contracts for the Sale of Goods: Admissions, Payment, Receipt. If the oral contract is not evidenced by a signed writing, whether or not the parties are merchants, and a party should admit in court by his pleadings or by his testimony or otherwise, that a contract for the sale of goods has been made, the contract will be enforced against him to the extent of the quantity of goods he admits.

Where the buyer makes full payment for the goods by cash or check and the payment is accepted by the seller, or where the seller makes full delivery and the buyer accepts the goods, the requirement of a writing is dispensed with, and whether or not they are merchants, the oral contract is enforceable against both. Where, however, the payment is partial and is accepted by the seller, or where the delivery is partial and is accepted by the buyer, the contract may be enforceable against both but only to the extent of the goods paid for or received and accepted. Thus, if the contract is for 1,000 units of a commodity for $1,000 and the buyer pays and the seller accepts $500, the oral contract is enforceable against both to the extent of 500 units. Where the buyer has paid $500 he is entitled to a delivery of 500 units, and where the seller has delivered 500 units he is entitled to $500 notwithstanding the absence of a writing. Where a fair and just apportionment cannot be made, the oral contract must remain unenforceable against both parties. If the oral contract is for the sale of a desk for $500 and the buyer has paid and the seller accepted $250, the contract is not enforceable and the buyer is entitled to a return of his money.

117. Contracts for the Sale of Goods: Specially Manufactured. Although there is no writing, no payment, no delivery, and although the parties may or may not be merchants, if the goods to be sold under the oral contract are to be specially manufactured for the buyer and are not suitable for sale to others in the ordinary course of the seller's business, and the seller, before the buyer has repudiated the contract, has made a substantial beginning of their manufacture or commitments for their procurement, the contract is enforceable against both parties [UCC Sec. 2-201(3)(a)].

118. Contracts for the Sale of Goods: What Are Goods? "Goods" means all things movable other than investment securities and things in action. The term includes money when it is treated as a commodity rather than a medium of payment. Things attached to or part of real property are goods if under the contract they are to be severed by the seller. Thus, timber, minerals, or even a building may be goods. Growing crops are also goods if they are to be severed by the seller or by the buyer.

119. Other Statutory Provisions. In a few states, including New York, statutes exist which provide in substance that an agreement not performable during the life of, or before the end of the lifetime of, the promisor, must be evidenced by a writing signed by the party to be charged. The New York statute provides that a contract not performable before the end of a lifetime is unenforceable unless in writing subscribed by the party to be charged.

The UCC provides in Sec. 1-206 that a contract for the sale of personal property beyond $5,000 in amount is not enforceable unless there is a writing which indicates that a contract for sale has been made at a defined or stated price, which reasonably identifies the subject matter, and which is signed by the party against whom enforcement is sought or by his authorized agent. This provision does not apply to contracts for the sale of goods or securities, nor to security agreements. It applies to the sale of accounts, contract rights, deposits or accounts maintained with banks, royalty rights, and transfers of interests or claims in and under policies of insurance.

In some states, it is provided that an agreement to make a will or to give a legacy or devise must be in writing. In New York, it is provided that a contract to bequeath property or to make a testamentary disposition of any kind must be evidenced by a writing subscribed by the party to be charged therewith or by his lawful agent.

Provisions exist which require agreements to arbitrate disputes to be manifested by a writing. The New York statute states that a written agreement to submit any controversy thereafter arising or an existing controversy to arbitration is enforceable without regard to the justiciable character of the controversy and confers jurisdiction on the courts of the state to enforce it and to enter judgment on an award.

120. Party to Be Charged. Where any provision of the Statute of

Frauds requires that a note or memorandum must be signed by the party to be charged, it need be signed only by the party against whom the agreement is sought to be enforced. It is not necessary that both parties sign. However, since it cannot be determined in advance, except in the case of a unilateral contract, who will be the party to be charged, each should require the signature of the other.

A signature may appear in the form of initials. It may appear anywhere on the document, in handwriting, print, or typewriting, as long as it was made to indicate that the writing was intended to be a note or memorandum of the contract. Of course, where it has been printed or stamped before the note or memorandum was made, parol evidence is admissible to show that it was intended to constitute a signature to a note or memorandum.

Where a statute requires a subscription rather than a signature, as do most provisions in New York, the document must be subscribed at the end of the writing.

121. Effect of Statute of Frauds. A contract which does not satisfy the statutory requirements of form is unenforceable and not void or voidable, and this notwithstanding that the particular provision may assert that it is void. In an action to enforce an oral agreement, or a written agreement or note or memorandum unsigned by the defendant, the failure by the defendant to plead as a defense the statutory requirement, will result in the enforcement of the contract against him. In this respect it is often said that the Statute of Frauds is an affirmative defense.

122. Effect of Statute: Restitution. Where a party seeks to repudiate a contract on the ground that the statutory provisions have not been complied with, after he has received the benefit of performance by the other party, he will be required to account for the benefits received. If the benefit is in form of money, he will be required to repay; if in the form of land, he will be required to pay for it or ordered to reconvey it; if in the form of services or goods, he must account for the value in money. Where an oral contract has been fully performed, neither party can plead the statute in an effort to recover what he has parted with.

123. Effect of Statute: Modifications. It is often inaccurately said that a written contract complying with the statutory requirements cannot be modified by an oral agreement. The modification of an agreement is itself a new agreement substituted for the old, and it results in a discharge of the former agreement. Thus, if the modification when made is not within any of the statutory provisions, it is enforceable though oral. If the modification is itself within the statute, it is unenforceable, and the original agreement remains in force and effect.

124. Effect of Statute: Divisible Contracts. A party to a contract may make two or more promises. If one or more promises is required to be evidenced by a writing and the others not, the question arises whether all promises are unenforceable. Generally, the question is resolved by determining whether the promises are divisible. If a promise not within the statute has its own separate consideration, it may be enforced, although the remaining promises are within the statute. If the contract is not so divisible, no one of them is enforceable unless all satisfy the statute.

125. Effect of Statute: Security. If security in any form is given for the performance of a contract unenforceable under the Statute of Frauds, the security may be enforced as though the contract complied with the statute.

126. Effect of Statute: Application of Payments. If a debtor owes more than one debt to a creditor and one of the debts is unenforceable against him because it arises out of a contract which fails to comply with the Statute of Frauds, and he makes a payment without a direction about application of the payment, the creditor may apply the payment to the unenforceable debt.

7. Consideration

127. In General. The mere fact that one person makes an oral or written promise to another does not alone create a legal duty to perform the promise. To make the promise enforceable there must be something to make the promise binding on the promisor, and that something has for many years been called consideration. Many different kinds of things have been held to constitute a sufficient consideration to make a promise binding, and there is no single rule or definition which will teach us all of the things which have or will have that effect. The Restatement, Contracts, tells us that consideration is something that is requested and given in exchange for a promise, something that is bargained for, but it recognizes that the courts have often found consideration to lie in things which are not requested or bargained for. On the other hand, not everything which is requested or bargained for constitutes a sufficient consideration. But if the statement that consideration is something that is bargained for is generally sound, it follows that consideration must be something that is regarded as such by both parties.

A study of consideration involves a study of the things the courts have found sufficient to justify the enforcement of a promise.

128. Contracts Under Seal. In the early common law, the contract under seal was the only one the courts recognized as binding. The fact that the seal made the instrument a formal document, and that it indicated deliberation and solemnity, appealed to the courts. The requirement of consideration did not exist. Today, however, by statute in most states including New York, the seal has virtually lost its significance and the substance of the agreement is more important than its form. It is now generally recognized that consideration is necessary to make a contract binding.

129. Benefit to the Promisor. Many promises have been held to be enforceable on the ground that the promisor received something in ex-change for the promise which was beneficial to him. In most cases, it appeared that what the promisor received in exchange for his promise was an economic benefit to him. But there are many cases in which the promisor receives nothing of economic value, yet it is held that the promise is enforceable. Thus, where A promises B that A will pay B if B will render or promise to render a service to C, A receives nothing of benefit. His desire is merely to make a gift to C, yet his promise is enforceable if B renders the service or promises to render it. This has, of course, been recognized, and it is often said that there can be no consideration for a promise unless there is some benefit to the promisor or some detriment to the promisee.

Damages or loss

130. Detriment to the Promisee. We have seen that benefit in the sense of economic advantage to the promisor has been held to constitute sufficient consideration for the promise, but that the lack of some economic benefit to the promisor does not necessarily mean that consideration is wanting. If detriment to the promisee is used in the sense of economic loss or disadvantage to the promisee, it is an insufficient test, for there are many cases in which the promisee suffers no such loss or disadvantage and yet may enforce the promise. The Restatement, Contract, takes the position that gain or advantage to the promisor or loss or disadvantage to the promisee do not affect the sufficiency of consideration. Thus, if A promises to pay B a sum of money in return for a delivery to A of a promissory note which is not enforceable against A, A's promise is enforceable. In surrendering an unenforceable note, B suffers no economic loss. Accordingly, many courts have held that the detriment to the promisee need not consist of economic loss, but that if it consists of a *legal* detriment to the promisee it is a sufficient consideration to support a promise. They have held that the promisee suffers a legal detriment if, in exchange for the promise and at the request of the promisor, he does what he was not legally obligated to do, or promises to do what he is not obligated to do, or refrains from doing what he has a legal right to do, or promises to refrain from doing what he has a legal right to do. Of course, in suffering one or more of these legal detriments, the promisee may also suffer economic loss or disadvantage, yet it is the legal detriment suffered at the instance and request of the promisor, and in exchange for the promise, which determines the enforceability of the promise.

EXAMPLES

1. A says to B, "If you climb to the top of that flagpole, I will pay you

five dollars." B climbs to the top of the flagpole. B suffered a legal detriment in doing something he was not bound to do. There is consideration for A's promise.

2. S says to B, "I promise to deliver to you my white horse, Domino, if you promise to pay me two hundred dollars." B promises to pay $200. There is a consideration for S's promise. B, in promising to do something he was not bound to do, suffered a legal detriment.

3. A promised to pay B a sum of money if B would refrain from smoking for a definite period of time. B refrained. There was a valid consideration for A's promise. B refrained from doing something that he had a legal right to do and thereby suffered a legal detriment.

4. A says to B, "If you promise not to climb the flagpole today, I will pay you five dollars." B promises. B suffered a legal detriment in promising not to do something he had a legal right to do, and gave a consideration.

Note that in each example the promisee suffered a legal detriment by surrendering or giving up a legal right at the request of the promisor and in exchange for the promise. A detriment suffered voluntarily by the promisee—that is, not at the request of the promisor—is not a legal detriment and hence not a sufficient consideration.

131. Promise for a Promise. In a bilateral contract, each promise may be a consideration for the return promise. The offeror makes his promise in his offer and calls for an acceptance in the form of a return promise. Thus, while the promises are not made simultaneously, they become effective simultaneously. If each promise is one to do something that the promisor is not already bound to do, or to refrain from doing something that the promisor has a right to do, each promisor will suffer a legal detriment and furnishes consideration for the other's promise. One promise will not be a consideration for the other unless the performance of the promise would be a consideration. This must be so since the thing that each is bargaining for is the actual performance of the promise and not only its making.

If the return promise is not in express words but may be implied from words used or from conduct, it is a consideration, provided, of course, that it is in accordance with the terms of the offer made. On the other hand, an illusory promise is not a promise at all, and it is not a sufficient consideration. If an offeree uses words which do not constitute a promise, and the offeror thinks a promise has been made, the offeree's words are mere illusion. If A makes an offer calling for a promise by B to perform in the future, and B says, "I'll perform if, when the time comes, I am inclined to do so," there is no present promise to perform in the future.

If one of the promises in a bilateral contract is conditional, it is a consideration, even if the condition may never happen. Such a promise, usually called an aleatory promise, depends on chance, but it is not necessarily a wagering contract condemned by law. Insurance contracts are a prime example.

EXAMPLES

1. *A* has purchased a quantity of railroad ties. Suspecting that the quantity is less than was represented, he enters into an agreement with *B*, the seller, by which *B* agrees to return $1 for each tie under the contract amount, and *A* agrees to pay $1 for each tie in excess. Only one party will have to pay, but each promise is consideration for the other.

2. *A* is engaged in a business venture. To minimize the risk of loss, he promises to pay *B* one-half of his profits if *B* promises to pay *A* one-half of *A*'s losses. Each promise is supported by a sufficient consideration.

Where a promise is conditional upon an event that cannot take place, the promise is illusory; it does not exist.

132. Promise for an Act or a Forbearance. Where a promise is made in exchange for an act or a forbearance, the act or forbearance is the acceptance. Thus, the promise becomes effective upon acceptance, but only the promisor is now to perform. The contract is a valid unilateral contract. The act or forbearance, if something the offeree was not bound to do, is a sufficient consideration to make the promise binding. If, however, what is requested in exchange for the promise is a promise to act or to forbear, and such return promise is made, the contract is bilateral.

There are many classes of cases in which the promisor requests a forbearance in exchange for his promise. The request may be that the promisee forbear the exercise of a privilege or a power, or refrain from bringing suit or from pressing a claim.

EXAMPLES

1. *T* is a tenant under a lease providing that the tenant may terminate the lease upon 30 days' notice. *L*, the landlord, hears that the tenant intends to exercise his power to cancel the lease. *L* offers to reduce the rental by a certain amount if *T* will forbear cancelling the lease for the balance of the term. *T* forbears as requested. The contract is valid. *T*'s forbearance is a sufficient consideration for *L*'s promise to reduce the rental. *T* did not merely do what he was already bound to do; he refrained from exercising a power given him by the terms of the lease.

2. *S* offers to sell his white horse, Domino, to *B* for $200. *B*, of course, has the power to accept. If *C* promises *B* to pay *B* $20 if *B* will refrain from

accepting S's offer, and B does refrain, there is a valid contract between C and B.

3. A promises that he will convey a specified parcel of real estate to B if B will forbear bringing suit against A on a certain claim. If B forbears, there is a sufficient consideration for A's promise. The result is the same whether B's claim was a valid one or whether it was based on some doubtful, colorable, or plausible ground, since in either case B has the right to sue and when he forbears suit he suffers a legal detriment. Some difficulty is encountered, however, when the claim has no basis in law or equity. If it is known to the promisee that the claim held is void or has no basis, his forbearance is not a consideration for the promise. But the promisee may act in entire good faith believing he has a valid claim when in law he has no claim. Many cases have held that so long as he acted in good faith whether or not his claim had any basis, he may enforce the promise. It is not necessary that the promisee show that if he had brought suit he would have succeeded in enforcing the claim. Most courts, including those in New York, have held, however, that if the claim was not even doubtful or plausible, there can be no basis for an honest belief that it is valid, and forbearance to sue or press the claim is not a sufficient consideration for the promise.

A promisor may request a promise to forbear in exchange for his promise, but actually receive forbearance. It is usually held in such case that the thing bargained for is the promise to forbear and not actual forbearance, and the promisor is not bound for lack of consideration.

133. Adequacy of the Consideration. We have seen that a consideration must be bargained for and given in exchange for the promise. If it is a consideration, it does not matter that it has no economic value or that it is worth less than the promise made. Once the courts have found that a consideration exists, they do not concern themselves with its relative value. The promisor must determine what he will receive in exchange for his promise, and if he bargains for something with little or no value compared to the value of his promise, he has no complaint.

The proposition that the courts will not look into the adequacy of the consideration is not applicable, however, to the case of mutual promises made to pay or exchange sums of money. Thus, if A promises to pay to B $5 and B promises to pay A $50, the contract is unconscionable and void. If, however, a bargain is made for an old and unique coin the value of which is not exactly fixed, a contract to pay for the coin a sum of money is excess of its face value is valid.

134. Performance of a Preexisting Duty. Whether the promisor requests in exchange for his promise a promise to perform, the performance of an act, or a forbearance, the promisee in return for the promise must not be doing anything he is already legally obliged to do. If he promises to perform an act or performs an act which he is under a preexisting legal duty to perform, or if he forbears performance of an act which he was legally obliged not to perform, he gives no consideration for the promise. The preexisting legal duty may be one owed by the promisee to the promisor under a previous contract, or it may be a duty owing by the promisee to a third party under a previous contract with him, or it may be a duty imposed on him by law. Where the preexisting duty is owing to the promisor, it is generally held that there is no consideration. Thus, if A employs B for a two-year term at a stipulated wage, and in order to prevent B from leaving his employ at the end of one year A promises to pay additional compensation, B cannot recover the additional compensation. By remaining in A's employ for the second year, B was only performing a preexisting duty under the original employment contract.

If we suppose that C makes a promise of compensation if B remains in A's employ for the second year, the result is not so clear. B's preexisting duty is to A and not to C, the promisor. Most of the cases have held that C's promise has no consideration to support it, since B is only doing in in exchange for C's promise what he was already obligated to do under his contract with A; but the Restatement, Contracts, takes the position that C's promise is enforceable, and some cases seem to support that position. They say that C is getting what he has bargained for—something owed not to him but to a third person.

A public officer who performs his duty in exchange for a promise does not furnish a consideration. However, where the performance the public officer renders goes in some respect beyond his official duties, he furnishes consideration.

In some cases involving construction contracts it has been said that the contractor has the alternative of either performing his contract or paying damages, and that if in exchange for a promise of additional compensation he elects to perform, the promise is binding. This is on the theory that the contractor furnishes consideration for the promise when he elects not to pay damages. Obviously, this is unsound. The contractor does not have a legal right or a lawful option to perform or pay damages. But in the case of the true option there is a sufficient consideration. Thus, if under his contract the contractor had the option to install wooden window sash or metal window sash, and in exchange for a promise to pay extra compensation he installs metal window sash, the promise is enforceable. Forbearance of the privilege to perform one way or the other is a sufficient consideration.

135. Preexisting Duty: Unforeseen Difficulty and Expense. Often a party to a contract, due to unforeseen difficulty or expense, or both, finds that continued performance will result in serious loss, and thereupon ceases performance. It is held in most cases that if he resumes or continues performance in exchange for a promise of additional compensation he does only what he was obligated to do initially, and the promise lacks consideration to support it. It is thought that to hold otherwise would encourage the contractor to assert unforeseen difficulty and expense. However, a few cases have enforced the promise where it was clear from the evidence that the promisor willingly promised additional compensation and the contractor acted honestly in that the difficulties and additional expenses were unforeseen and substantial. A few others have enforced the new promise on the ground that it resulted in a mutual rescission of the former contract. The latter view seems untenable. The new promise only proposes to change a single item in the original contract, not to substitute a new agreement for the old.

At common law, a modification of a contract was not enforceable unless supported by consideration and unless it complied with the Statute of Frauds. In New York, it is provided by statute that a modification of a contract or obligation is enforceable notwithstanding the lack of consideration if it is in writing and signed by the party to be charged. Under this statute, if the promise of additional compensation is in writing signed by the promisor, it is enforceable against him although there is no consideration to support it.

The UCC provides in Sec. 2-209 that an agreement modifying a contract for the sale of goods needs no consideration to be binding. This provision does not require the modification to be in writing, but if not in writing it may be unenforceable under the Statute of Frauds.

136. Past Consideration. We have seen that to furnish a consideration the promisee must suffer a legal detriment at the request of the promisor and in exchange for the promise. The promise must induce the promisee to act or to forbear. Often, however, a promise is made because the promisee has acted or has forborne action. In such cases, it is clear that the action taken or forborne is not bargained for by the promisor, and this has led to the frequent statement that past consideration is no consideration. In cases of past consideration, a promise is made because of some action previously taken by the promisee and not for the purpose of inducing some action. But in some cases, among which are the following, the courts have enforced the promise on the ground that the past consideration is so related to the promise that it may be said it, to some extent, induced the promise.

Statute of Limitations. Where A becomes indebted to B in 1952 and makes a new promise in 1956 to pay it, the new promise may be enforced by *B* in 1960, assuming that by statute a six-year limitation period is provided. The new promise is effective to give to the creditor a remedy he would not otherwise have had in 1960. The promise in 1956 causes the statute to commence running anew in 1956. Note that the creditor may enforce the debt even if the new promise is made in 1959, at a time when the original debt was already barred by the statute. The courts say that the past debt is a sufficient consideration for the new promise, thus indicating that, while the statute bars the remedy, the debt still has some legal effect. Where the debt has already been barred by the Statute of Limitations, the debtor need not pay it, and should he promise to do so he may limit the amount he will pay or make his promise conditional. Thus, if his debt is for $500 he may promise "to pay $250 and no more," or promise to pay $100 when he "sells his business," and the creditor's right will be limited to the terms of the promise. Where the debtor's promise is conditional, the statute commences to run against it as of the time the condition is fulfilled.

Discharge in bankruptcy. Another illustration of an enforceable promise based on a past consideration is the promise to pay a debt already barred by a discharge in bankruptcy. However, in many states the new promise must be in writing. In New York, the writing must set forth an express promise. Thus, no promise which may be implied from the part payment of interest or principal would be sufficient in that state.

Indorser, surety, infant, principal, victim of fraud. An indorser or surety who has been discharged by the creditor's failure to give notice of the default of the party primarily liable, or by an extension agreement, is held liable on a new promise to perform at least in cases where he suffered no real injury. One who, upon reaching the age of consent, makes a new promise to perform a contract made while an infant is liable without a new consideration having been given for such promise. The victim of a fraud who ratifies his contract by a promise to perform it after the discovery of the fraud is liable on his promise. A principal who ratifies the unauthorized contract of his agent by a promise to perform is liable on his promise.

In some of the situations mentioned above, a few courts state that the new promise is based on a previous moral obligation of the promisor, while others say that the consideration for the original transaction is a sufficient consideration for the new promise. However, whatever reasoning is used, it is clear that there is no new consideration for the new promise, and these cases are situations in which a new promise is enforced because of some past relationship between the parties.

137. Past Consideration: Past Performance. *A* requests that *B* perform an act. *B* performs the act expecting to be compensated for it, and *A* has knowledge of that expectation. The law implies a promise by *A* to pay for the performance. If *A* later makes a promise to pay *B*, he is promising to pay a debt which already exists. Of course, *A* is liable. However, some cases have held that *A* is liable on his new promise even where he had no knowledge that *B* expected to be paid for his performance. His liability is based on the fact that he requested the past performnace and that the past performance supports his new promise. Where the past performance was never requested, there is no basis at all for holding that a new promise to pay is enforceable, and the rule that past consideration is no consideration applies.

In cases where the consideration for a promise is partly past and partly future, no problem exists. Thus, if *A* states to *B*, "You have dug a well worth three hundred dollars on my property. If you will fence in my property I will pay you five hundred dollars for the well and for the fencing," *A*'s promise is enforceable if *B* fences in the property. The future consideration is sufficient even if the past consideration is ignored.

State statutes may, of course, affect the general rules of contract law in respect of past consideration. In New York, a signed written promise which recites a past consideration is enforceable if the past consideration was performed and if it would have been good consideration except that it was past.

138. Payment of Disputed Debt as Consideration. Where a debtor and a creditor enter into an agreement stating that if the debtor pays part of the creditor's claim the creditor will receive the payment in full satisfaction of his claim, the question is whether the debtor in making part payment furnishes a consideration for the creditor's agreement. Did the debtor do something he was not already bound to do? It seems clear that if the debt is admittedly due and owing, the debtor in paying a lesser amount does not furnish a consideration for the creditor's promise to receive it in full satisfaction, since the debtor is doing only what he is already bound to do. But where the debtor honestly disputes the existence of the claim, it is held that the payment will discharge the claim on the theory that the debtor is not obligated to pay the disputed debt until a court so decides.

139. Payment of Liquidated Claim as Consideration. A liquidated claim is certain in amount and not disputed by the creditor or the debtor. If the debtor pays to the creditor an amount less than the claim, and the creditor accepts the payment in full satisfaction, the claim is not discharged. The debtor in paying less than was admittedly due did only what he was legally obligated to do, and the creditor may recover the balance of his claim. There is no consideration for the creditor's agreement to receive the part payment in full satisfaction. This rule generally applies even where the agreement is bilateral—that is, where the debtor agrees to make a payment of a lesser sum and the creditor agrees to receive the lesser sum in full satisfaction.

140. Liquidated Claim: Delivery of Negotiable Instrument. It has been held in a few cases that a delivery by the debtor of a negotiable instrument for a lesser sum furnishes a good consideration for the creditor's promise. These cases hold that the creditor receives a benefit in that he can pass the instrument in the market, and the instrument carries with it a presumption of consideration. Actually, nothing can be passed in the market more easily than money, and if money in a lesser amount is paid there is no consideration. These cases do indicate, however, a reluctance on the part of some courts to apply the general rule. The better view is that the debtor's own note or check for a lesser amount than is admittedly due will not discharge the claim. The check should be deemed no more effective than cash, and the note, a promise to pay, should be no more effective than a payment.

Where a debtor sends his creditor a check for an amount marked "in full payment" without a previous agreement between the parties, and the creditor accepts the check and collects it, it is held that the creditor has agreed to receive it in full payment of the debt. The check is sent on condition that it be received in full payment, and if the creditor rejects the condition he should reject the check. When he has thus agreed to receive the check in full satisfaction, the question remains whether there is a sufficient consideration to bind him to his agreement. Where the original claim is liquidated, the debtor has done nothing more than he was already bound to do, and the claim is not discharged.

141. Liquidated Claim: What Is Sufficient Consideration? If the debtor pays a lesser sum and performs some additional act or delivers some other property, the seller's claim will be discharged. Thus, if the creditor accepts part payment of the debt and a delivery of goods, in full satisfaction, his claim is discharged. The debtor in delivering goods furnishes a consideration. Of course, the same result must be reached if the debtor delivers goods alone, or if he delivers a note for part of the debt together with security for the payment of the note. The security may consist of a third person's indorsement on the debtor's note, a pledge of personal property, or a chattel mortgage on the debtor's personalty. Also, the delivery by the debtor of a note of a third person is a sufficient consideration.

Not infrequently, the liquidated claim sought to be discharged is one which has not yet matured. If a claim for $100 falls due on June 15 and the creditor receives payment of $50 on the previous June 1 in full satisfaction, the claim is discharged. The debtor, in paying the lesser sum on June 1, when he was not obligated to pay, furnishes a consideration for the creditor's promise.

If the debt was due and payable in Chicago, and the creditor accepts in Atlanta a lesser sum in full satisfaction, the claim is discharged. The debtor was not bound to pay in Atlanta.

It is apparent from the foregoing that if the debtor does anything he was not originally bound to do, no matter how trivial it may be, the courts hold that the creditor's claim is discharged.

142.. Unliquidated Claims. An unliquidated claim is one for the payment of money the amount of which is not definite or certain. A claim for damages for breach of contract or for damages resulting from a tort is an unliquidated claim. Not only may the question of the amount of the creditor's claim be honestly disputed, but the debtor may in good faith also dispute his liability. Where the debtor pays the creditor any amount in full satisfaction of such claim, and the creditor accepts the payment, the claim is discharged. The amount of the claim or its existence being subject to an honest dispute, it cannot be said that the debtor in paying did only what he was already bound to do.

143. Accord and Satisfaction. Where pursuant to an agreement the debtor pays and the creditor receives an amount of money in full satisfaction of an unliquidated claim, the claim is discharged. It is generally said that there has been an accord and satisfaction, the accord constituting the agreement between the parties and the satisfaction the performance of the agreement resulting in the discharge of the claim. We have seen that if the creditor's claim is liquidated, the payment by the debtor of a lesser sum is not a sufficient consideration for the creditor's agreement to receive it in full satisfaction of the claim. Hence, the claim is not discharged. There is no accord and satisfaction. But if the debtor, in addition to the payment of money, should give or do something he is not under a preexisting duty to give or do, the acceptance in full of the debtor's performance will result in the discharge of the liquidated claim. There is then an accord and satisfaction.

144. Written Agreement to Discharge: Statutes. Some states now provide by statute that an agreement by a creditor to accept in full satisfaction a lesser amount than the liquidated claim is binding whether or not there is a consideration to support it. New York, for example, provides that an agreement to discharge an obligation, in whole or in part, shall not be invalid because of the absence of consideration if such agreement is in writing and signed by the party against whom it is sought to be enforced.

145. Accord Executory. Not infrequently, the agreement between the debtor and the creditor, although there is a sufficient consideration to support it, is not completely performed either because the debtor has failed to do so or because the creditor has declined to accept the debtor's performance. In such case, the debt is not discharged, and the creditor may recover his claim in full. The parties have entered into an accord but since there has not been a complete performance of the agreement there has been no satisfaction. It is commonly said that the parties intended that the performance of the accord should result in the satisfaction of the claim and not the agreement or accord itself, and until full performance takes place the original debt remains. The accord must be completely executed to sustain a plea of accord and satisfaction. An accord executory does not bar suit to enforce the claim in full.

An accord executory is an agreement that an existing claim shall be discharged by a performance other than the one required. Where the accord has been performed in part, the claim is discharged to the extent that performance has taken place. Thus, where a creditor agrees to accept in full satisfaction of a judgment for $5,000 cash in the amount of $1,000, delivery of goods of a value of $2,000, and an assignment of a patent right, and the debtor agrees to deliver the cash and the goods and to assign the patent right but delivers only the cash and goods, the creditor has received payment to the extent of $3,000 and may recover $2,000 as the balance of the judgment debt.

146. Enforceability of Accord Executory. The modern cases clearly establish that an accord supported by a sufficient consideration is a contract enforceable at the suit of either party. Where, however, the debtor has committed a breach of the accord, the creditor may fall back upon and enforce the original debt or claim, or he may, if he elects, sue for breach of the accord.

Statutes now exist providing that an accord executory will bar action on the original claim. Thus, if the accord is not performed, a remedy for nonperformance will be granted. In New York, it is provided that an accord by which the creditor agrees to accept a stipulated performance in discharge of a present claim or obligation and by which the debtor agrees to render such performance, is binding against either party if it is in writing and signed by him.

147. Executed Transactions. It is generally said that the doctrine of consideration applies to executory promises and not to executed transactions. A performance rendered without consideration will not be undone by the courts. A promise to make a gift is not enforceable for lack of consideration, but if the gift is made the courts allow it to stand. The subject of the gift cannot be recovered on the ground that no consideration was given for it.

148. **Composition Agreements.** We have seen that part payment by a debtor of a liquidated claim which is past due will not discharge the claim even if received by the creditor in full satisfaction. But where the arrangement is between the debtor and two or more of his creditors and they agree to accept lesser amounts in full satisfaction of their claims, the agreement is enforceable. The courts have said that each creditor's promise is consideration for the promise of each other creditor. It appears, however, that there is no consideration furnished by the debtor for the promise of each creditor. But whether or not there is any real consideration, it is universally held that a common-law composition is valid against all creditors who are parties to it. Those who do not so agree with the debtor may enforce their claims to the limit.

149. **Extension Agreement.** Where, after a debt falls due, the creditor agrees to extend the date of payment in exchange for the debtor's promise to pay the debt on the new date of maturity with interest, most courts hold that the creditor's agreement is supported by consideration. These courts take the position that the creditor receives a benefit in that he receives interest for the extended period, a benefit that he would not acquire if he did not assent to the extension. He receives an advantage by allowing his money to remain invested for the additional period of time. That benefit and advantage to the creditor is found to be the consideration for the creditor's agreement to extend the date of payment. However, by the minority view, followed in New York, the creditor's agreement is without consideration on the ground that the debtor has promised to do only that which he is already obligated to do. In New York, when a debtor is in default he must pay interest on his debt at the legal or judgment rate of 6%.

An extension agreement is a modification of an obligation, and, in New York, by statute, an agreement modifying an obligation is enforceable notwithstanding the lack of consideration if it is in writing and signed by the party against whom it is sought to be enforced. Where it is in writing and signed by the creditor, it is binding on him even if the debtor gives no consideration for the creditor's agreement. Where it is oral, the debtor must promise to do or to give something in addition to his promise to pay to make the agreement binding on the creditor.

150. Reliance on Promise. Is a promise binding where the promisee acts or forbears to act in reliance on a promise although the act or forbearance was not requested in exchange for the promise? The Restatement, Contracts, states: "A promise which the promisor should reasonably expect to induce action or forbearance of a definite and substantial character on the part of the promisee and which does induce such action or forbearance is binding if injustice can be avoided only by enforcement of the promise." In the case of past consideration, an act or a forbearance induces the making of the promise. In the case of reliance on a promise, the promise induces the act or forbearance. But in both cases the promisor does not request the act or forbearance, and it is not given in exchange for the promise.

151. Reliance: Charitable Subscriptions. A promise to make a charitable subscription is a promise to make a donation. There is no consideration for it in the sense that consideration must consist of an act or forbearance given in exchange for the promise and at the request of the promisor. Yet, charitable subscriptions are enforced everywhere. The thought that such promises should be enforced in the public interest has caused many courts to say that the promises must be enforced because of the reliance placed on them, and that such reliance is a sufficient consideration in that the promisor had reason to foresee that buildings would be erected and contracts made. Others have said that the promise is enforceable on the ground that the charity impliedly gives a return promise to carry out the program contemplated, such return promise constituting a sufficient consideration. Still others have taken the position that the promise of each subscriber is the consideration for that of each other.

152. Reliance: Substantial Act or Forbearance. It is clear that not every act or forbearance given in reliance on the promise will be deemed sufficient to enforce the promise. The reliance must have been induced by the promise, it must have been foreseen by the promisor, and it must result in a substantial change in position by the promisee. What is a substantial change of position is a question of fact which must be determined by the jury. No fixed standard exists for its determination.

EXAMPLES

1. S promises to deliver a horse to B. B walks to S's stable to pick up the horse. S's promise is not enforceable. B did not suffer a substantial change of position in reliance on S's promise.

2. S promises to convey land to B. S permits B to take possession and

B makes substantial improvements on the land. *S* must make the conveyance. *B* suffered a substantial change of position in reliance on the promise, and *S*, as a reasonable man, might have foreseen that *B* might take such action.

3. *A*, a mortgagee, promises to *B* that he will not foreclose the mortgage on *B*'s real estate. *B*, relying on the promise, makes expensive improvements to the property. *A*'s promise is enforceable.

4. *A*, in Maine, writes to *B*, in Oregon, that *A* will give to *B* a piece of land to live on. *B* breaks up his home and moves to Maine. *A*'s promise should be enforced. Although *A* intended to make a gift, *B*'s substantial action in reliance on the promise, and the fact that *A* might reasonably have expected such action, require that *A*'s promise be held enforceable without consideration.

A frequent example of liability based on reliance on a promise is that of a bailee who gratuitously promises to care for the property of the bailor. Of course, if the promisor never starts to perform his promise, there is no liability. But if the promisee delivers the property to the bailee and the bailee enters upon performance of his promise, he is liable for damage to the property resulting from his failure to fully perform. Often such liability may be predicated on a tort theory, but it need not be. The change of position by the bailor relying on the promise of the bailee is sufficient to enforce the promise.

EXAMPLES

1. If *A* gratuitously promises to collect a note for *B*, and receives the note, *A* is liable for failure to collect it. The change of position suffered by *B* when he delivers the note to *A* for collection is sufficient to make *A*'s promise enforceable.

2. *A* delivers his chattels to *B* upon *B*'s promise to store the same and to procure insurance on them. *B* fails to insure and the property is destroyed by fire. *B* is liable for failure to perform his promise. *A*'s delivery of the chattels and forbearance to take out insurance, relying on *B*'s promise, is sufficient.

153. Mutuality of Obligation. One of the most common statements in legal opinions is that both parties to a contract must be bound or neither is bound. If either party does not undertake a contractual duty, the other need not perform his duty. It is recognized, however, that this statement does not apply to the unilateral contract in which only one party assumes an obligation. If *S* says to *B*, "I will pay you fifty dollars if you deliver to me your white horse, Domino," and *B* delivers the horse to *S*, *S* is bound to pay $50 but *B* is not bound to perform. As we have seen, the contract comes into existence upon *B*'s delivery of the horse. *B*'s delivery is his acceptance of the offer and the consideration for S's promise. A promise by B to deliver will not constitute an acceptance of S's offer since the offer calls for an act and not a promise. If mutuality of obligation means merely that there must be a consideration for the promise, as indeed it does, then it is obvious that the unilateral contract does not fail for lack of such mutuality.

154. Mutuality: Promise to Buy One's Needs. A promise by B to buy all of a certain commodity that he needs in his business, given in exchange for a promise by S to sell, is enforceable. B's promise is a sufficient consideration for the return promise of S to sell. The promise is not one to buy what the promisor wishes to order; it is a promise to buy his needs or his requirements in his business. It is held that such a promise is not so indefinite or uncertain that it cannot be enforced. Of course, B may in good faith limit his business or even go out of business, but so long as he remains in business he must buy from S and none else. There is mutuality of obligation and the parties have a valid contract.

Where S promises to sell B all the coal that B may need during the next six months and B, in exchange, promises to buy from S all that B may use or resell during that time, the contract should be deemed enforceable. B's promise is to buy from S only, and he has given up the right to buy from others, thereby suffering a legal detriment. But some courts, including those of New York, have ruled that if B was not engaged in a business in which he had a need for coal, the contract is unenforceable. They say that his promise is illusory and there is a lack of mutuality in that he is not obliged to buy if there is no need, and if he is not obliged to buy the seller is not obliged to sell. These courts require that there be a need that may be reasonably estimated, and they say that this is possible only when the contract is made in connection with an established business.

In UCC Sec. 2-306 it is stated that a contract for the sale of goods which measures the quantity by the output of the seller or the requirements of the buyer means such actual output or requirements that may occur in good faith. Where the contract sets forth an estimate of the seller's output or the buyer's requirements, the seller may not tender nor the buyer demand a delivery of any quantity unreasonably disproportionate to the estimate. Where no estimate is set forth, the seller may not tender nor the buyer demand a delivery of a quantity unreasonably disproportionate to any normal or otherwise comparable prior output or requirements.

155. Good Consideration vs. Valuable Consideration. Good consideration is generally defined as consideration based on love and affection. While it has some significance in the law of conveyances of real property, it has no application in the law of contracts. Good consideration standing alone is not sufficient to support a promise. The love and affection of a husband for his wife will not render enforceable a promise to the wife which is not based on some other sufficient consideration. A promissory note delivered by the maker because of love and affection for the payee is not enforceable by the payee.

8. Illegal Bargains

156. When Is a Bargain Illegal? A bargain may be illegal because its making is forbidden or because its performance has been declared illegal. The illegality of the bargain may spring from the performance of one or the other party or of both, whether that performance has been or will be rendered.

Whether the contract is illegal because its making has been condemned or because a performance thereunder is illegal is not always a simple question. To make the determination we must look (*a*) to legislative enactments, to statutes and constitutions, and to the interpretations and constructions thereof by the courts (*b*) to the common law, the exceedingly large number of judicial decisions and opinions and the general rules drawn from them, and (*c*) to public policy, the prevailing practices of the people for their general welfare, which vary from time to time and from place to place.

157. Contracts Made or to Be Performed on Sunday. A contract made on Sunday or to be performed on Sunday is lawful in the absence of statute declaring it illegal. Most of the states have enacted statutes, but due to a lack of uniformity in terms and phraseology there is some variation in result from state to state. Some statutes prohibit servile labor, others condemn labor or business in one's ordinary calling. In some states, legislative enactments attack both labor and business on Sunday, while in others only labor on Sunday is illegal. Some statutes declare contracts made on Sunday or to be performed on Sunday illegal. Others, as that in effect in New York, attack only those to be performed on Sunday.

It appears, however, that no statute attacks contracts made on Sunday or to be performed on Sunday if the subject of the bargain is labor of charity or necessity, though there is some disagreement about what constitutes a labor of charity or necessity. It is generally agreed, however, that contracts made to further religious worship or for the relief of suffering or distress pertain to charity and are not affected by statute, and contracts made to preserve life, health, or property, such as contracts with physicians, dentists, hospitals, bargains for the purchase of drugs, or for the repair of bridges, highways, or water mains, are agreements of necessity if they cannot reasonably be postponed to a secular day.

158. Gambling Contracts. At common law, gambling transactions and wagers were not illegal. Today in most states statutes provide that wagers, bets, and gambling transactions are illegal.

The requisite of a gambling transaction is that the parties shall gain or lose upon the happening of an event in which neither has an interest except by the wager, and which event is not certain to happen. If A and B, about to play a game of golf, agree that if A loses he shall pay B $100, and that if B loses he shall pay A $100, the bargain is illegal as a wager or bet. Where the parties agree that, if A wins, B will sell and A will buy B's automobile for $1,000, and if B wins, B will sell and A will buy B's automobile for $1,500, the bargain is a wager or gambling transaction, since the value of the car is in no way connected with the outcome of the game, and the price depends on an event whose outcome is uncertain.

It should be noted that an insurance contract is not a gambling contract since the insured has an interest in the subject of the insurance and would suffer a loss by its destruction. Of course, if he has no insurable interest the insurance contract is void as a gambling transaction.

A lottery is a scheme for the distribution of property by chance among persons who have paid or agreed to pay a valuable consideration for the chance, and it is illegal whether called a lottery, raffle, gift enterprise, or by some other name. A contest or a competition is not a lottery, however, unless a price is paid for the opportunity to compete. Thus, where one pays the regular admission charge to a theater to witness a performance and wins a prize as the holder of a ticket bearing a number drawn by lot from the stubs of tickets sold, he did not participate in a lottery and is entitled to receive the prize. The admission fee was not paid for the privilege of participating in the drawing, but for the purpose of witnessing the show put on by the theater. But there are some cases which hold that if the customer would not have attended except for the chance of winning a prize, it is a lottery.

By statute in some states, money deposited in the hands of a stakeholder upon a bet or wager may be recovered by the loser if he has demanded its return before the stakeholder has turned it over to the winner.

Other states provide that the loser may recover the sum lost whether or not the stakeholder has turned the money over to the winner. Of course, if the event upon which the bet is made has not yet taken place, a bettor may withdraw and recover his money; he may repent prior to the consummation of the illegal act.

Where the parties agree to buy and sell personal property, such as shares of stock or grain, and it is provided that, if the market price shall exceed the agreed price as of a certain day, one shall pay the other the difference, and if the agreed price exceed the market price the other shall pay the difference, the transaction may constitute a wager on the rise and fall of the market price. Its illegality depends on whether the parties intend that a delivery be made even though the time of delivery is postponed. If there is to be no delivery of the property, it is a gambling transaction.

159. Usurious Bargains. Generally, usury is defined as the taking or agreement to take interest on a loan in excess of the maximum rate permitted by law. There (a) must be a loan or forbearance of money, (b) which must be repaid in any event, and (c) the borrower must pay something for the use of the money in excess of the interest allowed by law.

At common law, there was no limit to the amount of interest which could be exacted for a loan. Most states now have statutes setting forth the maximum rates of interest. Many states fix the maximum legal rates of interest but allow a higher rate by special contract. In Delaware, Kentucky, Maryland, New Jersey, New York, North Carolina, Pennsylvania, Tennessee, Vermont, Virginia and West Virginia the maximum legal rate and the maximum contract rate is 6 per cent. In other states, the maximum legal rate varies from 5 per cent to 8 per cent and the maximum contract rate varies from 6 per cent to 30 per cent. Thus, where interest is to be paid for the loan or forbearance of money but the parties do not fix the rate, the maximum legal rate applies. But where the parties fix the rate by contract, in a great majority of states a rate may be charged which exceeds the maximum legal rate. The rate so fixed by contract may be any rate of interest up to the maximum contract rate fixed by local statute.

In some states, as in New York, a bargain tainted with usury is absolutely void, and there can be no recovery by the creditor of either the principal amount of the loan or of interest. In others, no interest can be recovered; and in still others, the excessive interest alone is forfeited. Also, statutes exist in some states which authorize the recovery of usurious interest paid if action is brought within a prescribed time after such payment.

Often, devices are used to circumvent the usury laws. In the following examples, we assume a maximum legal and contract rate of 6 per cent.

EXAMPLES

1. *L* lends *B* $800 and receives from *B* a promissory note for $1,000, payable in three months with interest at 5 per cent. The loan is usurious since *B* is paying 5 per cent interest plus $200 for the loan of $800. The total payment exceeds 6 per cent on $800 for three months.

2. *B* borrows $1,000 from *L* and agrees to pay interest at 6 per cent. When the loan matures, they agree that *L* will extend the date of maturity 30 days and *B* will pay an additional $100. The $100 for 30 days is not a loan, but it is a forbearance and the transaction is usurious. The usury laws apply to loans and forbearances.

3. *L* lends *B* $100 on June 25 and receives from *B* his one-year promissory note for the amount with interest at 6 per cent, dated June 1. The loan is usurious. *B* is paying interest at the highest legal rate for one year but has the use of the money for less than one year.

4. *S* says to *B*, "I will sell you my tractor for three hundred dollars if you pay within thirty days, or for four hundred dollars if you pay in sixty days." *B* agrees to buy and to pay $400 in 60 days. The difference of $100 for 30 days exceeds the maximum rate of interest on $300 for that time, but the transaction is not usurious because there is a sale of goods and not a loan of money.

5. Not infrequently, a sale of goods will be used as a device to conceal a loan of money at an usurious rate. *S* sells *B* a painting worth $1,000 for $900, upon *S*'s agreement to buy it back from *B* at the end of one year for $1,100. The difference between $900 and $1,100 for one year exceeds the maximum rate of interest on $900 for one year, and the transaction is usurious.

6. *L* lends *B* $1,000 at the highest legal rate of interest. As part of the transaction, *L* requires *B* to buy from *L* a wheelbarrow, worth only $20, for $75. The transaction is usurious. It is merely a device enabling *L* to get for the loan of money more than the law allows.

7. *L* lends *B* $1,000, and *B* promises to repay $1,100 at the end of one year. The maximum rate of interest is 6 per cent. *L* contends the transaction is not usurious because he rendered services to *B* in connection with the loan which were of the reasonable value of $40. If *L* can establish good faith on his part and can show that the services he rendered were of the reasonable value of $40, the loan is lawful. But if it appears that the services were a device to obtain a higher rate of interest, the transaction is usurious.

Where a loan is made for a short term, not over one year, the lender may usually deduct interest in advance. By custom, such a loan is not usurious even though the lender has the use of the interest for a longer period than he should.

Generally, statutes permit such lenders as small loan companies and pawnbrokers to charge rates of interest higher than those applicable to other lenders. It is also generally provided by statute that corporations, and other organizations having the powers and privileges of corporations not possessed by individuals and partnerships, may not plead usury as a defense.

160. License Requirements. Statutes are common which require that a license be procured as a condition to the right to engage in the practice of a profession or a trade, or which deny to a corporation the right to conduct such practice. Lawyers, doctors, real estate brokers, architects, hotelkeepers, plumbers, peddlers, and stockbrokers are generally required to obtain licenses before they engage in their callings. If the license requirement or the denial of the right to practice exists for the protection of the public against incompetent or unreliable persons rather than merely to raise revenue, it is held that a contract made in violation of the statute cannot be enforced. In such cases, the unlicensed person or corporation cannot recover for services rendered in a profession or trade.

161. Bargains Obstructing Justice. Bargains which obstruct or interfere with the administration of justice are absolutely void. They consist of agreements compounding crimes, agreements ousting courts of jurisdiction, and agreements tending to encourage litigation.

A bargain made to conceal the commission of a crime or to not prosecute a person for the commission of a crime is illegal. But an agreement to make reparation for a crime is valid if it does not stipulate that prosecution for the crime shall be suppressed. Where the crime gives rise to a civil claim for damages, the settlement of the claim is valid because it does not of itself bar a criminal prosecution.

Since the state has an interest in its inhabitants and sees to it that their rights are protected and enforced, and that its courts shall be open for the redress of wrongs, no person may by agreement divest himself of his right of access to the courts. Such an agreement is illegal. There is a tendency, however, to relax this rule by statute. In New York, for example, an agreement to submit an *existing* controversy or one thereafter arising to arbitration is lawful and valid if the agreement is in writing.

Bargains tending to encourage litigation are violative of public policy and are illegal. Champerty and maintenance were crimes at common law. Champerty refers to the division or sharing of the proceeds of a sum, collected as a result of litigation, between the owner of the claim and another. But an agreement by an attorney to prosecute a claim on a contingent fee basis (that is, an agreement by an attorney to withhold a percentage of the recovery) is not champertous, at least where the amount withheld is not unconscionable. Most states hold, however, that a contract for a contingent fee under which the attorney agrees to bear the costs of litigation is champertous and void. Generally, statutes exist which prevent an attorney from buying a claim for the purpose of suing thereon, or from paying a consideration to or splitting his fee with a layman as a reward for procuring business.

Maintenance is the promotion of litigation of another. It is the stirring up of litigation by improperly encouraging another to commence litigation. Lawyers may not procure clients by agreements with persons who for profit procure clients and promote litigation.

162. Bargains Injuring Public Service. The efficiency of public service must be preserved, and all agreements tending to injure the public service by improper influence exerted on legislators and public officials violate public policy. Agreements affecting or tending to control the operation of government or appointment to public office, or tending to influence the course of legislation, or tending to procure pardons by corrupt means are condemned by the courts.

The most common agreement which may tend to injure public service is the lobby contract. If an agreement contemplates the use of lawful means in procuring favorable legislation or in blocking unfavorable legislation, the contract is valid. One may legally contract for the services of another to collect facts, prepare legislation, and explain the same to the legislature or a legislative committee, and he may pay for the services so rendered. But where the contract requires the use of bribery or other improper influence or means, it is contrary to the public interest. A promise to support or campaign for or make a campaign contribution for a legislator, if he will use his influence in certain legislation or if he will vote in favor of it, is void. The employment of a political leader to exert his influence on legislators is void.

Public officials who have the power to appoint to public office are required to exercise discretion in the public interest without thought of personal gain. Thus, an agreement by a public official to appoint a person to public office, if a consideration is paid for the appointment, or if a certain person will support the official in the next election, or if the person to be appointed will accept a lower salary than that fixed by law, is illegal.

163. Bargains to Defraud Third Persons. Bargains intended to operate as frauds on third persons or on the public violate public policy. An agreement between the seller of goods at auction and another person, by which the other is to bid up the goods and create a false appearance of competition, is void, and the "puffer" may not enforce his contract. An agreement by which one refrains from bidding, thus stifling competition, is also void.

An agreement to publish a libelous book or article is void. An agreement by a newspaper to sell its editorial influences is a fraud on the public and will not be enforced. A bargain by which one agrees to slander another, or to infringe on a patent or copyright or trademark, is void.

A conveyance of property made to defraud, hinder, and delay creditors is illegal. Thus, if A, a debtor owing $10,000, conveys all of his assets to B upon B's promise to reconvey the assets at a later date, the agreement is void. The bargain is entered into for the purpose of screening the assets from the creditors. The creditors may reach the assets in B's hands, but A may not enforce B's agreement to reconvey the assets.

Not infrequently, a debtor who enters into a composition agreement with his creditors by which he promises and undertakes to pay them a percentage of their claims, finds that he is unable to procure the signature of a certain creditor unless he secretly agrees to pay him a larger percentage of his claim. Such an agreement is void because it is fraudulent on the creditors who have no knowledge of it. It is generally held that innocent creditors who signed the composition agreement are not bound by it and may hold the debtor for the full amount of their claims.

164. Bargains in Restraint of Trade. In the early common law, any bargain which restricted or lessened competition or restrained a person's right to carry on his trade or calling was in violation of the public policy. It was generally held that such a restraint on a party diminished and lessened his means of earning a livelihood, exposed him to oppression, discouraged enterprise, lessened competition, and enhanced prices. Today, such a bargain is illegal only if it constitutes an *unreasonable* restraint of trade—that is, if the restraint is greater than is necessary in the circumstances and imposes a hardship on the party restrained. In determining whether a restraint is reasonable, the courts will consider the relationship of the parties to the contract, the extent of the trade, business, or profession which is to be restrained, the geographic extent of the restraint, the duration of the restraint, and whether the restraint is general or partial. It is commonly said that a general restraint is unreasonable but that a partial restraint may be reasonable.

The most common examples of cases which have come before the court are those in which (a) a seller of a business agrees not to compete with the buyer; (b) an employee agrees not to compete with his employer after his employment terminates; (c) a retiring partner agrees not to compete with the firm; (d) a buyer of property agrees not to use it in competition with the seller. Of these, the first arises most frequently.

X owns and operates a retail business in New York City. All of his sales are made in New York City. He enters into a contract for the sale of his business to Y. As part of the contract of sale, X agrees not to engage in a similar business anywhere in the state of New York. The restraint on X is illegal. It was unnecessary to the protection of the business acquired by Y that X should not compete anywhere in the state. The restraint is unreasonable in respect of the area covered.

Often, the business sold is of a professional nature. A dentist in a small town sells his practice and promises the purchaser that he will not thereafter practice dentistry in that town. The contract is legal. Where, however, one is about to engage in a business or profession in a particular locality, and he agrees, for a consideration paid him by another practicing that trade or profession in that locality, not to engage in that trade or profession in that locality, the bargain is illegal as an unreasonable restraint. There is no business or interest purchased which requires protection.

Often, where an employee agrees that he will not accept similar employment in a given area, the bargain is held illegal as unnecessary to the protection of the employer and a hardship on the employee because it lessens his opportunity to earn a livelihood. Thus, where one is employed as manager of a restaurant owned by a corporation which maintains restaurants in all the major cities of the state and agrees that upon the termination of his employment he will not secure other similar employment in any city in which the corporation maintains a restaurant, the agreement is illegal.

165. Effect of Illegality. In many cases, the courts have emphasized differences in the degree of illegality and have sought to justify remedies granted accordingly. A bargain which was wrong and illegal because of statute but was lawful prior to the statute was described as *malum prohibitum*. A bargain deemed morally wrong and evil, which evidenced moral turpitude even in the absence of prohibitive legislation, was described as *malum in se*. This difference in the degree of illegality was often made the basis for determining the availabilty of remedies. But many recent cases have taken the position that the distinction between bargains or acts *malum prohibitum* and *malum in se* is not a sound one.

As a general rule, an illegal bargain will not be enforced, and no action can be brought to recover what was paid or delivered in performance of the bargain. The courts will leave the parties just as it finds them. There are, however, many situations in which the courts grant a remedy to one or the other party. Sometimes a remedy is granted because it is found that the bargain is divisible and is illegal in part only, and the illegal part can be separated from the lawful part; or because the parties are not in *pari delicto*—that is, not equally guilty. Remedies are also granted even to a guilty party if public policy or the public welfare so requires.

166. Effect of Illegality: Divisible Contracts. Where the bargain consists of one promise for one consideration, and the promise or the consideration given is illegal, no remedy will be granted. Where several considerations are given for one promise and one or more but not all are illegal, a remedy is denied because it is impossible to determine which consideration induced the promise. Where the bargain consists of several promises, each given for a separate consideration, and the promises are severable, those lawful promises given for lawful consideration will be enforced.

EXAMPLES

1. S makes a bargain with B to sell B one horse, one plow, and a rifle, and B promises to pay $300. If the sale of the rifle is illegal, the entire contract is vitiated as illegal.

2. S and B make a bargain to sell and to buy one horse for $150, one plow for $100, and one rifle for $50. The agreement to sell the horse and the plow is enforceable. The sale of the rifle, if illegal, will not be enforced.

3. A agrees to plow B's field and to deliver a horse to B in exchange for B's promise to deliver a rifle to A. If the delivery of the rifle is illegal, the bargain is illegal in its entirety.

It should be noted that if, in the first example, S has delivered the horse, the plow, and the rifle, and B refuses to pay asserting the illegality of the bargain, S cannot enforce B's promise even though B derived a benefit from S's performance. The same result is reached in the third example if, after A has plowed B's field and delivered the horse, B refuses to deliver the rifle.

167. Effect of Illegality: Pari Delicto. Where the parties to a bargain are equally guilty, the courts will not generally grant a remedy to either whether the bargain has been fully performed on both sides, fully performed on one side only, or wholly unperformed. But where one of the parties is found to be less guilty than the other, and is not guilty of any serious moral turpitude, the courts will allow him to recover his consideration even if the other party has fully performed. In general, a party will be considered less guilty if the illegality stems from a legislative enactment which imposes a penalty upon the other party but not upon him. Also, a party will be deemed not equally guilty if public policy renders the bargain illegal but that policy is intended for his protection from the other party, as in the case of a bargain made for the services of a marriage broker.

168. Effect of Illegality: Illegal Purpose. Where a bargain is made for an illegal purpose, and the party who seeks to accomplish the illegal purpose has partly performed by paying part of the consideration but repents and demands its restoration, the illegal purpose not having yet been accomplished, a recovery is allowed by most courts.

Where an agreement is on its face free of illegal taint, but the intention of one of the parties is illegal, as where he intends to use the consideration received for an illegal purpose, the weight of authority in this country is to the effect that the innocent party may enforce the contract although he has knowledge of the illegal purpose, provided that he has done nothing to further it. The minority view, followed in New York, is that knowledge of the illegal purpose is sufficient to render the bargain illegal.

9. Interpretation and Parol Evidence Rule

169. In General. The words *interpretation* and *construction* are often used interchangeably, but, strictly, interpretation is used in relation to language used or an act performed, to determine its meaning. In the making of a contract, two or more people use words or perform acts, and one of them may give his expressions a meaning that differs from the meaning attributed to them by the other. The court must first determine which meaning in the circumstances must prevail, and then it must determine by the process of interpretation what that meaning is. By the process of construction of a contract, the court determines its legal effect and the legal relations of the parties. Words and expressions used in preliminary negotiations, offers, and acceptances must be interpreted before it can be determined what effect in law they have. For example, a meaning must first be given to a communication to determine whether it constitutes an offer before it can be decided whether the offeree had the power of acceptance; and the reply to the offer must be interpreted to determine whether it is an expression of acceptance or a counteroffer, before it is decided whether a contract exists.

170. Rules of Interpretation. Some of the standards of interpretation that have been stated in judicial opinions are the following:

(*a*) In determining the meaning of language used in a contract, whether oral or in writing, the transaction is to be treated as a whole. The meaning of particular language should not be determined out of context.

(*b*) Where language is susceptible of two interpretations, one lawful and the other illegal, the courts may give to the language the interpretation that will make it valid.

(*c*) Where provisions are conflicting, the conflict will be resolved by giving perference to specific language over general language, or, if the contract is in writing, by giving preference to hand-written portions or typed portions over printed portions.

(*d*) Where a contract includes words or phrases in sequence, the meaning of one word or phrase is affected by the others. Where one or more words or phrases are specifically listed and no general, inclusive, or catch-all language is stated, other things are excluded, even if similar.

(*e*) Where one party has chosen the language of the contract and the other merely assented to it, the court will adopt the interpretation less favorable to the user of the language. In other words, the language will be interpreted most strongly against the user of the language. It should be noted, however, that this rule is applied only when the court, having gone through the process of interpretation and weighed all the evidence submitted, is in doubt as to which of two possible interpretations should be adopted.

(*f*) Where language is susceptible of more than one interpretation, the courts in the process of interpretation will look to the language of the contract, the subject matter, the purposes or objects to be accomplished by the parties, to arrive at the intention of the parties. The language is not to be interpreted without regard to the surrounding circumstances.

(*g*) Technical words are to be given their technical meanings unless the context or usage indicates a different meaning.

(*h*) Where the parties, by their conduct subsequent to the making of the contract, indicate that they place a particular interpretation upon the language, that interpretation, if reasonably consistent with the language, will be adopted.

171. Proof of Surrounding Circumstances. It is necessary for the court before it can give a meaning to the language to receive evidence of the surrounding circumstances. It will consider the parties, their relationship, their object and purpose, and the situation in which the language is used. Proof of the surrounding cricumstances is admissible whether or not the contract is apparently complete on its face. Such proof does not violate the parol evidence rule since its purpose is not to vary the terms of the writing but rather to explain them. Where the terms are not ambiguous, evidence of surrounding circumstances is not admissible.

172. Proof of Preliminary Statements and Negotiations. Statements and negotiations which take place prior to or simultaneously with the making of a written contract regarded by the parties as their complete agreement, which agreement is sometimes called an integration, are admissible for the purpose of interpreting language of the contract. Such evidence is admitted for the purpose of determining the meaning of language and not for the purpose of varying or contradicting its terms.

173. Proof of Usage and Course of Dealing. A usage of trade is any practice or method of dealing having such regularity of observance in a vocation or trade as to justify an expectation that it will be observed with respect to the contract in question. The existence of the usage is to be proved as a fact. A course of dealing is a sequence of previous conduct between the parties to the contract which is fairly to be regarded as establishing a common basis for the interpretation of their expressions. A course of dealing between the parties and a usage in the trade in which they are engaged or of which they should be aware may supplement, qualify, or give particular meaning to the terms of their contract (UCC Sec. 1-105).

Thus, proof of usage is admissible for the purpose of interpreting language. However, one must offer affirmative proof that he intended the language to be governed by the usage and that the other party knew of his intention, or that each assented that the usage govern, or that each party knew of the usage or it was generally known by persons in similar circumstances. Of course, where one intends a meaning inconsistent with the usage and the other knows of that intention, the usage will not govern.

174. Interpretation Where Contract Silent on Terms. Often a court is called upon to supply terms not provided for in the contract. For example, parties frequently fail to express the time or place of performance. Where the parties fail to provide for the time of performance, it must take place within a reasonable time after the making of the contract. What constitutes a reasonable time is a question of fact to be determined according to the circumstances of the particular case. Thus, where a seller must send goods to a buyer and no time for sending them is fixed, he must send them within a reasonable time. Where, however, the contract is one for the loan of money and no time is fixed for repayment, the debtor must repay on demand.

Where each party is to perform and the performances may take place simultaneously, in the absence of contrary intention expressed in the agreement the performances are to take place concurrently. Accordingly, where a seller is to deliver goods to the buyer and no time of delivery or payment of the price is fixed, payment and delivery are to take place simultaneously within a reasonable time after the contract is made.

If the performance by one party must take place over a period of time and performance by the other may take place in a moment, the performance of the first party must take place before the second is required to perform, unless the parties have expressed an intention to the contrary. Thus, in a contract for personal services, the employer is not to pay until the employee has fully performed unless the parties have expressly provided otherwise.

In the case of a contract for the sale of goods which is silent on the place of delivery, the seller's place of business is the place of delivery, if he has one, and if not, his residence. But where the goods are identified and known by the parties to be at some other place, that place is the place of delivery. Where a contract for the sale of goods does not state a price, or if the price was left to be agreed upon and they fail to agree, the price is a reasonable price at the time of delivery (UCC Secs. 2-305, 2-307, 2-308, 2-309).

175. Parol Evidence Rule. When the terms of a contract are set forth in a writing which the parties regard as the complete agreement between them, that is, an integration, evidence of prior agreements, statements, promises, or negotiations, whether oral or in writing is not admissible for the purpose of contradicting or adding to or varying the written contract.

Whether the writing is intended to operate as the complete agreement is a question of fact which may be determined by resort to any material evidence even if it be oral. A determination that it is the complete contract has the effect of nullifying and discharging any inconsistent oral or written agreements, understandings, or statements that previously took place, or oral agreements made at the same time.

If language in the integregation is ambiguous, the court must interpret it, and the parol evidence rule does not prohibit any relevant evidence of understandings or statements for that purpose. Such evidence does not vary or contradict the integration; it merely explains it. Also, evidence tending to prove lack of consideration, fraud, duress, undue influence, illegality, or mistake is not barred by the rule. Such evidence is offered to show that the integration is either void or voidable, rather than to vary or contradict it. The rule does not prohibit evidence justifying a rescission.

Sec. 2-202 of the UCC provides that a contract for the sale of goods evidenced by a writing which the parties intend to be the final expression of their agreement with respect to the terms included therein, may not be contradicted by evidence of any prior agreement or of any contemporaneous oral agreement, but it may be explained or supplemented by course of dealing, usage of trade, or by course of performance. It may also be explained or supplemented by evidence of consistent additional terms unless the court finds the writing was intended as a complete and exclusive statement of the terms of the agreement. This section rejects the notion that the agreement must be ambiguous to allow evidence of course of dealing, usage of trade or course of performance. It also rejects the assumption that because the writing is final on some matters it is final on all terms.

176. Parol Evidence Rule: Condition Precedent, Incomplete Agreement. An oral agreement made prior to or simultaneously with the integration by which the writing shall not become binding until a future event, is admissible in evidence if there is nothing in the agreement inconsistent therewith. The purpose of such proof is to show that the agreement is conditional; that no obligation arises if the event does not occur. Thus, where A and B enter into an agreement for the purchase and sale of a definite quantity of hides at a fixed price, evidence of a prior oral agreement between them that the buyer's obligation to perform was conditional upon a third person's approval of the quality of the hides is admissible.

If the writing is found not to be an integration, evidence of prior oral or written promises or statements, and oral promises or statements made simultaneously therewith, are admissible to show the complete agreement.

10. Conditions

177. In General. A condition is a fact or an event upon the existence of which a legal relationship depends. The right of one or the other of the parties may depend on an event or a fact before it will entitle him to a remedy. If S makes an offer to B to sell his white horse Domino for $50 and B accepts the offer, B has the right to delivery and S has the right to payment. But if S delivers the horse upon B's promise to pay $50 if and when C will buy B's carriage, S's right to payment is based on a fact or an event that may never happen. S's right is, therefore, conditional upon the purchase by C. The purchase by C is a condition precedent to S's right to collect the price from B.

178. Conditions Precedent and Subsequent. A *condition precedent* is an event or a fact that must occur after the contract is made in order to give a right to immediate performance or a remedy for the failure to immediately perform. (a) A promise to pay if John Doe, architect, certifies in writing that the work is properly done, (b) a promise to pay if John Doe approves of the quality of the goods, and (c) a promise to pay for goods delivered if they meet with approval of the buyer, are illustrations of a condition precedent. In each there is no enforceable right unless the event specified occurs.

A *condition subsequent* is a fact or an event occurring after the breach of the contract, which operates to terminate the right to immediate performance. Here the right to performance exists, but the happening or failure to happen of the fact or event terminates the duty to perform. Examples frequently given are (a) the provision in a fire policy that in the event of a fire loss and a rejection of the insured's claim the failure of the the insured to sue within a prescribed time shall result in the termination of the company's liability, and (b) the sale or return transaction in which goods are sold and delivered to a buyer who may return the goods instead of paying the price.

Not infrequently, the condition subsequent is an event which is to occur after the contract is made but before a breach. Thus, where S and B enter into a contract on May 15 which provides that S is to deliver certain goods to B on June 15 and B is to pay upon delivery, and that if the government fails to issue a permit by June 1 the contract is to become null and void, the issuance of the permit is subsequent to the making of the contract and the failure of the event terminates the agreement.

179. Concurrent Conditions. Where the agreement requires that the parties render their performances simultaneously, the promise of each person is conditional upon performance by the other party. Accordingly, where a contract calls for payment of the price upon delivery of goods, the duty to deliver the goods is conditional upon payment of the price, and the duty to pay the price is conditional upon delivery of the goods. Delivery and payment are to take place concurrently.

180. Promise vs. Condition. A condition is a fact or an event which creates no right or duty. It is not an assurance or an expression of intention that there will be a performance. A promise creates a duty in the promisor and a right in the promisee. It expresses an intention that some performance will be rendered. A promise is made by one of the parties; a condition is agreed upon by both parties or it is inferred by law. The failure to perform a promise is a breach of contract. The failure of a condition does not give rise to a duty, and it creates no rights.

A particular performance may be brought about by a promise or a condition. If A wants B to perform an act, he may secure B's promise to do so by contract, or he may make B's performance of the act a condition precedent to A's performance.

181. Dependent and Independent Promises. In the case of a bilateral contract, the mutual promises may be dependent or independent. Where the promises are to be performed concurrently, performance or a tender of performance of each is conditional upon performance or tender of performance of the other, and each promise is said to be dependent on the other. If the promises are to be performed at different times so that the first is to be performed only after performance of the second, the first is dependent and conditional upon performance of the second. It seems more understandable to refer to the promises, or the duties they create, as conditional or unconditional rather than dependent or independent.

182. Personal Satisfaction as a Condition. X makes a promise to render a certain performance and Y, in exchange, promises to pay if X's performance meets with his satisfaction. Clearly, Y's satisfaction is a condition of his duty to pay. If Y is not satisfied with the performance, X is not guilty of a breach since he has not agreed to satisfy Y. Where, however, X promises to perform to Y's satisfaction and Y, in exchange, promises to pay, X is guilty of a breach if Y is not satisfied with his performance. Notwithstanding that Y's promise is not expressly conditional in the latter situation, the courts hold that in each case Y's duty to pay is conditional upon his satisfaction with X's performance. It would seem, therefore, that if Y is honestly dissatisfied with X's performance, no matter how unreasonable his expression of dissatisfaction may be, he should not be required to pay. But the courts so hold only in the case where the object of the contract of the parties is to gratify personal taste or fancy, or to serve personal convenience or individual preference. In such case, it is not proper to investigate the question whether the expression of dissatisfaction is unreasonable or arbitrary. The only requirement is that it be honest, genuine, and not feigned. If Y's dissatisfaction is real, and not assumed merely to rid himself of his duty to pay, it is of no consequence whether in the circumstances he ought to be satisfied.

183. Personal Satisfaction: Objective Test. Where, however, X's performance involves no personal taste, fancy, or judgment, but is one of mere operative fitness or mechanical utility, it is held that it may be measured by objective tests, and that if in the circumstances a reasonable man would be satisfied, Y ought to be satisfied and he must pay. In this class of case, it is entirely proper not only to determine whether Y's expression of dissatisfaction is honest and real or feigned, but also to determine whether a reason has been given and, if so, what it is. An insufficient reason, though honest, will not excuse Y's duty to pay. Thus, in such cases, by a process of interpretation the courts conclude that "personal satisfaction" means satisfaction of a reasonable man; the condition of Y's duty to pay is not his personal satisfaction but the satisfaction of a reasonable man.

Where there is doubt whether the language means that Y's duty is conditional upon his personal satisfaction or upon the satisfaction of a reasonable man, the courts will adopt the latter. Moreover, courts hesitate to decide that language means personal satisfaction where the performance rendered is of such a nature that its value will be completely lost unless paid for. In such case, a condition of personal satisfaction will be found only if the language used is so clear as to mandate such result.

184. Approval or Certification as a Condition. Not infrequently, a contract provides that approval or certification by a third party is a condition to a promisor's duty. In a contract for the construction of a building the builder promises to erect a building according to the plans and specifications, but often the promise to pay is made conditional upon a certificate of an architect or engineer that the work has been performed according to the plans and specifications, or that it has been performed to his satisfaction. Where the certificate is withheld fraudulently or in bad faith, all courts hold the condition ineffective and require payment. The same result is reached where there is a failure or a refusal to make the necessary inspection of the work. Where, however, the architect or engineer acts honestly after a fair inspection, the condition is upheld.

Where a contract for the sale of goods requires approval of the goods by a third person as a condition to the buyer's duty to pay the price, a dishonest or unreasonable disapproval or withholding of approval by the third person results in a discharge of the buyer's duty to pay. To hold otherwise would make the buyer the guarantor of the honesty and reasonableness of the third party. However, where it appears that the third person acts in collusion with one of the parties to the contract and disapproves of the goods to relieve that party of the burden of the contract, the requirement of approval is waived and the contract enforced.

185. Nonperformance of Condition as Failure of Consideration. When we speak of a *failure of consideration* we mean that a promisor has not received what he bargained for. We do not mean that there is *no consideration* for his promise. In a bilateral contract, each promise to perform is consideration for the exchange promise, and the contract is binding. Where, however, one promisor fails to perform his promise there is a failure of consideration which will excuse performance by the other promisor. The thing bargained for is not only the promise but also the performance of the promise. In the case of a promise by A to perform in exchange for a promise by B to pay a sum of money, the promises are made in exchange for each other but each promisor also bargains for the performance of the promise. Thus, if A tenders performance and B fails to pay, there is a total failure of consideration and A's duty to perform is discharged. B's failure to pay or tender payment is a breach of the condition to A's duty to perform, which discharges A's duty.

186. Partial Failure of Consideration. Is a party justified in refusing to perform his promise if the other party has only partly performed his duty? It is generally held that, if the performance rendered is substantial, the other party must fully perform, but he may recover damages resulting from the partial failure of consideration. One party to a bilateral contract cannot enforce the promise made to him unless he has performed a substantial part of his own promise. In other words, the duty of one promisor is conditional upon substantial performance of the consideration he bargained for.

187. The Doctrine of Substantial Performance. In determining the legal effect of a partial failure of performance, the character and extent of the partial failure and its importance to the party who has bargained for a complete performance are prime considerations. Whether one is privileged to reject a partial performance depends on whether the partial performance was a substantial performance. If it was a substantial performance, there is no right to refuse it. Where a substantial performance has not been rendered, and there is justification for believing that it will not be rendered because the time for performance has passed or because the defects cannot be cured, the performance can be rejected, and the duty to render the exchange performance is discharged. The rule of substantial performance may apply to many kinds of contracts, but the most common example is the building contract.

188. Substantial Performance: The Building Contract. Ordinarily, the building contract is bilateral, the builder promising to build and the owner promising to pay. As in other bilateral contracts, the parties bargain not only for promises but also for the performances of the promises. If the builder fails to build there is a failure of consideration for the owner's promise to pay and his duty to pay is discharged.

Where the contract clearly states that a defect in the builder's performance, no matter how slight, shall constitute a material breach, the owner may reject any defective performance. The courts then say that full and complete performance by the builder is a condition of the owner's duty to pay. However, due to the nature of the performance to be rendered under a building contract and the difficulty involved in conforming to the many details specified, it is unusual that the contract contain language making any deviation from its terms a material breach. In the usual case, the courts say that substantial performance by the builder is the condition of the owner's duty to pay. Thus, if the defect in performance is slight or trivial, the builder has substantially performed and is entitled to the price. But he must account for the minor defects in his performance. Substantial performance is not full performance but something less; there is a breach of duty by the builder, small and unimportant, but it entitles the owner to his damages.

189. Substantial Performance: Trival or Material Breach. There is no formula to decide whether a breach is material or so trivial that we may say there has been substantial performance. The question is one of fact. The extent of the performance rendered, the degree of deviation from the terms of the contract, the value of that part which was not performed, and the extent the injured party may be adequately compensated for the breach, are important factors. Also important are the purposes and desires of the innocent party and the extent to which the defective performance or the nonperformance frustrates those purposes and desires. Courts have been influenced, also, by the hardship and oppression that may result from a rejection of the defective performance. Where the contract is one for the sale of ordinary goods, a rejection of the goods on the ground that the seller's performance is defective in part leaves them in the seller's hands for possible sale to others. But in the case of a building contract a rejection of the builder's performance may result in total loss. For this reason, the courts have been somewhat more lenient in the case of building contracts than they have been in cases of mercantile contracts.

It is generally held that if the builder's breach is willful and deliberate, no action may be brought for compensation even if the breach is so trivial that it may be said he has substantially performed. The doctrine of substantial performance is intended for the protection of those who have faithfully and honestly attempted to perform in full. Yet, it is clear that not every deviation, even though intentional, should defeat the contractor. If, in a given case, a contractor makes a substitution of materials in the honest belief that those called for in the specifications are less suitable to sound construction, he should not be denied compensation, and there is authority to that effect. This would indicate that the purpose of a willful departure from the terms of the contract and the value of the substitution to the owner should be considered.

In any case, the parties may by appropriate stipulation in their contract make any deviation from the letter of the contract such a material breach as to justify rejection of the tendered performance.

190. Substantial Performance: Installment Contracts. In the case of a contract to sell goods in installments, delivery by the seller and acceptance by the buyer are concurrent conditions. A tender of delivery of an installment by the seller is a condition of the buyer's duty to accept that installment and the buyer's duty to accept is a condition of the seller's duty to deliver. The failure of either party to perform as agreed in respect of one installment is not necessarily such a breach as will authorize the other to reject or cancel the whole contract. The UCC states in Sec. 2-612 that where there is an installment contract for the sale of goods requiring delivery of goods in separate lots to be separately accepted, failure to deliver an installment, or a tender of a nonconforming installment is a breach of the entire contract if it impairs the value of the whole contract. If it does, the buyer may reject or cancel the entire contract. Thus, the mere failure to make a proper delivery or to accept a delivery does not ncessarily give to the injured party the right to regard the entire contract as having been broken or his duty to further perform as having been discharged. The failure may or may not affect the value of the whole contract according to the circumstances. If it does not, the injured party may not elect to treat the entire contract at an end.

191. Substantial Performance: Time of Performance. Where a contract *expressly* provides that one party's performance *at a stated time* is a condition of the other's performance, all courts hold that the time of performance is of the essence of the contract. Thus, where A agrees to charter B's vessel if it arrives for loading on March 1 and the vessel does not arrive until March 2, the failure of the express condition relieves A of his duty to charter. But a mere promise to render a performance on a stated date does not alone make the time of performance of the essence of the contract and the failure to perform on that day does not necessarily discharge the duty of the other party.

192. Substantial Performance: Time of Performance, Sale of Land. In a contract for the sale of real property, a provision which calls for a conveyance of the land at a fixed time or for payment of the price at a fixed time does not make the time of performance of the essence of the contract. Failure of the seller to convey at a stated time does not discharge the purchaser's duty to pay, and failure of the purchaser to pay on the date specified does not discharge the seller's duty. But performance within a *reasonable time* is of the essence of all such contracts. The failure to perform within a reasonable time after the agreed day is a material breach. Thus, there is a substantial performance if the delay is not unreasonable in the circumstances, and such breach does not result in a discharge of the duty to render the counterperformance. Such a delay will, however, give rise to a claim for the resulting damages.

193. Substantial Performance: Time of Performance, Mercantile Contracts. Generally, the time for performance of mercantile contracts is of greater importance than of contracts for the sale of real property. A longer delay in performance is usually countenanced in real estate contracts than in other types. Indeed, it is usually said in the case of contracts for the sale of goods or for the sale of securities that the time of performance is of the essence of the contract, and that the failure of the seller to perform on the agreed date will justify a rejection of the subject matter by the buyer and result in the discharge of the buyer's duty to pay.

194. Substantial Performance: Time of Performance, Building Contracts. Building contracts usually prescribe a date for commencement of construction and a date for its completion. Unless the parties expressly provide that commencement or completion by the agreed date shall be a condition of the owner's duty to pay, a provision that is not usually included in such contracts, the courts generally hold that time is not of the essence. Since it is generally understood that performance by the contractor is subject to delay for many reasons, and since the building, as fast as it is constructed, becomes the owner's property because it becomes part of the owner's land, the courts hold that a reasonable delay by the contractor will not discharge the owner's duty to pay. But a delay, however short its duration, gives the owner the right to recover the resulting damages.

However, by apt and clear language the parties may make the time of performance of a building contract of the essence, and if the party in default cannot offer a justifiable excuse for the delay, or if on the facts it does not appear that the other has waived the delay, it will be enforced by the courts.

195. Waiver of Conditions. Where a seller is to make a delivery of goods upon a payment or tender of payment by the buyer of the price, his duty to deliver is conditional. But if he delivers the goods without a payment or tender of payment, he waives the condition and performs a duty he was not obliged to perform. It is not necessary that the buyer give the seller a consideration for the elimination of the condition. It is not a contractual modification by mutual assent; the waiver results from the action of the seller alone.

The same holds true in the case of a contract for the sale of land by which the seller is to convey title on a certain day. The conveyance on the agreed day may be the condition of the purchaser's obligation to pay, but the condition may be waived by the buyer. He waives not the conveyance but the condition that it be made on a specified day.

Where a seller promises to deliver goods "if the buyer pays the price on or before March first," and there is a failure to pay the price by that date, the seller is discharged of his duty to deliver the goods. Should the seller, nevertheless, deliver the goods, the condition of payment by that date is waived, but there is no waiver of payment.

In building contracts, an engineer's or architect's certificate is frequently made a condition of the owner's duty to pay. The owner agrees to pay for the work done and not for the certificate. Thus, the certificate is not part of the consideration for the promise to pay. It is merely a condition of the promise which the owner may waive by a suitable statement or by payment without having received the certificate.

196. Waived Condition May Be Reestablished. One who has waived a condition upon which his duty to perform is based may reinstate the condition in respect of his duty to perform in the future by giving notice of such intention. Such notice will not, however, destroy the effect of his waiver of the condition prior to the communication of notice.

197. Waiver of Condition Is Not a Waiver of Damages. A voluntary waiver of a condition upon which one's duty to perform is based eliminates the condition. If the condition is performance by the other party, and the condition is waived, nonperformance by the other party is still a breach of contract. Thus, where a purchaser is to pay for real property upon the delivery of the deed by the seller, the condition of the purchaser's duty to pay is delivery of the deed. If the purchaser pays the price before such delivery, he waives the condition of delivery but not the seller's failure to deliver, and he may pursue a remedy for the seller's breach.

11. Breach of Contract

198. In General. Most contracts impose a duty to perform some time after the contract is made. Others may require that performance take place immediately. As a general rule, there can be no breach of contract unless there is nonperformance of a duty to be performed immediately. Where the obligation is to perform in the future, it would seem that there is no breach until the time of performance arrives and the conditions, if any, of performance have been fulfilled.

Ordinarily, neither party to a contract expressly agrees that he will not hinder or prevent in any way the performance by the other of his contractual duties, but every contract imposes such a duty. A breach of that duty is a breach of contract. Also, it is the duty of a contracting party not to prevent the performance or fulfillment of any condition to his own duty to perform.

199. Total Breach and Partial Breach. A breach is generally said to be "total" when there has been a repudiation of the contract or nonperformance of so material and important a duty that it justifies the injured party in terminating the contract. A partial breach is one that is not so material. For either breach, an action may be brought at once by the aggrieved party to recover his damages. But where the breach is partial, the aggrieved party is not justified in stopping his own performance or refusing to perform, and he cannot regard such breach as a breach of the entire contract. The party who has committed the partial breach may continue to render the performance under his contract. Where the breach is total, the aggrieved party can collect damages for breach of the entire contract. A repudiation of the contract is a total breach, and if a party repudiates his contract before he is to render performance, the breach is usually called an anticipatory breach.

200. Anticipatory Breach. The majority rule today is that a breach of contract may take place long before the date performance is to commence. Such a breach takes place upon an unconditional repudiation of the contract by words or by act. A clear and positive statement by A to B that A will not or cannot perform his contract when the time for performance arrives is a repudiation. There is also a repudiation by A if A, having contracted to sell his horse, Domino, to B, now sells it to C.

Upon an anticipatory breach, an action for damages may be brought at once. The breach results from a manifestation of an intention not to perform in the future. The injured party may bring action immediately upon the repudiation, regarding it as having terminated the contract. He may instead wait for the time of performance, regarding the contract as binding on both parties, and base his action on the failure of the defendant to perform his contractual duties as agreed. If the injured party elects to wait for the date set for performance, ignoring the repudiation, he must not only accept performance by the repudiator if it is rendered at that time, but he must also keep himself in readiness to perform, for he does not regard the contract as terminated.

The UCC, Sec. 2-610, provides that where either party repudiates a contract for the sale of goods before performance is due, and the loss of that performance will substantially impair the value of the contract, the aggrieved party may (a) wait for performance for a commercially reasonable time, (b) resort to any remedy for breach of contract even though he may have indicated that he will wait for performance or has urged a retraction of the repudiation, and (c) in either case suspend his own performance while he negotiates with or awaits performance by the other party.

201. Anticipatory Breach: Injured Party Has Fully Performed. Where both parties to the contract are yet to perform at the time of repudiation by one, it is said that the aggrieved party has a right to regard the contract as terminated, that he may sue at once for the anticipatory breach, and that this right is afforded him so that he will not be required to keep himself in readiness to perform. Thus, if the injured party has already performed in full at the time of repudiation, or was not required to perform because the contract was unilateral, it is unnecessary to protect him by giving him an immediate right of action. He cannot be prejudiced by waiting for the date when the repudiator is to perform before bringing action. This reasoning has led to the statement, frequently made by the courts, that if the injured party is not then under a duty to perform, he cannot regard the repudiation as an anticipatory breach.

EXAMPLE

1. L lends $1,000 to B and B executes and delivers his promissory note for $1,000 to L payable 6 months after date. At the expiration of three months,

B makes a clear and positive statement to L that he will not pay the note. L must wait until the date of maturity of the note before bringing action. The courts hesitate to allow recovery of money before it is due. Money due in the future does not become due upon the debtor's statement that he will not pay it.

2. A and B enter into an agreement whereby A promises to deliver his tractor to B on June 1 and B promises to fence in A's property on July 1. A delivers the tractor as agreed. B on June 15 states that he will not fence in A's property. A must wait until July 1 and, if B does not perform on that day, A may bring action for damages. At the time of B's repudiation, A had fully performed.

3. S and B, on May 1, entered into a contract by which S promises to deliver a tractor on June 1 and B promises to pay $200 as the price on July 1. On May 15, B repudiates the contract. S may bring action for anticipatory breach. Many cases hold that B's duty to pay money is not of itself sufficient to deny recovery for anticipatory breach where S is still under duty to perform at the time of B's repudiation.

4. S, a seller, and B, a buyer, enter into a bilateral contract on June 1 for delivery of goods by S on July 1 and payment of the price by B on August 1. On June 15, B notifies S that he will not perform the contract. B's repudiation makes it unnecessary for S to tender performance, and enables S to bring action at once for an anticipatory breach. Here the contract was bilateral, and at the time of B's repudiation S had not rendered any performance.

202. Anticipatory Breach: Restitution as a Remedy. Where there has been an anticipatory breach, the injured party is entitled to the remedy of rescission just as he is in cases of total breach of contract by failure to perform a present duty. As a remedy for anticipatory breach, rescission is less objectionable than the remedy of damages. Damages must be fixed by looking to the future, to the day on which performance was to be rendered. The remedy of rescission presents no problem. The injured party upon rescission is entitled to restitution, the return of what he has given, or its value.

203. Anticipatory Breach: Retraction of Repudiation. One who has repudiated his contractual duties prior to the time set for performance may retract his repudiation by notice that he will perform his duties. Such a retraction restores the duties of both parties, and places them in the same position they occupied before the repudiation. This power of retraction is denied, however, where it appears that the injured party has changed his position relying on the repudiation. If an employee has repudiated his contract of employment and the employer has hired another, or has commenced suit based on the repudiation, there can be no retraction by the employee.

In respect of a contract for the sale of goods, the UCC in Sec. 2-611 provides that the repudiating party may retract his repudiation unless the aggrieved party has since the repudiation canceled the contract or materially changed his position or otherwise indicated that he considers the repudiation final. Sec. 2-609 states that the aggrieved party, upon the retraction, may demand in writing adequate assurance of performance and if he does not receive the same within 30 days after receipt of his notice he may regard the contract as having been repudiated.

204. Anticipatory Breach: Lack of Uniformity. The rule that a clear and positive repudiation of a contract, made by one party and known to the other, is a breach although it takes place before the time fixed for performance, is generally followed in this country. Some states have imposed limitations on the rule; others have extended it quite liberally. In New York, there has been recognition of the rule in cases of contracts to marry, contracts for personal services, and contracts for the sale or manufacture of goods. However, an action for damages for breach of a contract to marry is no longer maintainable in that state.

12. Rights of Third Parties

A. THIRD-PARTY BENEFICIARIES

205. In General. A contract creates rights and duties enforceable by the contracting parties. If one party refuses or fails to perform his promise, the other may bring action against him for the breach. One may enforce a promise to perform because it was made to him and because he gave a consideration in exchange for it. Both parties may alter, rescind, or discharge their contract without the consent of any third party. The contract is a private matter to the contracting parties; there is a "privity" of contract between them. For these reasons, it had been said many times by judges and writers that only the parties to the contract, those in privity, can acquire rights under it, and that third persons who are strangers to the contractual relationship have no standing to assert rights under the contract.

Thus, where, in a contract between A and B, B promised A, for a consideration supplied by A, to render a performance to C, it was thought that only A, the promisee, could enforce B's promise: that C was a stranger to the relationship and to the consideration and had no right to B's performance. However, the courts gradually came to recognize that A intended to benefit C and exacted the promise from B for that purpose, and that C should have an enforceable right against B.

206. Third-Party Beneficiary. A party who will be benefited by performance of a promise, though he is not a promisee and gives no consideration for the promise, is called a third-party beneficiary. Such a beneficiary is either a creditor beneficiary, a donee beneficiary, or an incidental beneficiary.

207. The Creditor Beneficiary. The beneficiary is a creditor beneficiary if, at the time the promise is made, the promisee owes the beneficiary a legal debt or obligation, and if the promise is made to extinguish that debt or obligation in whole or in part. Where *A* owes a debt to *C*, and *B*, for sufficient consideration given by *A*, promises to *A* that he, *B*, will pay a sum of money to *C*, *A*'s purpose in procuring *B*'s promise is to confer a benefit upon *C*. *C*, a creditor of *A*, is a creditor beneficiary, and acquires a direct right against *B* on his promise. Note that no promise is made to *C*. *A* is the promisee and he, also, acquires a right against *B* on the promise.

It is not necessary, however, that a debt be owing by the promisee to the beneficiary at the time the promise is made. If the promisee contemplates a debt or obligation to the third party in the future, the third party becomes a creditor beneficiary when he becomes a creditor of the promisee. Thus, *B* may promise *A* that *B* will pay *A*'s future debts. When *C* becomes a creditor of *A*, he can enforce *B*'s promise.

In most of the creditor beneficiary cases, the creditor has a monetary claim against the promisee. But the creditor may have in a given case the right to receive from the promisee some other performance, such as a delivery of goods or personal services. If the promisee intends that his duties to the creditor be extinguished by some performance by the promisor, be it a delivery of like goods, other goods, or the payment of money, the creditor is a beneficiary.

Not infrequently, the undertaking of the promisor must be interpreted in order to determine whether the promise to the promisee is to pay the debt or debts of the promisee or whether it is a promise to reimburse or indemnify the promisee against losses to a third party. A promise to indemnify the promisee is not a promise to pay the creditor.

208. Creditor Beneficiary: Assuming Grantee of Mortgaged Realty. An example of the creditor beneficiary relationship is one that arises from the sale of mortgaged real property. *A*, the owner of land, borrows money from *D*, and executes and delivers to *D* a bond by which he promises to repay the loan, together with a mortgage on *A*'s land as security for the payment of the bond. *D* is a creditor of *A* and now has an interest in *A*'s land. *A*'s interest in the land is usually called an equity of redemption. *A* now sells the land to *B*, who assumes payment of the mortgage debt; that is, he promises *A* that he, *B*, will pay the mortgage debt. *A* exacts *B*'s promise to benefit *D*. *D* is a creditor beneficiary and acquires a personal right against *B*. If the mortgage debt is not paid and *D* forecloses, and the amount realized on the foreclosure sale is not sufficient to satisfy the mortgage debt, *B* is liable to *D* for the balance. Of course, *A* is also liable on his bond. By selling the land, *A* does not rid himself of his personal liability on his bond.

209. Creditor Beneficiary: Nonassuming Grantee of Mortgaged Realty.
An interesting situation develops when *B*, in the example above, makes
no promise to *A* but sells the land to *C* and exacts from *C* a promise to pay
the mortgage debt. Many courts hold that *D* is a creditor beneficiary and
has a right against *C* because *B* exacts the promise from *C* for the benefit
of *D*, and that while *B* is not personally obligated to *D* he nevertheless
has a liability to *D* in the sense that *D* has a power over *B*'s land by reason
of the mortgage. It would seem on principle that this reasoning is not
sound. *B* no longer has an interest in the land upon the sale to *C*, and *D*'s
power is no longer one over *B*'s land. Some courts, including those of New
York, have recognized this and require that *B* be personally indebted to *D*,
the mortgagee, in order that *D* acquire a right against *C* on the promise.
They conclude that only *B* acquires a right against *C* on his promise.

210. Creditor Beneficiary: Other Examples. Other examples of the
creditor beneficiary relationship are those arising upon the sale of a business where the purchaser promises the seller that he will pay the outstanding debts; those in which a contractor gives an owner a bond promising to
pay materialmen and laborers; those in which a new partner enters a partnership and promises to pay a share of the debts incurred prior to his
admission to the firm. In these cases, it is immaterial that the identity of the
beneficiaries is not disclosed when the promise is made.

211. Creditor Beneficiary: Statute of Frauds. The promise made to
the promisee for the benefit of a third party is enforceable though oral. The
promise to pay the debt of another under the Statute of Frauds is a promise
to pay the debt of a person other than the promisee. If the promise is made
to the third party, the creditor, it is required to be in writing. In the
beneficiary case, it is made to the debtor.

212. The Donee Beneficiary. The third party is a donee beneficiary if
the promisee intended that the benefit of the promised performance should
be conferred upon the third party as a gift. Thus, in order that the donee
beneficiary acquire a right against the promisor, it is not necessary that
there be a legal debt or duty running from the promisee to the beneficiary.

If the beneficiary of a life insurance policy is other than the insured, he
is a donee beneficiary. There is no requirement that the beneficiary pay
premiums or that he be the promisee. The company promises the insured
that it will pay the proceeds of the policy to the beneficiary, and the
promisee, the insured, intends that the proceeds be paid the designated
beneficiary as a gift. All states allow an action by the beneficiary against
the company.

In a contract between an employer and a union, there may be certain items of performance by the employer for the benefit of workers who are members of the union. Such persons are donee beneficiaries. Where a contractor promises an owner that he will pay the wages of workmen at a stated rate, the workmen are donee beneficiaries. Contracts made by a governmental authority, such as a municipality, for services to be rendered for the benefit of inhabitants, have been held enforceable by the inhabitants as donee beneficiaries.

Many cases have arisen in which there is a blood or family relationship between the promisee and the beneficiary of the promise. For example, A withdraws his objection to the marriage of his daughter, C, in consideration of a promise by her future father-in-law and mother-in-law to pay her an annuity of $5,000 per year for life. If payments are not so made, it is held that the daughter, C, can recover on the promise as a donee beneficiary. Also, where A in consideration of services rendered to B receives a promise from B to pay A's wife a stated sum of money, the wife is a donee beneficiary and may enforce B's promise.

Some courts, notably those of New York, have based the family relationship cases upon a "moral obligation" running from the promisee to the beneficiary which entitles the beneficiary to support of the promisee. It is not clear how far the New York courts will go in finding a moral obligation as the family relationship becomes more removed. It seems, however, that the intent of the promisee should be the determining feature, not the degree of relationship between the promise and the beneficiary. The fact that there is a blood or family relationship may evidence the promisee's intention that the third party receive a gift, but the absence of such relationship will not alone negate such intent. In this respect, the New York decisions do not reflect the prevailing rule in this country.

213. The Incidental Beneficiary. It is clear that not every third person who would be benefited by the performance of a promise may enforce it. If there is no motive or intent on the part of the promisee that the third party receive performance in satisfaction of a debt owing him by the promisee, or as a gift, the third party is an incidental beneficiary and has no right to enforce the promise. Only the promisee has that right.

EXAMPLES

1. A promises to sell and deliver goods to B, and B promises that he will buy an automobile from the X Company and deliver it to A. There is no intent on the part of A that a gift should be made to the X Company, and A owes no debt or obligation to that company. Of course, the performance by

B of his promise will benefit the company in that it will increase its business, but that is not sufficient to give the company an enforceable right against *B* for nonperformance of the promise.

2. *C*, *D*, and *E* are creditors of *A*. For a sufficient consideration given by *A*, *B* promises *A* that he will put sufficient funds in *A*'s hands to enable *A* to pay the creditors. *C*, *D*, and *E* have no right against *B* on his promise. Performance by *B* of his promise will not alone satisfy the claims of the creditors. The debts will stand until *A* turns the money over to them. *A* does not intend that *B*'s performance satisfy *A*'s debts. *C*, *D*, and *E* are incidental beneficiaries.

214. Identification of Beneficiary. A beneficiary acquires no right to sue on a promise until he has become identified. But identification at the time the promise is made is not necessary; it is sufficient if the beneficiary becomes identified at least by the time of performance. Thus, where *B* promises *A* that he will pay *A*'s future debts, it is impossible to identify the future creditors at the time of the promise. When *A* acquires creditors, they may enforce the promise. Further, should a class of persons be designated beneficiaries, any person in the class may enforce the promise although he is not specifically identified when the promise is made.

B. ASSIGNEES

215. In General. We have seen that a donee or creditor beneficiary may enforce a promise not made to him and for which he furnishes no consideration. There is another third party, also a total stranger to a contract, who may acquire rights under that contract. He is an assignee, a person to whom a right to performance is assigned by a party to a contract.

Not every right or claim held by a party is assignable by him. Statutes exist which prohibit the assignment of certain claims against a government—the right to a federal pension and the right of a public officer or employee to future wages. While we do not deal herein with tort claims, it may be noted that claims for injuries to persons are not assignable. But, whatever the nature of the claim, once an action is brought to enforce it and the claim is reduced to judgment, it becomes a debt and is assignable.

The contract right most frequently assigned is the right to receive a payment of money, but rights to other types of performance, such as the right to receive delivery of a deed or a delivery of goods at a specified place, are just as freely assignable.

216. Assignment of Rights. Where a contract right is one for the payment of money, it is freely assignable unless it is clearly provided in the contract that the right to payment shall not be assigned. The debtor's duty to pay is not personal to the creditor; it cannot be said that it was intended that the debtor pay the creditor personally. Thus, money claims are freely assignable and upon payment by the debtor to the assignee of the claim the debtor is discharged. The same result is reached where the contract right assigned is one to receive a delivery of goods or of a deed to real property. Unless a contrary intent clearly appears, the obligor cannot have intended to deliver the goods or deed to the obligee personally.

Where the contract right is that of an employer to receive the services of his employee, the employee has contracted to render his services to the empolyer only and to no other. An assignment by the employer of his right would place the employee in a position where he would be required to render his services to the assignee, a duty he was not bound to perform by his contract. Indeed, the employee might initially have been unwilling to render services to any other person. Thus, it appears that the assignability of a contract right may be affected by the nature of the contract which gives rise to the right.

Further, in an employment contract, the employee's personal performance of his services is a condition to his right to receive payment. His right to receive payment is coupled with his duty to personally perform. An assignment of his right to receive payment is not effective unless he has personally performed the services required. Once the services have been performed, the employee is free to assign his right to compensation. Hence the assignability of a contract right may be affected by the fact that the right is coupled with a duty to perform.

A buyer, we have seen, may assign his right to receive a delivery of goods, but such assignment must not in any way affect the seller's duty to deliver. Hence it may not require the seller to deliver at a different place, or in any other way make his duty to deliver more burdensome. Nor can the buyer and the assignee arrange for such change without the consent of the seller. The UCC provides in Sec. 2-210(2) that all rights of either the buyer or the seller of goods may be assigned except where the assignment would materially change the duty of the other party or increase materially the burden or risk imposed on him by his contract, or impair materially his chance of obtaining return performance.

217. Assignment of Duties. An assignment of a duty signifies that the assignor intends another, the assignee, to perform the duty and that he, the assignor, shall be relieved of it. Whether or not the duty must be personally performed, the person charged with the duty cannot assign it to another without the assent of the person entitled to receive performance. An attempted assignment is actually a repudiation of the duty, and it results in a breach of contract.

Thus, if *A*, a famous tenor, has agreed to sing at *B*'s theater, he cannot assign his duty to sing. Similarly, a seller cannot assign his duty to deliver goods. Neither person may rid himself of his duty to perform by transferring the duty to another. Duties are not assignable. But if *B*, the owner of the theater, or the buyer assents to the assignment, he thereby agrees to accept performance of the duty by the assignee in place of performance by the assignor, and the assignor is discharged of his duty.

218. Delegation of Duties. We have seen that an assignment of a duty is an attempt by the assignor to rid himself of the duty by transferring it to the assignee. The law does not permit this to be done without the consent of the person entitled to receive performance of the duty.

A delegation of a duty must be distinguished from an assignment of a duty. If *D* is under a contract duty to pay a sum of money to *C*, or to deliver goods to *C*, or to deliver a deed to *C*, *D* may not assign his duty without the assent of *C*. But *D* may, without *C*'s assent, delegate his duty to *E*. Note that *D*'s duty is not one that he must personally perform. Upon delegation, *E* is to perform the duty for *D*, not in place of *D*. The duty to perform remains with *D*, and if *E* does not perform it as required by the contract, *D* is liable to *C* for breach of contract. The duties mentioned should be compared with a duty to paint a portrait, to render a performance at a theater, or to perform some other personal service. These duties must be performed personally. *C* exacts these duties of *D* because he wants *D* to personally perform them. Such duties may not be assigned or delegated without *C*'s consent.

Sec. 2-210 of the UCC provides that a party to a contract for the sale of goods may perform his duty through a delegate unless otherwise agreed or unless the other party has a substantial interest in having him perform personally the acts required by the contract. No delegation of performance relieves the party delegating of any duty to perform or liability for breach.

219. Assignment of Contracts. Frequently, the expression "assignment of contract" is encountered. If by such language the assignor intends to transfer to the assignee his duties as well as his rights, as we have seen, the assignment will not have that effect. His contract rights may pass to the assignee, but his duty to perform will not pass without the assent of the person entitled to receive performance of the duty. If, however, his duty is not to be personally performed by him, the assignment operates as a delegation of the duty. In at least one situation the matter is now controlled by statute. The UCC, Sec. 2-210, provides that an assignment of a contract to sell goods is an assignment of rights under the contract, and, unless the circumstances or language indicate the contrary, it is a delegation of the duties of the assignor. The assignee's acceptance of the assignment constitutes a promise by him to perform the duties. The promise is enforceable against the assignee by the assignor or by the other party to the contract as a creditor beneficiary. The section further provides that a prohibition against assignment of the contract is to be construed as barring only delegation of duties; it does not bar assignment of rights unless the circumstances so indicate.

220. Defenses Against Assignee. As a general rule, the assignee takes a claim subject to all defenses available against the assignor even if he is an innocent purchaser of the claim for value and without notice of any defense. This rule exists to protect the obligor against being put in a worse position by an assignment. If the original contract was void, the assignee acquires no rights. If it was voidable by the obligor, the assignment does not destroy the power to avoid it. In short, the assignee is in no better position than the assignor.

221. Estoppel Against Obligor. Where the obligor, to enable the assignor to assign his claim, makes a statement in writing to the effect that he has no defenses or counterclaims against the assignor, and the assignee purchases the claim in good faith relying on the statement, the obligor will be estopped from asserting any defense or counterclaim against the assignee. Even an oral statement to that effect made to a prospective assignee, which induces him to take the assignment, will result in an estoppel.

222. Successive Assignments of Same Right. Where an assignor assigns a right he is divested of it, and it passes to the assignee. If, thereafter, the assignor attempts to assign the same claim to another, no right passes to that other since the assignor had no right to pass. The prevailing rule in this country is that the first assignee in time acquires the right. Some states follow the English rule that the assignee for value and in good faith who first gives notice to the obligor of the assignment acquires the right.

Under either rule, if the obligor pays the assignor without notice of any assignment, or if he pays the second assignee without notice of the first assignment, he is discharged. If the obligor pays the second assignee without notice of the first assignment, and the second assignee accepts payment knowing of the first assignment, the second assignee will be deemed a trustee of the fund and will be required to turn it over to the first assignee. The obligor is, of course, discharged.

223. Implied Warranties of Assignor. It is usually held that an assignor impliedly warrants by the assignment that he will do nothing to prevent the assignee from collecting. Thus, if after the assignment, but before notice of the assignment is given to the obligor, the assignor discharges the obligor by release, acceptance of payment, or accord and satisfaction, the assignor is liable for money damages to the assignee. The assignor also impliedly warrants the genuineness and validity of the claim unless he expressly negates such warranty. He makes no implied warranty that the obligor will pay or perform.

224. Partial Assignment. The modern rule is that while the assignor may assign parts of his claim to different assignees as though the parts were separate claims, an assignee of one part cannot maintain a proceeding to enforce it unless he joins as parties to the suit all persons having a right to the obligor's performance.

225. Assignments for Security. Often an assignment is made to secure the assignee against a debt or obligation owing him by the assignor. When the assignor performs his duty the security reverts to the assignor. If the assignor does not perform as required, the assignee may realize on the assigned claim—that is, collect it from the obligor—and apply it to the obligation owing by the assignor. If there is a surplus, it must be turned over to the assignor.

226. Assignment for Collection. Not infrequently, assignments are made so that the assignee may collect the claim for the assignor. Unless statute provides otherwise, the assignee is permitted to sue in his own name. Indeed, it has been held that a statute requiring suit by the "real party in interest" does not prevent the assignee from suing in his own name. Where the assignee collects the claim, he holds the fund in trust for the assignor.

227. Form of Assignment. Any communication, oral or written, by the assignor to the assignee, evidencing an intention to transfer a right against an identified obligor, is effective as an assignment. The law sets forth no required form. Usually, however, the assignment is in writing. Where the right to be assigned is evidenced by a writing, a delivery of the writing, or indorsement and delivery, together with language indicating an intent to assign, is sufficient.

13. Discharge of Contracts

228. In General. A contract is discharged when the duty to perform it has been discharged by some fact or event after the contract is made. These facts or events may consist of any of the following: performance of the contract, breach of the contract, agreement between the parties, or operation of the law.

A. DISCHARGE BY PERFORMANCE OF CONTRACT

229. Discharge by Full and Complete Performance. Full and complete performance of the contract in respect of the nature, quantity, quality, and time of performance, results in the discharge of the contract. A partial performance does not operate to discharge the contract. One who materially deviates from the terms of his contract cannot recover, but if his partial performance has been accepted and retained, he can recover its value. Since, however, partial performance constitutes a breach, this right to compensation is subject to a claim for damages.

Where a contract is unilateral and calls for the payment of money, or where it is bilateral and the performance in exchange for the payment of money has been completely rendered, the payment of the amount due will discharge the contract. If in such case the payment is sent by the debtor, there is no discharge unless and until it is received. But, where the agreement requires that the payment be sent, or the creditor has so directed, the payment is made when sent, and the contract is discharged even though the payment is never received.

230. Payment by Instrument of Debtor. The delivery to the creditor of an instrument for the payment of money, negotiable or nonnegotiable, which is signed by the debtor as maker or drawer, will not operate as a discharge unless the creditor agrees to receive the instrument as absolute payment. Ordinarily, the instrument is only a means of payment, a conditional payment, and in the absence of such agreement by the creditor the payment is not made and the contract not discharged until the instrument is honored. The result is the same even if the debtor's instrument is a check certified at his request. Where, however, the creditor procures the certification of the debtor's check, there is a discharge of the debtor's duty to pay.

231. Payment by Instrument of Third Person. The delivery to the creditor of an instrument for the payment of money will discharge the underlying obligation of the debtor if the instrument has been signed by a bank as maker, drawer, or acceptor, and if there is no recourse on the instrument against the debtor—that is, if the debtor has not placed his signature on the instrument. In any other case, the underlying obligation of the debtor is not discharged but merely suspended until the instrument is due, and if it is not paid action may be brought on the instrument or on the underlying obligation of the debtor (UCC Sec. 3-802).

232. Application of Debtor's Payment. If the debtor is under duty to make several payments to the creditor, such duty arising from various transactions with the creditor, the debtor may direct that any payment made by him be applied to a particular debt. Thus, the debtor may decide which debt shall be discharged by his payment. If no direction is given by the debtor, the creditor may apply the payment as he sees fit, except that no application may be made to an illegal debt, to a debt which has not yet matured, or to a debt whose existence is disputed. A creditor who holds both secured and unsecured claims may apply the payment to an unsecured one. Where one of the debts has already been barred by the Statute of Limitations, the creditor may apply the payment to the debt barred. The statute does not affect the debt; it bars only the remedy. He may even apply the payment to a debt unenforceable under the Statute of Frauds. If one of the debtor's debts carries interest and another does not, the creditor may apply the payment to the non-interest bearing debt.

If the debtor has given no direction and the creditor has made no application, the courts will make the application that they deem fair and reasonable. Generally, the courts will make application to overdue interest rather than to principal, to unsecured rather than to secured debts, and if all are unsecured, to the oldest debt.

233. Tender of Performance. A tender of performance is not performance. It is an offer to perform coupled with the ability to perform. Standing alone, it does not result in a discharge of the duty to perform. One who is under a duty of immediate performance is not relieved of that duty by making a tender.

If performance of a duty cannot be rendered without the cooperation of the other party, it is necessary that the other cooperate and accept the tender. Where the performance to be rendered is a service or a delivery of goods, it cannot be completely performed unless the service or the goods are accepted. Thus, a tender of the service or goods makes it incumbent upon the other to accept, and if he fails to accept, the duty to render the service or deliver the goods is discharged. It is the failure to accept the tender, and not the tender alone, which results in the discharge. Similarly, the duty to pay a sum of money requires the cooperation of the creditor. The payment cannot be made unless the creditor accepts it. Here, his refusal to accept does not result in a discharge of the debtor's duty to pay. The creditor is not entitled to collect interest after the tender, but if he is later willing to accept payment of the principal the debor must pay.

B. DISCHARGE BY BREACH OF CONTRACT

234. In General. It is commonly said that a contract may be discharged by a party's total or partial failure to perform, by a party's renunciation of his duty to perform, or by a party's act which impedes or makes it impossible for him to perform.

235. Total Breach. One party's total failure to perform, which in the circumstances is not excusable, subjects him to liability for damages and gives to the injured party the immediate right to regard the contract as terminated or discharged and himself relieved of any duty to further perform.

236. Partial Breach. Where the breach consists of a partial failure to perform, whether the injured party may be equally precipitate in treating the contract as terminated and his duty as discharged depends on whether the breach is a trivial one or a material one. Where it is trivial or minor, there having been a substantial performance, the injured party is not discharged of his duty to perform. He is required to accept the defective performance and to continue the performance of his own duties, but retains the right to be compensated for the damages resulting from the breach. For a discussion of the rule of substantial performance see § 187 et seq.

237. Renunciation. Where one renounces his duties and liabilities under a contract by a clear and positive indication by words or conduct that he will not perform when his performance is due, the injured party may regard such indication as an anticipatory breach of contract discharging him from his duty to perform, or he may treat the contract as remaining alive and regard the failure to perform at the agreed time as the breach resulting in his discharge. A discussion of anticipatory breach appears in § 200 et seq.

238. Party's Prevention of His Own Performance. Not infrequently, one party performs an act or enters into a transaction which makes performance of his contractual duty impossible, thereby subjecting himself to liability for damages and bringing about a discharge of the other party's duty under the contract. Thus, if *A*, the owner of a garage, agrees to store *B*'s car in that garage for one year and within that period sells the garage, *A*'s breach subjects him to liability for damages and discharges *B*'s duty to perform.

239. Nonperformance of Condition. Often one party's duty to perform is subject to a condition; that is, he is not under a duty to perform until the condition is fulfilled. In such case his duty is subject to a condition precedent, and if that condition is not fulfilled within the time required, his duty to perform is discharged by nonperformance of the condition. Where the condition precedent is performance by the other party, his duty is discharged by the other party's failure to perform. Where the parties to the contract have agreed that their performances shall take place concurrently and in exchange for each other, their performances are concurrent conditions and a tender of performance by one must take place before the other comes under a duty to perform.

Where by the terms of the contract one party's performance is to take place before the other's, we have seen that the performance to be rendered first is a condition precedent to the other performance. Thus, where *S* agrees to deliver goods on Monday and *B* is to pay the price on Friday, the delivery of the goods is a condition precedent to *B*'s duty to pay the price. *S*'s duty to deliver is not conditional upon *B*'s duty to pay, but the performances are nevertheless in exchange for each other, and if *S* can show that *B* will not pay, *S* should not be required to deliver. There is a prospective failure of consideration for *S*'s undertaking and he should be discharged from his duty to deliver. Moreover, *S* has a right to damages without tendering delivery of the goods. He must, however, show strong proof that *B* will not be able to perform. Even the insolvency of *B* is not conclusive proof that he will be unable to pay.

240. Prevention by One of Performance by Other. Where one party performs an unjust act, making it impossible or substantially more difficult for the other to perform his duty, the duty is discharged. Thus, where an owner has contracted for the erection of a building on his land and then refuses to allow the contractor to come upon the land, the contractor's duty is discharged. Also, where the owner, knowing that the contractor is negotiating with a third person for the necessary building materials, induces the third person not to sell to the contractor, the contractor's duty should be discharged.

C. DISCHARGE BY AGREEMENT

241. Rescission. The parties may, by mutual assent, discharge their mutual rights and duties under their contract. If any right to receive a performance continues after such agreement, there is no complete rescission between the parties and the performance must be rendered.

Where the contract between the parties is unilateral—that is, only one party is under a duty and only the other has a right—a mutual assent to rescind is without a sufficient consideration to support it, and does not alone operate as a discharge. Where the contract is bilateral, each party has rights to give up, and a mutual assent to rescind the contract operates immediately as a discharge.

The mutual assent to rescind is not required to be evidenced by a writing under the Statute of Frauds. It may be orally concluded even if the rights and duties sought to be discharged arose out of a contract required to be in writing. Where, however, the discharge of one contract results from the making of another contract substituted for it, the new contract may be required to be in writing under the Statute of Frauds even though the former was not.

242. Release. A release, sometimes called a special release, is a statement in writing by which one party discharges another from a particular duty. At common law, to be effective as a discharge, the release was required to be under seal or given in exchange for a consideration. Most states have abolished the effect of the seal but still require a consideration to validate the release. However, statutes in some states provide that a signed release in writing operates as a discharge. In New York, a signed release needs no consideration to support it. Other forms of release are the mutual release by which two or more persons who owe duties to each other extinguish or discharge those duties, and the general release by which a creditor or obligee discharges each and every duty owing him by the obligor. The UCC in Sec. 1-107 provides that any claim or right arising out of an alleged breach can be discharged in whole or in part without consideration by a written waiver or renunciation signed and delivered by the aggrieved party.

243. Gift. Where, as in New York, a written release signed by the creditor or obligee is made sufficient to discharge a claim even without consideration, the creditor or obligee makes the discharge as a gift.

In New York, a receipt indicating "payment in full" of the claim, delivered by the creditor, may be evidence of an intent to discharge the balance by gift if the sum paid is less than the amount due. However, in many states the delivery of the receipt is not of itself sufficient evidence of such intent.

244. Substituted Contract. A contract is frequently discharged when the same parties make a new agreement relating to the same subject matter. The new agreement substituted for the antecedent one must, like any other contract, satisfy the requirements of a valid and enforceable contract. The making of the new contract, if its provisions are not exactly those in the former contract, operates as a discharge of the prior contract. The failure to perform the new contract does not revive the old.

245. Novation. A novation is an agreement by which the duty of one party to a contract is assumed by another with the consent of the person entitled to performance of the duty. Thus, where X owes a duty to Y, Y may enter into an agreement with Z by which Z agrees to perform the duty and X is to be discharged. It amounts to a substitution of Z's duty for X's duty with the consent of Y. Of course, Z consents to the substitution upon making of his promise to perform the duty. It is generally held that X's consent is not necessary.

246. Accord and Satisfaction. We have seen that part payment of a liquidated debt, payment of which is due, is not a sufficient consideration for the creditor's promise to accept it in full satisfaction of the debt, and the creditor may bring action for the balance. But where the debtor, not being bound to do so, performs an act, renders any service, or delivers goods, he furnishes a consideration and the debt is discharged. If the liquidated debt is not yet due, the receipt by the creditor of a lesser sum will discharge the claim, the payment by the debtor before the due date being a sufficient consideration for the creditor's promise to receive the lesser payment in full satisfaction.

Where the creditor's claim is unliquidated, the debtor in paying any amount furnishes a sufficient consideration, and the creditor's receipt of the payment in full satisfaction discharges the claim.

For a more complete discussion of discharge by accord and satisfaction, see § 138 et seq.

247. Terms of Contract. The terms of the contract itself may provide for discharge of the rights and duties of the parties thereto upon lapse of time or upon the happening of a specified event. Common provisions effecting a discharge are those which state that a lease shall terminate upon a sale of the leased property by the landlord, or that a contract shall terminate upon the death or bankruptcy of one or either of the parties, or that performance shall be excused in the event of fire, strike, war, and so on.

248. Account Stated. It is quite common that persons doing business with each other enter into a series of transactions resulting in an open running account, and that they may not know at any particular time what the state of such account is and which one is debtor or creditor. However, where the debts owing by each are certain and liquidated, it may be readily determined by arithmetic what amount is due and by whom. If the parties make the correct arithmetic computations and strike a balance, there is an account stated.

Where the running account is made up only of liquidated debts and a balance is struck, there is usually an express or an implied promise by the debtor to pay that balance. But in such case there is no sufficient consideration for the debtor's promise since, if the reckoning is accurate, he is promising to do only what he is already obligated to do. Yet, the promise is held enforceable even without consideration. However, where there has been error in striking the balance due, the mutual assent was to a balance thought to be correct and the promise is not enforcable. The account stated is only evidence of the balance due; it is not conclusive on the parties.

Where the running account includes one or more unliquidated debts and a balance is struck by agreement, the balance is reached without regard to the accuracy or validity of the unliquidated debts, and the promise to pay such balance is enforceable. Though this is often called an account stated, it is also the compromise of a dispute, or where the balance is paid, it is an accord and satisfaction. In the case of a running account consisting only of liquidated items, the balance struck by mutual assent is not a compromise, since there is no dispute about any of the items. It is merely an accord, and when the balance is paid there has been an accord and satisfaction.

D. DISCHARGE BY OPERATION OF LAW

249. Impossibility of Performance: In General. When one is sued for nonperformance of his promise, he may interpose as a defense that the happening of an event has made it impossible for him to perform, that his purpose in making the contract has been frustrated by an event, or that an event has made it impossible for the other party to render the agreed performance in exchange for his. Thus, he may offer as justification for his nonperformance the fact (*a*) that he cannot perform, (*b*) that the promise given in exchange for his cannot be performed, or (*c*) that it is impossible to achieve his purpose in making the contract. Note that the defense in (*b*) is actually failure of consideration because he will not receive the performance to be rendered in exchange for his own. In (*c*) the defense is not that it has become impossible for either party to perform, but that it has become impossible for him to realize the benefit or advantage he bargained for and his purpose in making the contract has been frustrated. All three defenses indicate that something has become impossible due to a supervening event. The event may be the destruction of the specific subject matter of the contract, the death or illness of a necessary person, the destruction or nonexistence of a condition or means of performance, the enactment of a law, the act of a government, or an interference by a contracting party.

250. Destruction of Subject Matter. Often the performance of a promise becomes absolutely impossible because of the destruction of a specific thing. Where A contracts for the sale to B of a specific pile of lumber for an agreed price, title to pass to B upon delivery, both parties understand that if the subject matter is destroyed A's promise to deliver cannot be performed. They make no contractual provision covering that eventuality; they merely assume that the specific pile of lumber will continue to exist. Thus, if the lumber is destroyed without the fault of A, his duty to deliver is discharged. B then takes the risk of nondelivery, the risk that he will not receive what he bargained for. But the fact that he will not receive the agreed exchange for his promise to pay discharges him from his duty to perform his promise, not because it is impossible for him to pay but because of the failure of consideration, and if he has paid all or part of the price he may recover the payment. A, the seller, must bear the loss since by the agreement title was not to pass until delivery.

It has often been said that since both parties contemplate the continued existence of the specific goods, the duty to deliver is subject to the implied condition that they will continue to exist, and if the condition fails because they cease to exist the seller is discharged.

In the case of a contract for the construction of a building, the destruction of the partially completed building will not relieve the contractor of his duty since it has not become impossible for him to perform. He may still erect the building, though it will be more expensive for him to do so. Where he must complete the structure by a certain date and he can no longer do so because the partially completed building is destroyed, the delay may well be excused, but the duty to reconstruct must be performed.

251. Destruction of Means of Performance. Not infrequently, the performance of a duty requires the continued existence of some physical condition or some means of performing the duty. If the performance cannot be made unless the condition or means continues to exist, the nonexistence or destruction of the means or condition will discharge the duty. One who contracts to tow a vehicle across a particular bridge is discharged from his duty if the bridge has collapsed. One who contracts to supply water from a particular well is excused from performance if the well dries up. The duty to sell goods to be manufactured in a particular factory is discharged by destruction of the factory. One who contracts to furnish water for irrigation, without specifying the source, is not discharged by a drought.

252. Death or Illness of a Necessary Party. Where the continued life and health of a party is necessary because of the nature of the performance to be rendered by him, his death or disabling illness discharges the duty to perform. Thus, where the contract requires that one render a personal service, his death or illness discharges his duty to perform. On the other hand, if his promise is merely to pay a sum of money, performance is not discharged by death or illness.

In an employment contract, the death of either the employer or the employee makes further performance by the deceased impossible. If at the time of the death of an employee he has already performed services, the employer is not discharged from his duty to pay for them. But the employer is not bound to accept or pay for services offered by the representative of the employee's estate, since by contract he is entitled to the services of the employee personally in exchange for his promise to pay, and to the extent that the employee does not perform there is a failure of consideration.

The death of the employer in a case where his duty is to personally direct, supervise, and control the services of the employee makes it impossible for the employee to render the agreed service. The employee's duty to perform is discharged. The duty to pay is not rendered impossible by the employer's death, but there is a failure of consideration for his promise to pay since the employee cannot perform as agreed, and the duty to pay is discharged.

A contract by which one promises to care for and support another for a stated period of time is discharged by the death of either, or by the prolonged illness of the person rendering the service. But there is no discharge of the duty to provide care and support in the event of illness of the party to receive such service since it is one of the risks assumed.

Not infrequently, the person whose continued life and health are essential to performance of the contract is not a party to the contract but a third person. Where A contracts with B for B's services as an accompanist to *C*, a famous singer, the death or extended illness of *C* will operate as a discharge of the contract between *A* and *B*. The death or disabling illness of *B* will also discharge the contract between *A* and *B*. The death of *A* should not, however, discharge the contract, since neither *B*'s agreement to accompany *C* nor *A*'s agreement to pay is rendered impossible.

253. Performance Involving Danger To Life or Health. There are a number of cases in which the performance of a promise involves a danger to the life or health of the promisor which was not contemplated when the agreement was made. It is generally held that if the danger is great, considering the nature of the required performance and the extent of loss resulting from a breach, the duty to perform is discharged. Thus, where one who has contracted to paint a building discovers that there is a serious danger that it will collapse, he is discharged from his duty to perform. On the other hand, a duty to repair a building known to be in such a state that collapse is possible is not discharged. The duty is to eliminate the danger. One who has contracted to render a performance in a particular locality is discharged from his duty if the outbreak of a communicable disease in that locality creates a great danger to life and health. However, it is not necessary that there be a danger to the life or health of a contracting party. One may be discharged from his duty to perform if performance may constitute a danger to the life or health of third parties. It has been held that the owner of a vessel is discharged from a contractual duty if his performance will imperil the safety of his passengers.

254. Subsequent Legislation. A duty, the performance of which is lawful at the time the contract is made, will be discharged by legislation rendering performance a violation of law. A carrier's duty to transport goods at a particular rate is discharged by legislation creating a higher rate. An ordinance prohibiting the erection of wooden buildings discharges a contractual duty to erect such a building.

255. Outbreak of War. A contract made with a resident of another country may be rendered illegal by the outbreak of war with that country. Since performance is illegal, the duty to perform is discharged.

256. Act of a Government. An act of governmental authority which makes impossible the performance of a contractual duty results in a discharge of the duty. Thus, a duty to manufacture and sell goods is discharged by a government requisition requiring the seller to deliver his entire output to the government. The duty of a carrier to transport goods to a particular destination is discharged by a confiscation of the goods by government inspectors. The duty to sell property will be discharged by the acquisition of the property by a government under its power of eminent domain even though the seller must receive just and fair compensation for his property.

257. Interference by Contracting Party. Where the performance of a contractual duty by one party is prevented or made more difficult or more expensive by the other party to the contract, the nonperformance is not a breach. Indeed, one is not permitted to take advantage of a nonperformance for which he is responsible. The duty to perform is in such case discharged. Some courts have said that the duty to perform is conditioned upon the absence of interference by the other party. Others have said there is an implied promise not to interfere with the performance by the other party.

258. Frustration of Purpose. Each party to a contract has reason for entering into a contractual relationship with the other. If the happening of an event frustrates the purpose of one party, that party's duty to perform is discharged, and the other party's duty is discharged by the failure of consideration. A enters into an agreement of lease with B. A enters into possession and commences to pay rent. A's purpose was to sell liquor on the premises, and this was known to B. A law is now passed which makes the sale of liquor unlawful. Although such enactment does not render it impossible for A to pay rent, it does frustrate A's purpose in leasing the premises. Recent cases indicate that the tenant's duty to pay rent is discharged by the legislative act, the sale of liquor on the leased premises being the basis or essence of the lease. But where the parties do not regard the sale of a particular commodity as the basic purpose of the lease, the legislative prohibition will not discharge the lessee's duty to pay rent. Similarly, where the leased premises are destroyed without the fault of the lessee, it not impossible for him to pay rent, but his purpose is frustrated and his duty to pay rent is discharged.

259. Performance Commercially Impracticable. Where, under a contract to sell goods, a seller's delay in delivery, or nondelivery of all or part of the goods is occasioned because it has become commercially impracticable to perform as agreed due to (*a*) the occurrence of a contingency the nonoccurrence of which was a basic assumption on which the contract was made or (*b*) compliance with a foreign or domestic governmental regulation or order, there is no breach of duty by the seller if he complies with the following requirements: (*1*) Where only part of the seller's capacity to perform is affected, he must allocate production and deliveries among his customers fairly and reasonably; and (*2*) he must give the buyer seasonable notice that there will be delay or nondelivery, and, when allocation is required, he must so notify the buyer of the estimated quota available to the buyer (UCC Sec. 2-615).

This Code provision deals only with the matters of the seller's delay in performance and his failure to perform fully in respect of the quantity of the goods. It makes no attempt to mention the specific contingencies which make full and complete performance commercially impracticable, but the Official Comment to the Section indicates that severe shortage in the goods contracted for due to unforeseen shutdown of sources of supply, local crop failure, war, or embargo which causes marked increase in cost or which prevents the seller from acquiring the necessary goods, comes within the scope of the Section. If, however, it appears that the parties have made full performance by the seller a condition of the buyer's duty, the provisions of the Section are not applicable.

260. Impossibility of Performance of Condition Precedent. Often a party being sued for nonperformance of his duty defends on the ground that a condition precedent to his duty has not been performed. We have seen that when the duty to perform is subject to a condition precedent, there can be no breach of duty unless the condition is performed. But is the performance of the condition precedent excused where it has become impossible? A building contract provides that payment by the owner shall be made upon the production of an architect's or engineer's certificate that the work was done in accordance with the contract, plans, and specifications. Due to the death, insanity, or other disability of the architect or engineer, it is impossible to produce the certificate. It is held that the production of the certificate is excused. It is true that it is of paramount importance to the owner that the building be erected as agreed, but the certificate is only evidence of such performance, and if other evidence that the work has been properly done is available, it is sound to dispense with the requirement of the certificate rather than to deprive the contractor of payment.

In many cases, the performance to be rendered as a condition precedent has been bargained for by the other party. The duty to perform the condition precedent may be discharged by impossibility, but this does not subject the other party to a duty to perform. Thus, where S agrees to deliver specific goods to B and B agrees to pay ten days after delivery and those goods are totally destroyed by fire, S's duty to deliver is discharged but B need not pay the price. While the delivery of the goods is a condition precedent to B's duty to pay, the delivery is also in exchange for payment, and nondelivery results in a failure of consideration which discharges the duty to pay. It is not just to require B to pay something for nothing. The owner who must pay the contractor if it has become impossible to produce an architect's certificate bargained essentially for work and labor, and he suffers no substantial loss or harm by the requirement to pay. These parties have received essentially what they bargained for. They are not paying something for nothing.

261. Restitution. Where a party has received payment in advance for his performance but his duty to perform has been discharged because of impossibility, he is under a duty to restore the advance payment. Accordingly, one who has contractd to render personal services and has been paid in advance must make restitution if it becomes impossible for him to render the services because of prolonged disabling illness. If he has rendered some performance before such illness, he may retain the reasonable value of his services but must restore the balance. Where a party has rendered part performance and is discharged from his duty to further perform because of impossibility, he is entitled to the reasonable value of the performance rendered.

Where there is no excuse for failure to complete performance, there can be no recovery for performance rendered before the breach, and damages must be paid for the breach. Thus, a contractor under a contract to erect a building is not discharged by the destruction by fire of the uncompleted structure, and he is not entitled to recover compensation for the work done. Indeed, he is bound by contract to complete a building, and unless he does so he is liable in damages.

262. Act of God. In the law of impossibility of performance, the courts have recognized that the supervening events which make performance of a duty impossible are often caused by the hand of man as well as by an act of God, and that the cause of the impossibility to perform is not the determining feature. Impossibility caused by an act of God does not always result in a discharge of duty. A party's duty to deliver 10,000 bushels of beans "growing on his farm" is discharged if the crop is destroyed by flood or storm. But a duty to deliver 10,000 bushels of beans, without specifying the source, will not be discharged because of a flood or storm. In the latter case, it is commonly said that impossibility is not an excuse. Actually, there is no impossibility at all. The duty to deliver may be performed by acquiring the commodity anywhere. In each case, an act of God is the cause of nonperformance, yet only in the first does it result in a discharge of the duty.

263. Implied Condition. It was often said at common law that impossibility of performance did not result in a discharge of a duty because a contracting party could by suitable provision protect himself from any eventuality. Some courts repeat the common-law rule but assert that there are certain exceptions to its operation, and they base the exceptions on a theory of implied conditions. They say that where the performance of the contract depends on the continued existence of a person or thing, or the parties contemplate the continued existence of a person or thing, the death or disabling illness of the person or the destruction of the thing discharges the duty to perform. They imply a condition that the person will continue to exist and remain in good health, or that the thing will continue to exist, and conclude that, if the person or thing ceases to exist or the person becomes so ill that he is incapable of performing his duty, the condition fails and the duty is discharged. Thus, if the contract is to paint a house or to construct a wooden building, or to render personal services, there is an implied condition that the house or the employee will continue to exist, or that no law will be passed making the erection of a wooden building unlawful. If, in any of these cases, the condition fails, the duty to perform is discharged. While difficulty is encountered where the contract does not contain language which can be so interpreted, the theory of implied conditions is used to reach a just result, and to that end it serves a useful purpose.

264. Subjective vs. Objective Impossibililty. Subjective impossibility is the personal inability of a party to perform a duty which others can perform. A debtor may be unable to pay because he has no funds and can procure none. His duty to pay is not excused by such impossibility. Only objective impossibility will discharge a duty. There is an objective impossibility when the performance cannot be made by the promisor or by anyone else.

265. Bankruptcy. The decree of a bankruptcy court granting to the bankrupt a discharge of his provable debts (except those not affected by a discharge) operates to discharge the debtor from the duty to pay. The mere insolvency or inability of a debtor to pay does not result in a discharge.

266. Material Alteration. A material alteration of a contract made or authorized by a party thereto without the consent of the other discharges the other from his duty to perform. The innocent party may, however, if he so elects, hold the guilty party to the contract as altered or to the contract as originally made. A material alteration is one which changes the legal effect of the contract. Alterations in the amount to be paid, the time of delivery, the time of payment, and the place of performance are deemed material.

14. Remedies for Breach of Contract

267. In General. The law recognizes a duty to perform a contract and affords a remedy for its breach. The remedy most frequently sought is the judgment for money damages, the only remedy recognized by the courts at common law. In equity the remedies of specific performance, rescission, and injunction are often granted, but only in cases where the plaintiff can show that the law courts cannot award damages or that the remedy of money damages is inadequate. If the remedy at law is adequate, equity will not take jurisdiction.

268. Damages at Law. The remedy of money damages is not granted to penalize the defendant. The judgment for money damages is granted to enable the plaintiff to secure compensation for a loss suffered by him by reason of the defendant's breach. In determining whether the plaintiff is entitled to damages at all or whether he is entitled to the sum prayed for, the law courts apply certain rules or yardsticks designed to meet the particular case.

269. Rule for the Measure of Damages: Employment Contracts. Where there has been a breach of contract by an employer, the employee may recover the agreed salary for the unexpired portion of the employment contract. However, if the employee secured other employment of a similar nature and rank during the unexpired portion of his contract, or if it can be shown that he could have secured such employment in the same general area during that time, the compensation that he received or could have received will be deducted from his damages. Sums that were earned or that could have been earned by him in employment of a dissimilar rank and dignity will not be deducted. Expenditures to be made by the employee as incidental to performance of the unexpired portion of his contract are to be deducted. Thus, where A employs B as a salesman for

129

one year at a salary of $600 per month, B to bear all costs of travel, and A wrongfully fires B at the end of the ninth month of employment, B's damages are $1,800 less the traveling expenses he would have borne for three months and any compensation he may have earned or could have earned during the three-month period in employment of similar rank and dignity in the same general locality. Where the employee is guilty of a breach, the employer may recover the difference between the employee's compensation and the cost of procuring another to perform the services.

270. Rule for the Measure of Damages: Construction Contracts. In the case of a contract for the construction of a building, a breach by the builder during the process of construction will entitle the owner to a judgment for money damages measured by the actual cost of completion. Where the breach by the builder is a trivial or minor one resulting from inadvertence or oversight, so that it may properly be said that the builder has made substantial performance, the owner may recover for the breach the difference between the value of the building as completed and the value it would have had if constructed according to the letter of the contract. Where the breach by the builder is a material one, the cost of replacement is the measure of damages. Where the builder has failed or refused to commence performance, the measure of damages is the difference between the contract price and the cost of construction by another builder. Should the builder delay completion beyond the date fixed by the contract, the owner may recover the amount by which the building has declined in value during the delay, or the reasonable rental value for the period of delay, according to whether the building was being constructed for resale or for occupancy.

Should the owner commit a breach by repudiating the contract during construction, the builder may recover the agreed price, less installments received and less the cost to the builder of completion. Thus, where the builder is to construct a building and the owner is to pay $25,000, a repudiation by the owner after having paid $15,000 will entitle the builder to $10,000 minus what it would cost him to complete the building.

271. Rule for the Measure of Damages: Contracts to Sell Goods. Sec. 2-708 of the UCC provides that the seller's damages for the buyer's repudiation or nonacceptance of the goods is the difference between the market price at the time and place of tender and the purchase price, together with any incidental damages but less the expenses saved by the seller in consequence of the buyer's breach. If this measure of damages is inadequate to put the seller in as good a position as performance by the buyer would have done, then the seller may recover the profit he would have made if the buyer had fully performed, together with incidental damages and a due allowance for costs incurred by the seller. However, the buyer is entitled to a credit for payments he has made or for the proceeds of a resale of the goods by the seller.

Under Sec. 2-710 of the UCC, "incidental damages" to the seller are those suffered in connection with the return or the resale of the goods, or otherwise resulting from the buyer's breach. Included are the commercially reasonable costs to the seller in stopping delivery, in transportation, and in the care and custody of the goods after the buyer's breach.

Where there is a breach by the buyer before the time set for his performance, the seller's damages shall be based on the market price prevailing at the time the seller learned of the repudiation [UCC Sec. 2-723(1)].

The buyer's damages for nondelivery or repudiation by the seller are measured by the difference between the market price at the time the buyer learned of the breach and the contract price, together with incidental and consequential damages but less expenses saved. Market price is determined as of the place of tender, or where the breach occurs after arrival of the goods, as of the place of arrival (UCC Sec. 2-713). The buyer's incidental damages include his expenses reasonably incurred in inspection, receipt, transportation, and care and custody of goods rightfully rejected. His consequential damages include any loss which the seller had reason to know would occur and could not have been prevented by the buyer.

272. Duty to Mitigate Damages. Where there has been a breach of contract, the aggrieved party must make all reasonable efforts to keep his damages as low as possible. For example, one who is employed for a specified period of time and who is wrongfully discharged is under a duty to seek similar employment in the same general locality for the balance of the employment period. His recovery is lessened if he can secure such employment and fails to do so. If, however, he makes reasonable effort to secure other employment, the expenses incurred in the attempt are included as damages.

273. What Damages Are Recoverable. The rule universally followed in this country is that a defendant is liable only for those damages which flow as a natural and proximate result of the breach of contract. Many courts, stating the same rule in a different way, have held that only those damages contemplated or foreseen at the time of the contract are recoverable. Damages which are not the natural and proximate consequence of the breach, or which are not contemplated or foreseen when the contract was made, are called indirect or remote damages.

EXAMPLES

1. A enters into a contract to replace a roof on B's dwelling. The roof installed is defective and water leaking into the dwelling damages the walls. The damage is the natural and proximate consequence of the breach. It could have been foreseen as the result of the breach.

2. S agrees to sell and deliver to B a quantity of raw materials. S fails to deliver and B is unable to procure such materials elsewhere. As a consequence, B closes down his factory for 10 days. Since S has no reason to believe the raw materials are not available elsewhere, he cannot foresee that the factory will close down. Hence, losses sustained by the shutdown will not be recovered.

3. A, a salesman, contracts with the X Railroad Company for carriage from Pittsburgh to New York. A has appointments in New York with certain of his customers. A is carried to Harrisburg, but further transportation fails and A is unable to keep his appointments. A cannot recover for his loss of business since the X Railroad Company had no reason to know of the appointments.

Special damages, which are ordinarily remote and indirect and hence not recoverable, may become recoverable if notice is given when the contract is made that the contract is made for a special purpose or that in the event of a breach certain damages will be sustained. Such damages are then contemplated and foreseen as a result of the breach. Notice given after the making of the contract but before the breach is not sufficient to accomplish this result.

274. Damages Must Be Certain. Damages resulting from a breach of contract are not recoverable unless there is a sufficient basis for estimating their amount with reasonable certainty. Reasonable certainty does not, however, mean absolute certainty or mathematical accuracy and precision. The best estimate and approximation in the particular circumstances may be sufficient. In this respect, the courts know that a breach of contract is the cause of the difficulty, and the person guilty of the breach may not be permitted to insist too strongly that the damages are not clear and certain.

A situation arises very frequently in which it is asserted that the breach has caused a loss of prospective profits. Where A and B enter into a partnership for a term of 10 years, and after the fifth year B withdraws from the firm, it is held that A may recover as damages his loss of profits for the remaining 5 years, and evidence of profits the firm earned during the first 5 years may be considered as an indication of A's loss of profit. Future profits may be shown by past experience and it is sufficient if the evidence shows the extent of damages as a reasonable inference although the result is only approximate. If, however, B repudiates the partnership agreement before

the firm enters into business, the loss of profits is too conjectural and specu-
lative. It is not certain that there would have been any profit at all.

275. Cost of Litigation as Damages. Not infrequently, a breach of
contract by one party causes the other to become involved in litigation
begun by a third party. If such event can be foreseen at the time the contract is made, the amount of a judgment rendered and the expenses of the
litigation may be recovered as damages. Thus, where A has contracted to
furnish B a machine suitable for B to use in a manufacturing process, and
the machine is defective and causes injury to X, an employee of B, B can
recover from A the amount of any judgment recovered by X against B
together with the expenses of litigation incurred by B.

276. Liquidated Damages. Parties often insert into their agreement
a provision fixing the amount of damages to be paid in the event of a breach
of contract. If the amount of damages fixed is a reasonable estimation of
the actual damages, and if the actual damages are incapable or difficult of
accurate forecast, the provision for liquidated damages will be enforced.
However, if the actual damages caused by the breach could have been accurately estimated, and the liquidated damages provided for exceed the
actual damages, the provision will be stricken down as a penalty. In cases
of doubt, the courts have usually held the provision a penalty.

Where a contracting party makes a deposit of money or property as
security for his performance and agrees that, upon his failure to perform,
the other may retain the deposit as liquidated damages, the agreement
will be enforced if it is a reasonable estimation of the actual damages.

The UCC, Sec. 2-718, provides that a contract for the sale of goods
may fix as liquidated damages an amount which is not unreasonable in the
light of the harm caused by the breach, the difficulty of proof of loss, and
the inconvenience or nonfeasibility of otherwise obtaining an adequate
remedy.

277. The Remedy of Specific Performance. The remedy of specific
performance is a remedy granted in a proper case by a court of equity
upon proof that there is no adequate remedy at law. Where the remedy
at law for damages is available and adequate, an equity court will not act.
In granting the remedy, the equity court orders the defendant to render
precise and exact performance of his promise, and if he refuses to comply
with the court's order he is incarcerated for contempt and is kept in custody
until he does comply with the order. Whether the remedy will be granted
rests in the discretion of the equity court, and in determining whether it
will act the court will invoke certain well-established maxims. Examples

of these are "He who seeks equity must do equity"; "He who comes into equity must come in with clean hands"; and "Equity aids only the diligent." Specific performance will not be granted in favor of one who is guilty of fraud, bad faith, undue influence, or duress. Equity will deny a prayer for specific performance where it appears that the consideration for the promise is so grossly disproportionate that it makes enforcement unconscionable. In the exercise of its discretion, equity will not aid one who is guilty of laches—that is, who has delayed his suit too long.

278. Contracts to Sell Unique Personal Property. Where a contract is made for the purchase of a work of art, a rare book, a patent right, or shares of stock not available in the open market, and the seller fails to make a delivery of the same, the buyer's remedy at law is inadequate and equity will grant specific performance. In the case of ordinary property such as wheat, coal, or lumber, the damage resulting from a failure to deliver is readily reducible to money, and a money judgment is substantially adequate relief.

Where the buyer refuses to accept delivery of the unique personal property and to pay the price thereof, there is some disagreement among the courts whether the buyer may be compelled to specifically perform. Some courts hold that the seller has an adequate remedy at law for the buyer's breach; others say that the seller is entitled to specific performance since the buyer has such a right and there should be mutuality of remedy.

Sec. 2-716 of the UCC provides that specific performance may be decreed where the goods are unique or in other proper circumstances. It was intended under this section to do away with any requirement that the goods be specific, indentified, or ascertained at the time the contract is made. Also, the language "in other proper circumstances" is intended to liberalize the attitude of the courts. "Uniqueness" is no longer the sole test whether the remedy shall be granted.

279. Contracts to Sell Real Property. In the eyes of the law, all real property is unique. One piece of land may appear to be the same as another, but in respect of location each parcel is unique. Thus, a contract for the sale of real property will be specifically enforced at the suit of the purchaser, but whether it will be so enforced at the suit of the seller depends on the attitude of the courts of the particular jurisdiction on the question of mutuality of remedy.

280. Contracts for Unique Personal Services. Courts of equity will not decree specific performance of contracts for skilled or unskilled personal services. The services of a famous painter, an opera singer, a professional baseball player, or an acrobat are skilled and unique in the sense that the particular service to be rendered by each such person is not the same as that of any other engaged in the same calling. However, courts of equity will not order them by mandatory injunction to specifically perform their contracts. First, such a decree involves involuntary servitude; and second, an equity court cannot control the quality of the performance of an unwilling promisor. Also, for the latter reason, equity courts have refused to order the performance of contracts where such decree would require the equity court to supervise the work. A common example is a contract for the erection of a building. Thus, the equity court will not act as a foreman, superintendent, stage manager, or director.

281. The Injunction as a Remedy. A prohibitory injunction, or restraining order, is an order granted as a remedy for breach of contract which compels one to refrain from doing a certain act. It is a preventive or prohibitory order granted by a court of equity in cases where there is no adequate remedy at law. While a court of equity will not compel one to perform a service, it may, nevertheless, issue an injunction to prevent a person from rendering the same service to another. In a well-known case, a family of acrobats who had agreed with the owner of a theater to perform *exclusively* at his establishment for six weeks, were restrained by injunction from performing at a rival theater during the six-week period. In an equally well-known case, a professional baseball player who contracted to play for one major league club *exclusively*, repudiated his contract and attempted to play for another club. An injunction was issued to restrain him from rendering his services to the other club during the pendency of his original contract.

The injunction has been granted in many cases to restrain the breach of an express negative covenant. For example, there have been many cases in which one who sells his business agrees with the buyer that he will not open a competing business in a prescribed area for a stated time. The injunction is issued to prevent the violation of his negative promise. Similarly, one who by contract has agreed not to erect a certain type of structure on his property will be restranied by injunction from violating his promise.

282. The Remedy of Rescission. Where there has been a material breach of contract, the injured party may elect to rescind the contract and regard himself discharged from the duty to further perform. If the aggrieved party has partly or fully performed at the time of his election to rescind, he may recover the value of the performance he has rendered.

283. Remedies Barred by Statute of Limitations. Statutes of Limitations in the various states prescribe periods of time within which claims must be prosecuted in the courts. The law requires that claims be enforced with diligence, and in prescribing these periods of limitation the state legislatures have given consideration to the nature of the claim or right so that the time within which action must be brought varies with the particular cause of action. The time period begins when the cause of action accrues to the claimant, and if he fails to prosecute his claim within the time provided his remedy is barred. Where action is brought after the statutory period has expired, the defendant must plead the statute as a defense to the action or he will be held to have waived its benefit.

A promise to pay a debt before the statutory period has expired will "toll" the statute, that is, cause it to begin anew from the date of the promise, notwithstanding the fact that the promise is not supported by consideration. The promise need not be express; an acknowledgment of the debt from which a promise to pay may be implied will have the same effect. A payment on account of interest or principal, or the delivery of security for the debt, will also toll the statute.

Where the debt has been barred by the statute an express promise to pay it, an acknowledgment implying a promise to pay it, a delivery of security for the debt, or a voluntary payment on account of interest or principal will revive the debt and render it enforceable. However, statutes exist which require a promise to pay a debt barred by the statute to be in writing signed by the promisor.

It may be noted that the Statute of Limitations does not run (that is, it is suspended) as to a claimant who suffers a disability to sue, for example, because of infancy or insanity, and also as to a debtor or obligor who is beyond the jurisdiction of the state and therefore not amenable to the process of its courts.

Table of Problems

Topic	Problems
Offer and Acceptance	1 – 21
Reality of Assent	22 – 31
Infancy	32 – 39
Statute of Frauds	40 – 57
Consideration	58 – 78
Illegality	79 – 86
Parol Evidence Rule and Interpretation	87 – 92
Conditions	93 – 103
Breach of Contract	104 – 109
Third-Party Beneficiaries	110 – 117
Assignments	118 – 123
Discharge of Contracts	124 – 135
Remedies	136 – 140

Problems

1. *A* offered by mail to sell *B* his farm for $10,000. *A*'s letter was mailed on July 5 and received by *B* on July 8.

(*a*) Assume that *B* wrote *A* on July 9, inquiring, "Won't you take less?" *A* replied by letter on July 13, "No." *B* then mailed a letter to *A* on July 17, stating, "I accept your offer of July 5." *A* refused to have any further dealings with *B*. Assuming that July 17 was a reasonable time within which to have replied to the offer of July 5, is there a valid contract between *A* and *B* for the sale of the farm? Explain.

(*b*) Assume that *B*, on July 10, sent a telegram to *A* in which he accepted the offer of July 5. *A* never received the telegram. Would a valid contract have been formed between *A* and *B* for the sale of the farm? Give your reasons.

(*c*) Assume that *A* had intended to ask $10,500 for the farm but inadvertently used the $10,000 figure in his letter. *B* accepted the offer but *A* refused to sell for less than $10,500. Is *B* entitled to enforce the contract for $10,000? Explain.

(*d*) Assume that *B* was not interested in *A*'s offer, and gave *A*'s letter to *C* to accept if he were interested. *C* sent a letter to *A* in which he said, "I accept your offer." *A* refused to convey the land to *C*. May *C* recover from *A* for breach of contract? Why?

2. On April 1, 1965, Root mailed the following letter to Heaton: "I hereby offer to sell you my painting 'Blue Boy' which you have seen in my art gallery for $5,000, cash on delivery, provided, I receive your acceptance on or before April 10. (Signed) Root."

(*a*) April 9, Heaton mailed a letter of acceptance which was received by Root on April 11.

(*b*) April 5, Root died. April 7, Heaton mailed a letter of acceptance which was delivered to Root's office on April 9.

(c) April 8, Heaton received a telegram from Root revoking his offer. Heaton, nevertheless, sent a letter accepting Root's offer which was delivered to Root at 3 p.m. on April 10.

(d) April 8, Root received a letter from Heaton as follows: "I accept your offer but will have to give you my 60 days note for $1,000 as part payment. (Signed) Heaton."

Was there a contract in *each* of the above separate situations? Why or why not?

3. A, by telegram dated Buffalo, November 3, 1965, offers to sell to B in New York, a house and lot belonging to A in Buffalo. The telegram reads: "I will sell you premises 203 Main Street, Buffalo, for $10,000 subject to a $6,000 mortgage. Your answer must be here on or before November 10."

On November 4, B replies by letter, "Will you not take $9,000, subject to a $5,000 mortgage? I enclose check for $500 as evidence of my good faith."

A receives the letter on November 5. He replies immediately by letter, "I cannot accept your proposal." B receives this letter on November 6, and on the same day writes to A, "I accept your original offer." Twenty minutes after B mails this letter he receives a telegram from A reading, "Disregard my offer. I have sold the property."

4. Comment on the following statements:

(a) The revocation of a general offer to the public is legally effective when the revocation is made in the same way as the offer was made, even as against a party who, having no actual notice of the revocation, may thereafter attempt to accept it.

(b) Usually the advertisement "I am holding my car at $1,500" is construed by the courts to be a general invitation to deal, even though the specific price is stated, rather than a legal offer to sell.

(c) When an offer made in jest is accepted by the offeree who honestly believes the offeror to be serious, a valid contract is entered into, despite the fact that a reasonable man would recognize that the offer was not meant to be serious.

(d) When a municipality advertises for bids to perform a certain project, the advertisement constitutes an offer to contract.

(e) If an offer is made by A to B, and unknown to B, A dies before B's acceptance, A's death causes the offer to lapse.

(f) If X sends an offer to Y via mail and says nothing as to how Y should reply, and Y replies via messenger, no contract is formed, even though the messenger gives actual notice of the acceptance to X within a reasonable time after the offer was made.

(g) If an offer specifies that it must be accepted in a specified way, acceptance, to be valid, must be made in the manner required.

(h) An offer intended for a particular person cannot be accepted by another.

(j) A person accepting a written offer without reading it is not bound by his acceptance.

5. On October 20, 1967, Jones wrote to Smith: "What will you sell me 450 kegs of nails for, in the course of a month, cash down?" On October 23, 1967, Smith replied: "We will sell you 450 kegs common assorted nails at $3.62 per keg of 100 pounds each, cash." On October 27, 1967, Jones again wrote to Smith: "Nails have advanced so much I am almost afraid to buy; but will you send me as soon as possible 303 kegs common assorted nails and I will send you a check on Exchange Bank." Jones sues Smith for non-delivery of the nails. Judgment for whom?

6. On November 7, 1966, the defendant wrote to the plaintiff: "Kindly advise us by wire to be received at our office on November 9 if you will buy 1500 creosote barrels between now and January first, at 96¢ each, delivered in carload lots." The plaintiff received the above letter on November 9. At 7:30 p.m. the same day he sent the following telegram to the defendant: "We accept your offer of 1500 barrels as per yours of the 7th." This telegram was received by the defendant at 10:36 a.m., November 10, shortly after the defendant had sold the barrels to another party. The plaintiff sued to recover damages for non-delivery of the barrels. Can the plaintiff recover?

7. Tait received a pamphlet from Green advertising hosiery packings at $2.00 per 1,000. He wrote them on October 1, 1962: "Send me 30,000 hosiery packings at $2.00 per 1,000, shipping 5,000 by November 15 and the balance as ordered by me. Bill when shipped." Green replied on October 4, by mail: "We acknowledge your order of October 1. We cannot ship packings to your order, billed on shipment, at that price. There will be an extra charge of 25 cents per 1,000 for this accommodation." Tait wired: "Will not pay extra charge. Can get extra packings elsewhere without extra charge for accommodation. Hope you will see your way clear to ship as ordered." Green did not reply to this wire, but on October 20, shipped 5,000 packings at $10.00. Tait, having ordered packings elsewhere, rejected the shipment. Green sued for breach of contract. Can he recover? Why?

8. On March 30, 1963, Williams wrote to Fox offering to buy for $2800 Fox's motor cruiser, *Domino*, then stored in Longley's boat yard. The letter ended, "If this is satisfactory you may, upon your acceptance, draw a draft on me for the price and tell Longley to overhaul and repaint her at my expense." Fox first saw this letter on April 16, 1963, when he returned from a month's business trip. The same day he drew a draft on Williams for the price, placing the draft with his bank for collection, and on April 17 he went to the boat yard for the purpose of arranging for over-hauling and painting, only to find that the cruiser and been destroyed by fire the previous night. On the afternoon of April 16, 1963, Williams sent Fox a night letter saying, "Please wire me your decision on *Domino* as I cannot keep my offer open after noon the 18th." Fox first saw this on his return from the boat yard on the afternoon of April 17, when he immediately wired Williams, "Your offer accepted yesterday. Draft on way." Fox's draft was presented to Williams at 11 a.m. on April 18, but he refused to pay. What are Fox's rights? Why?

9. A, on October 1 at 1 p.m., writes the following letter to *B*: "Will sell you my black horse, Domino, for $150." At 1:15 on the same day, *B* sent the following telegram to *A*: "Will pay $150 for your black horse, Domino." *A* received this wire at 4 p.m. on October 1. At 9 a.m. on October 2, *A*'s letter is received by *B*. *B* now demands the horse and offers $150. *A* refuses. Is there a contract? Why?

10. Davies wrote to Offord as follows: "If you will discount bills for the firm of Watson and Co. I will guarantee the payment of such bills to the extent of $3,000." Certain bills were discounted by Offord and were duly paid. After $1,200 in bills were discounted and paid, Davies notified Offord that he would not guarantee any more bills. Offord, however, discounted other bills and they being unpaid, sued Davies on the guaranty. Is Davies liable? Why?

11. Defendant, on or about August 1, 1966, signed a paper which reads as follows:

> "Brooklyn, New York
> August 1, 1966
> "Undersigned hereby authorizes the publishers of the *Butchers' Advocate* to insert our advertisement to occupy ¼ page in *Butchers' Advocate* for one year and thereafter until publishers have order to discontinue the advertisement, for which we agree to pay $8.00 (eight dollars) per insertion.
> Safety Auto Trolly
> J. W. Berkof"

Butchers' Advocate proceeded under this authorization to publish advertisements for defendant. Some time during September defendant notified the *Advocate* to discontinue the ads, but the *Advocate* nevertheless continued to insert them in each issue for the balance of the year. The *Advocate* sues to recover $416 for the insertion of the ad for one year. What result? Why?

12. Corlies, a merchant, furnished White with specifications for the fitting up of a suite of offices at 57 Broadway, and requested him to submit to Corlies the price at which he would do the work. On September 28 White delivered his offer to Corlies. Corlies then wrote a letter to White dated September 29 in which it was stated: "Upon your agreement to finish the fitting up of offices at 57 Broadway in two weeks from date you may begin at once." White did not reply to this letter, but upon its receipt White purchased lumber and began work. On the next day White received a countermand of the letter of September 29. White sues for breach of contract. May he recover? Why?

13. Glover brings action against War Veterans Post 58 to recover a reward of $500 offered "to the person or persons furnishing information resulting in the apprehension and conviction of the persons guilty of the murder of M. L. B." Notice of the reward was published in a newspaper on June 7. A day or so later one *P*, a man suspected of the crime, was arrested, and the police received information that the other murderer was *W*, a boy friend of the daughter of Glover, the plaintiff. On June 11 the police visited Glover, who advised them that *W* and his daughter left the city on June 5 and furnished them with the names and locations of relatives whom the daughter might be visiting. The police apprehended *W* at the first address given them. *W* and *P* were convicted of murder. Glover claims the reward but admits he first learned of the offer on the day after he furnished the information to the police. Is Glover entitled to the reward? Why?

14. Sears, the owner of Domino, a racehorse, wrote to Blair on March 1: "As you undoubtedly know, Domino won the race at Danville last week. She made me very happy and a little richer. However, I have decided to retire from the racing scene and Domino is now for sale. I offer to sell her to you for $20,000 cash, delivery at my stables. I will keep this offer open for 20 days from the date of this offer. I hope you see your way clear to buy a great horse." On March 5, Blair wrote, "Yes, Domino is a great horse and I like your proposition, but I would prefer paying $10,000 in cash and $10,000 in 60 days. Can you accommodate me?" On March 10,

Sears wrote, "No credit. The deal is off." On March 17, Blair wrote, "I accept your offer of March 1." Is there a contract? Why?

15. (a) A, a grower of coffee, offered in writing to sell to B, a dealer in coffee, a large quantity of Colombian coffee. The offer recited that it would be kept open for four months. Three and one-half months after the offer was made, B duly communicated his acceptance to A. Is there a contract? Why?

(b) Suppose in (a) that the contract was concluded by telephone, and that A mailed to B a confirmation of the oral contract embodying its terms, but containing an additional term in conspicuous language indicating that the coffee was being sold "as is" and "with all faults." B contends that the additional term is not part of the contract since it negatives the implied warranties of merchantability and fitness for purpose which normally attach in the coffee trade. A contends that the additional term is part of the contract since B did not object to it within a reasonable time after he received it, as the evidence shows. Which contention is sound? Why?

16. (a) A offers to sell to B his used automobile for $400 cash. B replies, "I accept your offer, but I want thirty days within which to pay. Please advise." A does not respond. Is there a contract? Is the 30-day credit period part of the contract?

(b) Suppose in (a) that B replied, "I accept your offer for four hundred dollars cash. Deliver car immediately." Is there a contract? What are its terms?

(c) A, a manufacturer of hardware, mails to B an offer to sell a quantity of goods. B accepts by wire. When does a contract come into existence? Why?

(d) A sends to B a wire offering to buy goods if they are promptly shipped by B. B replies by wire promising to make a prompt shipment. Is there a contract at common law? By statute?

17. Over a period of time the Fletcher Corporation bought from Thomas Smith and Sons 15 separate lots of canned goods. On each invoice the following notice was stamped in red: "All disputes regarding this sale are to be settled by arbitration." The Fletcher Corporation retained all the invoices, paid by voucher checks, and at no time in its dealings with Thomas Smith and Sons made any reference, oral or written, to the arbitration notice on the invoices. On the goods covered by the last invoice a question arose as to the quantity of the goods received. The Fletcher Corporation refused payment and Thomas Smith and Sons demanded that the dispute be submitted to arbitration in accordance with the notice on the invoice. Can

the seller require the Fletcher Corporation to arbitrate on the ground that the latter's silence as to the arbitration notation implied acceptance thereof?

18. Plaintiff is the publisher of a newspaper. The defendant subscribed for the paper for two years, paying the entire cost when he executed the subscription. After the two-year period expired, the plaintiff continued to send the newspaper although the defendant did not again subscribe for it. The defendant admits that he continued to receive the paper at the post office where he picked up his mail, and that he brought it to his home and read it. He also admits that he received bills at the end of each of the two years and that he refused to pay them, advising the publisher that he had not renewed his original subscription. Is the defendant liable for the cost of the paper over the two-year period? Why?

19. Wicks deposited a parcel for safekeeping in a checkroom maintained by the X Railroad. He received from the person in charge a card. The card, a piece of pasteboard 3 inches long and 2 inches wide, bore on its face in red letters one-quarter inch high, the word, "Contract," and beneath that word in fine but legible print appeared a statement to the effect that "The X Railroad shall not be liable for loss or damage of any parcel beyond $10." When Wicks received the card he placed it in his pocket. He did not read it nor was he asked to read it by the person in charge. When he called for the parcel he was advised that it had been delivered to another person. He sues for $100, the value of his parcel. May he recover? Why?

20. Wells shipped $5,000 worth of goods from New York to San Francisco. Upon delivery of the goods to the carrier for transit Wells received a bill of lading covering the shipment. The bill contained a clause limiting the liability of the carrier for loss or damage to the goods in transit to the sum of $50, unless upon shipment a higher value on the goods was declared by the shipper. Wells did not read this language nor was he asked to read it by the carrier. The shipment was lost in transit. Wells sues the carrier to recover $5,000. The carrier, as a defense, sets up the clause in the bill of lading. Wells asserts he is not bound by the clause, and that since he never agreed to it it did not become part of his contract. May Wells recover $5,000? Why?

21. Martin Meehan and his sister Anastasia lived in the same house. When Anastasia died, Martin was appointed the administrator of her estate. While acting as such, he died. X was appointed administrator of his estate,

and Z was appointed administrator of the remainder of the estate of Anastasia. After the death of Martin, there was found among his private papers in a desk owned by him a non-negotiable promissory note signed by Anastasia and payable to Martin. X presented the note to Z for payment out of the estate of Anastasia. Z refused to make such payment. May X recover for the benefit of the estate of Martin? Why?

22. One Walter J. Gwynne, in person, falsely represented to William R. Phelps that he was Baldwin J. Gwynne, a man of financial responsibility, residing at Cleveland, Ohio. Relying upon the truth of this statement, Phelps delivered to him upon credit a quantity of jewelry. Gwynne in turn sold it to Dennis C. McQuade, who bought it in good faith, for value and without notice of any defect in title. Learning of the deception practiced upon him, Phelps brought an action in replevin against McQuade to recover the goods. Judgment for whom and why?

23. Plaintiff brings action to recover bonds given in exchange for other bonds. His complaint alleges that his bonds, issued by the Union Traction Co., were given in exchange for certain bonds of an Irrigation District in reliance upon false representations made in a prospectus issued by the defendant, and that the defendant knew the representations were false and fraudulent and made them with the intent to deceive. The evidence showed that, while the statements were false, the defendant made them in good faith and without knowledge of their falsity. Plaintiff is willing to return the bonds he received and demands a return of the bonds he delivered. The defendant contends that the complaint alleges fraud, that the plaintiff has failed to prove fraud, and that therefore the remedy he seeks should be denied. What result? Why?

24. Plaintiff was the owner of a plot of vacant land on Elmwood Street and an adjoining plot of land on Highland Avenue with houses on it. The immediate neighborhood is devoted exclusively to residences. Defendant sought to purchase a portion of the plot of vacant land, stating that he desired to purchase the same for residence purposes. The representations of the defendant that he intended to build dwellings on the land he wished to purchase were repeated during negotiations and the plaintiff relying thereon gave him a deed to a portion of the plot for $5,525. The day following the delivery of the deed the defendant instructed his architect to prepare plans for a garage to occupy the entire lot sold him, and less than two weeks thereafter he entered into a contract for the construction of a garage. Plaintiff claims to have been deceived by the defendant's representations and demands a reconveyance of the property sold and offers to

restore to the defendant the price paid. Is plaintiff entitled to the remedy she seeks? Why?

25. Plaintiff brings action to recover damages for fraud and deceit, claiming to have been induced to buy 50 shares of stock of the par value of $100 each of the American Oriental Co. The defendants are directors of the corporation. Sale of the stock was made through Charles D. Barney & Co., bankers. Barney & Co. prepared a circular or prospectus which consisted of a letter of the president of American Oriental to Barney & Co. Evidence shows the following statements in the prospectus were false: (a) that the San Francisco plant for refining crude oil was well built, fully completed, and had a capacity of refining 2,000 barrels a day; (b) that there was an abundance of crude oil in California; and (c) that there was a profitable oriental market for the sale of refined products. The prospectus contained the names of the directors. No evidence was given to show that the defendant directors had knowledge of the falsity of the statements. Indeed, they testified they believed the statements to be true.

The trial court charged the jury that it was the duty of the defendants, when they, as directors, approved of the circular, to ascertain the truth of the statements made and that if they had the opportunity but failed to do so, they are just as liable as if they had actual personal knowledge that the statements were false. On the question of damages for fraud, the trial court charged the jury that if they believed the plaintiff was entitled to recover, the damages should be measured by the difference between the value of the stock at the time of the purchase and the value of the stock as it would have been at that time if the representations were true. The jury found a verdict for the plaintiff for $6,000. On appeal, what result? Why?

26. Plaintiff purchased shares of stock in the defendant corporation. He claims he was induced to buy them by fraud and misrepresentation. He rescinded the contract, tendered a return of the shares, and then sued to recover the price he paid. After the action was brought, dividends were declared and paid and the plaintiff accepted and retained them. He alleges that the dividends were paid out of capital and that he accepted them not as dividends but as a partial return of the purchase price and that at trial he would offer them as credit to the defendant. Evidence was given to show that, before the dividends were paid, a representative of the plaintiff notified some of the defendant's officers that dividends were not earned and if declared they would be paid out of capital and that he would advise stockholders, including the plaintiff, to accept them as monies on account to reimburse them partially for their losses on the purchase of stock. The lower court held that by acceptance and retention of the dividends the

plaintiff treated the contract as in existence and so defeated his claim to rescission. On appeal, what result? Why?

27. (*a*) X and Y live in State Z. X lends money to Y under an agreement providing for payment of interest at the highest lawful rate of interest in State Z. Both X and Y believe at the time of agreement that the highest legal rate is 4 per cent. Actually, it is 8 per cent. When interest becomes due, X learns that 8 per cent is the highest rate permissible, demands payment of interest at 8 per cent, and on Y's refusal, sues for such interest. Y's defense is that the contract is void because of mutual mistake as to the law as to the rate of interest. What rule would you apply? Explain.

(*b*) In January 1967, John Porter insured a ship for one year with the Reliable Mutual Insurance Company, against loss at sea, with a provision that the policy could be canceled on arrival of the ship at port. On June 1, 1967, Porter and the insurance company, both believing that the ship had arrived in port before then, entered into a agreement canceling the policy. Both were then ignorant of the fact that the ship had been lost at sea prior to June 1. On learning of its loss, Porter brought action to set aside the policy cancellation. Is Porter entitled to have the cancellation set aside? Explain.

28. A, an architect, at B's request, mailed to X, Y, and Z, contractors, plans and specifications for a proposed building to be erected for B with a request for bids reading in part as follows:

> "All bids must be received at the office of the undersigned on or before 12 o'clock noon on May 2, 1966. Contract in standard form of American Institute of Architects to be executed by owner and contractor immediately upon acceptance of bid.
>
> (signed) A, Architect"

Y and Z mailed bids of $303,000 and $298,000, respectively. X sent by messenger a bid for $269,000. All bids were received before noon on May 2. At 12:15 p.m. on May 2, A left his office to meet with B at the Merchants' Club, where the bids were opened. Both A and B expressed surprise at X's bid, A saying he had estimated the cost to be $300,000. B, at 1:30 p.m., mailed a letter to X accepting his bid. At 12:30 p.m., X discovered an error of $30,000 in adding his detailed estimates, so that the correct total was $299,000. X immediately went to A's office, where he arrived at 12:45 p.m. A arrived at 1:45 p.m. X revoked his bid. A told X of B's letter. X refused to sign a contract or to build. B's letter was delivered at X's office on May 3. Is X liable to B? Why?

29. Clyde submitted a bid on the construction of a school building. His bid was the low bid and it was accepted. The following day he discovered that he had omitted from his calculations a $5,000 item and he gave immediate notice of withdrawal of his bid. He was met with refusal and he now brings action to have the contract rescinded on the ground of mistake. Should he succeed? Why?

30. As to each of the following, state whether the threat used by A to obtain B's consent to a contract which was valid in all other respects leaves the agreement valid, or makes it void, or makes it voidable:

(a) A threat to sue B for a debt erroneously believed to be owing.
(b) A threat to have B prosecuted criminally for an actual defalcation.
(c) A threat to publish defamatory matter concerning B's wife.

31. Action by Smith against Lenchner on a $1200 note. Lenchner was the principal stockholder of the LC Corporation, a security business. Smith owned one share of the stock of the corporation. Lenchner contends that a sale of the business was pending and that Smith threatened to block the sale unless Lenchner paid him $1200; that Lenchner did not have the cash and gave Smith the $1200 note. Smith claims that he had bought his one share of stock for $1200; that he was uncertain of the ability of the prospective purchaser to pay for the business; and that he sold his one share to Lenchner and took Lenchner's note. Lenchner's defense is duress. May Smith recover on the note? Why?

32. Connelly subscribed for a correspondence course in "Complete Steam Engineering" in the City of Rochester at the offices of the International Text Book Co. His offer stated that he was 21 years of age, though in fact he was not yet an adult. It was accepted by the office of the division superintendent of the Company in Scranton, Pa., and a copy of the contract was sent to Connelly. His contract required that he pay $5 per month until the sum of $75.20 was paid in full. August 20, the date on which he became an adult, he had paid $10 on the contract. Thereafter and on December 5 he made another $5 payment. He made no payments thereafter and pursuant to the contract the Company declared the entire balance due and payable, and demanded a return of the books loaned to Connelly. He returned the books. The Company sues in New York for the balance due and Connelly pleads infancy as a defense. The Company contends that (a) the contract was for a necessary; (b) the defendant is estopped from pleading his infancy because he misrepresented his age in procuring the contract; (c) the defendant ratified the contract when some three and one-half months after he became an adult he made a $5 payment; (d) the

contract was made in Pennsylvania and there is no proof that infancy is a good defense there. What ruling on each of the Company's contentions? Why?

33. Kane, an infant aged 20 years, was the owner of a parcel of real estate. He borrowed $3500 from Radford and gave to Radford his bond by which he promised to repay the $3500, together with a mortgage on his real estate as security for the performance of his promise. When Kane became an adult he disaffirmed the bond and mortgage by a notice duly given to Radford, and sold his real estate. Radford now claims a lien on the proceeds of the sale, contending that Kane was obliged to return to Radford the money borrowed as a condition to his right to disaffirm. Kane concedes that if he still had the money borrowed he would be under duty to return it, but asserts that he had spent and squandered it before coming of age. Is Radford's contention sound? Why?

34. Action was brought by the plaintiff, a minor aged 17 years, on a contract for the purchase of a bicycle. The agreed price was $45, $15 of which was paid by the minor on the purchase. The remainder was to be paid at the rate of $1.25 per week. The infant bought the bicycle in June, used it until September 20, and then returned it to the seller, demanding a return of the payments made. The seller accepted the bicycle but refused to refund the money paid. At the trial, he produced evidence showing that the use of the bicycle and its deterioration in value exceeded the sum paid.

(a) May the infant plaintiff recover the amount paid? Why?

(b) Where the deterioration in value exceeds the amount paid, may the infant be held liable for the difference? Why?

35. P was 17 years of age. He entered into a contract with S, an adult, to buy a radio from S for $350. P paid $100 at the time of the purchase and agreed to pay the balance in five monthly installments of $50 each. P told S that he, P, was 22 years of age.

Answer the following questions giving a statement of the rule of law involved.

(a) P used the radio for two weeks. At the end of that time he decided he did not want to keep it as he had broken it so that it would not function. He offered to return the damaged radio to S and asked for his $100 down payment. Is P entitled to the money?

(b) Assume that S learned that P was only 17 and that S demanded the return of the radio, offering to give back P's payment. May S obtain the radio over P's objection?

(*c*) Assume that *P* kept the radio but defaulted on the last payment. May *S* recover the $50 payment from *P*'s father?

36. Richards, 20 years of age, entered into the produce business and bought a truck from ABC Motors on credit for the list price of $2,600, to be used by him in making deliveries of produce to his customers. At the time he purchased the truck he falsely represented himself to be 22 years of age. When the obligation to ABC Motors matured, Richards defaulted. In an action brought by ABC Motors, Richards pleads infancy as a defense and offers to return the truck. Judgment for whom and why?

37. The sum of $29,000 was obtained from 10 different banks upon checks forged by one Saunders. The defendants offered a $5,000 reward for the apprehension of the forger. Plaintiff was a lad 17 years of age. His mother received for safekeeping from a friend a package containing $25,475 in bank notes. She suspected that something was wrong and directed her son, the plaintiff, to inform the Merchants Bank and one Mr. Austin. He gave them the informaton and the bank president and Austin came and took the money. Several persons including the plaintiff made claim for the reward and they agreed to submit their respective claims to arbitration. The arbitrator awarded the plaintiff $1,000 and this sum was paid to his guardian. When the plaintiff arrived at full age he had an accounting with his guardian, received the $1,000 and released him. Some two years later, he brought action against the defendants to recover such part of the $5,000 reward as the $25,475 recovered bore to the $29,000 lost, less the $1,000 he received. The defense sets forth the arbitration and the accounting between the plaintiff and his guardian. The plaintiff asserts that the settlement with his guardian had no reference to his claim in this action, and that at the time of such settlement he had fully determined to recover the balance of the reward. He admitted that for two years after he became of age he made no claim for the balance of the reward. May the plaintiff recover? Why?

38. Select all of those phrases which state a correct legal conclusion. Note that some of the questions may contain more than one correct statement.
     (*a*) A contract for the sale of a motorcycle to a minor can be enforced by:
          (1) The minor.
          (2) The other party against the minor.
          (3) Both parties.
          (4) The other party against the minor's parents.

(5) None of these.

(*b*) Assuming that the terms of the following contracts were reasonable in all respects, the following provisions could be enforced against a minor:

    (1) A lease of lodgings to be used by the minor during the next school term.

    (2) Employment of a janitor to care for an apartment building owned by the minor.

    (3) Rent due on a house used as a dwelling for the minor and his wife.

    (4) Purchase of food—the minor lives with his parents who support him.

    (5) None of these.

(*c*) Assuming that the contract is one which a minor may disaffirm, his election may be made:

    (1) Only while he is still a minor.

    (2) Only during a reasonable time after reaching his majority.

    (3) Only within a reasonable time after making the contract.

    (4) At any time.

    (5) None of these.

(*d*) A minor will be deemed to have validly disaffirmed a contract:

    (1) Only if he expressly informs the other party to that effect.

    (2) Only if he obtains an order of a court to that effect.

    (3) If he expressly disaffirms the sale of real property during his minority.

    (4) If he fails to affirm before he reaches his majority.

    (5) None of these.

(*e*) If the minor wishes to disaffirm a contract for the purchase of luxury goods which is reasonable and fair in all respects:

    (1) He must return all of the goods.

    (2) He must return all of the goods which he may possess at the time of his disaffirmance.

    (3) He must pay the reasonable value of goods he actually consumed or from which he received benefits.

    (4) He must return only those goods which he desires to return.

    (5) None of these.

(*f*) A minor who has purchased a motorcycle on the installment plan will be deemed to have affirmed the purchase if, after he has reached his majority:

    (1) He retains the motorcycle and continues to use it for six months.

    (2) He fails to disaffirm at that time.

(3) He signs a new note for the balance.

(4) He promises orally to pay the balance due.

(5) None of these.

(g) A minor purchasing a motorcycle on the installment plan, representing to the seller that he was of legal age, and having the appearace of one who was at least 23:

> (1) May effectively plead his minority as a defense to a suit for the balance of the purchase price.
>
> (2) Will be deemed to have waived his right to disaffirm.
>
> (3) Will be required to restore, so far as possible, what he has received if he seeks to recover the amount paid in equity.
>
> (4) Will be liable for any resulting damage based on a tort action of deceit.
>
> (5) None of these.

39. Amos, an infant, sold his riding horse to Stokes for $250. Stokes resold the animal to Bates who paid value for it without knowledge that Amos was an infant and at one time owned the horse. Amos disaffirms his contract with Stokes and sues to recover the horse from Bates. May he recover? Why?

40. A entered into an oral contract with B, in which contract A agreed to sell an unimproved city lot to B for $2,500.

(a) Assume that B paid A $500 at the time the agreement was made. A later refused to convey the lot to B but offered to return the $500. B refused to accept the money and brought action for specific performance of the contract. What result?

(b) Assume that no payment was made, but that A wrote B a letter three months after the agreement was made. In this letter, which was signed, he outlined the terms of the contract. If A later refused to perform the contract, could B enforce it against A? Explain.

(c) Assume that B paid A $2,500, and that A gave B a deed to the lot. The lot is now worth $4,500. A wants to return the money to B and get the lot back. May he do so? Explain.

41. Hart enters into a contract to sell Blackacre, a house and plot of land, to Evers for $12,000. Relying on his oral contract, Evers enters into possession of the property and makes substantial improvements thereon. Hart brings action to eject Evers from the property on the ground that the contract is unenforceable under the Statute of Frauds. Evers counterclaims for specific performance of the contract. Judgment for whom? Why?

42. Brown orally employed Smith as foreman of Brown's flour mill, the employment to continue as long as Smith was physically able to perform the duties, at a salary of $600 per month. About three years later they quarreled and Smith was dismissed, although he had always performed his services faithfully, and was still able and willing to do so. Smith sues Brown for breach of contract. Can he recover? Why?

43. Lawrence and Brennan, mining engineers in New York, in a telephone conversation with Steel, a metallurgical chemist who resided in Chicago, hired him to take charge of their refinery in Mexico for one year at a compensation of $750 per week. It was agreed that they would reimburse him for his traveling expenses, but that his employment would not begin until he actually arrived at the plant. Three months after his arrival there, Steele is discharged without sufficient cause. He sues for breach of contract. Has the employer an adequate defense?

44. Plaintiff and defendant were engaged as partners in the business of manufacturing and selling toys in the City of New York. On April 20, 1965, they entered into a verbal agreement whereby the defendant sold to the plaintiff his interest in the business theretofore conducted together with the good will thereof. The plaintiff states that it was part of the agreement that the defendant "would not again enter into or carry on the business of manufacturing and selling toys in the City of New York until the last installment of the price was paid, and that in April, 1966, the defendant did enter into the business of manufacturing and selling toys in New York City." Defendant states that on April 20, 1965, he executed and delivered to plaintiff as the purchase price a note payable in 27 monthly installments. Does the defendant have a defense? Why?

45. Barber, wishing to start a business of his own, borrowed $3,000 from Platt. He agreed to repay in one payment two years later. The entire agreement was oral. Whey payment fell due, Barber refused to pay. Platt sued for breach of contract. Has Barber a legal defense to this suit? Explain.

46. Moss is a stockholder, director, and vice-president of the X Corp. He orally agreed with Smith that if Smith purchased 6,000 shares of stock in the X Corp. and paid to the corporation $15,000 as the price, that he, Moss, would personally pay Smith $15,000 should the stock become worthless. Smith made the purchase and paid the price. Later his shares become worthless and he brought action for $15,000 against Moss. Moss sets up the Statute of Frauds as a defense. What judgment? Why?

47. In each of the following cases discuss the enforceability or non-enforceability of the contract if the party against whom the action is brought pleads as a defense that the contract, in order to be enforceable, is required to be in writing:

(a) A customer who has an account at a store calls up the manager and says: "I am sending my brother down. He needs a suit. Let him select any suit he likes, provided it does not cost over sixty dollars, and charge it to my account." The brother selects a $55 suit which he takes away with him. The customer refuses to pay the bill and is sued.

(b) A tenant on September 15 orally rents an apartment at an annual rental of $1200, payable monthly in advance for one year beginning October 1. He takes possession and pays his rent regularly, but on June 30 he vacates. On July 3, the landlord sues him for the July rent which became due on July 1.

(c) Brown, having been discharged in bankruptcy, orally promises Jones, one of his old creditors, that if Jones will trust him with $5,000 worth of merchandise in his new business, he will pay him the entire old debt of $10,000. Jones gives him the merchandise. Brown pays him $5,000, $2500 of which is on account of the old debt and $2500 on account of the new debt. Subsequently, Brown fails to make any further payments and Jones sues Brown for $10,000.

(d) A wealthy man orally promises his niece that if she will retire from the operatic and concert stage, and sing in public only at such charitable benefit performances as he shall designate, he will pay her a stipulated income for life. After having paid such income for three years, he refuses to make any further payments, and she sues.

48. Henry, who operates a chicken farm, says to his neighbor, Perry: "I am called to Cailfornia on family business. I will sell you this farm and everything on it for fifteen hundred dollars. That includes my lease on the plot across the road which has two years more to run. The owner has agreed to have you as a tenant in my place. You need pay nothing now. Pay five hundred dollars in six months, five hundred dollars a year hence, and the balance in eighteen months. I will give you a list of my customers. They are all A#1. I'll make good for anyone that doesn't pay you." Perry accepts and enters into possession of the farm. He repairs the chicken houses and makes other improvements. Six months later, Henry returns and repudiates the entire transaction. Perry tenders him $450 (representing $500 less his losses on uncollectible accounts against Henry's former customers), which Henry refuses. Henry brings action to eject Perry from the farm. May Perry successfully resist on the strength of his

agreement with Henry, notwithstanding that it was oral? Discuss fully all aspects of the matter.

49. On April 15, 1966, a landlord made the following agreement with a prospective tenant of a store: the lease to be for the period beginning May 1, 1966 and terminating April 30, 1967. The tenant agreed to purchase certain fixtures forming part of the real property at their fair value, any dispute to be settled by a third party. The tenant gave to the landlord a check for $50 in part payment of the purchase price of these fixtures. The tenant also agreed to buy from the landlord some office furniture for $750. The tenant was to act as agent to collect the rents of the apartments in the building during the period of the store lease. The landlord was to lease to the tenant's parents an apartment in the building for one year, and the tenant agreed "to make good" if they did not pay the rent.

Under what four provisions of the Statute of Frauds would the agreements have to be in writing in order to be wholly enforceable, and why?

50. (a) S and B enter into an oral contract for the sale by S to B of a color television set at the price of $750. S sends to B a signed written confirmation of the oral agreement, naming both parties, describing the subject matter, setting forth the time and place of payment and delivery, but omitting the price. B, not a merchant, receives the confirmation and makes no comment in respect of it. Later, B brings action against S for breach of contract, S having refused to perform although B was ready and willing to do so. May B recover? Why? May B establish by parol evidence the agreed price?

(b) Suppose that, in (a), S tendered a delivery of the set to B but B rejected it. May S enforce the contract against B? Why?

51. (a) S and B, merchants, orally contract for the sale by S to B of 5,000 bushels of wheat at a price of $10,000. S then sends to B a signed written confirmation naming the parties to the oral contract, setting forth its terms, including the subject matter and the price. B receives the confirmation on March 15 and makes no comment concerning it. S tenders a delivery of the wheat on April 30, the date specified for delivery in the oral contract and the written confirmation, but B rejects the tender. S sues B for breach of contract. Does B have a defense? Why?

(b) Assuming that the written confirmation omitted the quantity of goods agreed upon orally, is B liable for a breach of contract? Why? Is S bound to the terms of the written confirmation? Why?

(c)(1) Suppose that, in (a), there was no written confirmation of the oral contract, and S delivered to B 1,000 bushels of wheat and B accepted the delivery. Is the oral contract enforceable against B? To what extent?

(2) Suppose S made no delivery but B made a payment of $4,000 on account of the price. Is the oral contract enforceable against S? To what extent?

(3) Is it important in (1) and (2) above whether S and B are merchants? Why?

52. Jones inspected a new truck, decided to buy it, and instructed the dealer to remodel the chassis and construct a special body for it, suited for peculiar conditions on Jones' farm, and to deliver it at Jones' farm the following week, at which time he would make a down payment of $400 on the purchase price of $1600. The dealer accepted the proposition and complied with the instructions, but on delivery Jones refused to accept the truck. The dealer sues for $300, representing his loss of profit on the deal. Has Jones any defense? Discuss.

53. Mrs. Nelson, socially prominent, expected to attend the Charity Bazaar, the outstanding social event of the year. She agreed to purchase from the Designing Company on elaborate costume to be made for her according to her directions as to color, design, etc. The agreement was oral and the price was $650. Two days before the Bazaar she discovered that Mrs. Blank expected to attend. Being unwilling to associate with Mrs. Blank socially, Mrs. Nelson decided not to attend and refused to accept or pay for the costume. The Designing Company sues for the agreed price. Can it recover? Why?

54. Raabe entered into a contract with S & W, contractors, to supply lumber for ten houses in which the contractors were to do the woodwork for Jenks and Stokes, owners. The lumber was to be delivered in installments and payment for the lumber was to be made by S & W upon delivery by Raabe at the buildings. Raabe refused to deliver the third installment of lumber until paid in full for prior deliveries. Jenks and Stokes then called on Raabe, explained that they were the owners of the buildings and they wanted them finished, and said that if Raabe would deliver the rest of the lumber they would see Raabe paid, and that if S & W failed to pay, Jenks and Stokes would pay and deduct the amount from what they owed S & W. Raabe, relying on the promise of Jenks and Stokes, delivered the balance of the lumber, but is unpaid to the extent of $2800. Are Jenks and Stokes liable for the amount? Why?

55. Green borrows Black's motor cruiser, *Domino*, and being unfamiliar with the waters in the area, he strikes a submerged object and damages the

vessel. Green contracts with White, a boat builder, to repair *Domino*. White completes the work, but Green is unable to pay him and White refuses to deliver the boat. Black calls White on the telephone, stating: "If you will deliver *Domino* to me I promise that I will pay your bill if Green does not do so." White delivers the vessel to Black but remains unpaid. He sues Black. May he recover? Why?

56. Green entered into an option agreement to purchase certain tracts of land. Before the expiration of the option period, Green exercised the right of election granted therein by giving the seller written notice that he would purchase the property. Subsequently, and before the expiration of the option period, Green entered into an oral agreement with R whereby Green agreed to sell and R agreed to purchase from Green all of Green's interest in and to said option agreement; and

(*a*) to pay the consideration fixed by the option and to perform all of the terms and conditions of said option agreement; and

(*b*) to form a corporation which was to take title to said property; and

(*c*) to cause said corporation to issue 25 per cent of its capital stock to Green, and further agreed to pay to Green the par value of the stock at any time the market value of said stock should be less than 50 per cent of the par value of the stock; and

(*d*) to cause the corporation to employ Green for a period of five years at a salary of $20,000.

R was to retain a controlling interest in the capital stock of the corporation. Green performed his obligations under the agreement, but R refused to perform. Green brought suit and R set up the Statute of Frauds as a defense. Are the oral promises of R enforceable under the Statute of Frauds? Explain.

57. Catherine McKenna was the owner of real property. Her son, John, brings action against her daughter, Mary, alleging that while his mother was lying on her death bed she gave to Mary a deed to the real property upon Mary's agreement to hold the property for the life of Catherine, and upon Catherine's death, to hold the property for herself and her brother, share and share alike, divide the income between them, and upon sale of the property to divide the proceeds equally. After Catherine's death Mary refused to carry out the terms of the trust. John's action is for the declaration of a trust for the benefit of John and Mary. It was not alleged whether the trust was oral or in writing. Mary's defense is that there was no trust created and that the deed was for Mary's benefit alone. At the trial it was asserted in Mary's behalf that the trust was oral and hence unenforceable under the Statute of Frauds. What result? Why?

58. Action to foreclose a mortgage for $5,000 given by Duncan to Schreyer and by Schreyer assigned to Vanderbilt. It is asserted that Schreyer is liable for any deficiency on the ground that he guaranteed the mortgage debt.. Vanderbilt entered into a contract with Schreyer to erect certain buildings in New York City. The agreement called for payments by Schreyer as the work progressed. One provision stated that when the houses were topped out Schreyer was to assign to Vanderbilt the $5,000 mortgage held by him. When the houses were topped out, Schreyer offered to assign the mortgage but Vanderbilt insisted that Schreyer guarantee payment. Upon Schreyer's refusal Vanderbilt stopped work on the houses. To get the buildings finished, Schreyer guaranteed payment of the mortgage. Vanderbilt then completed performance. When the mortgage was not paid, the action was brought. Schreyer defends on the ground that there was no consideration for his promise of guaranty. What result? Why?

59. X Corporation entered into a contract with Y Corporation to construct concrete ramps and runways at an airfield. X Corporation contemplated when the agreement was made that, to set the ramps and runways, approximately 600,000 tons of dirt would have to be removed. When X Corporation commenced work it discovered that 1,200,000 tons of dirt had to be removed. It immediately stopped work and proposed to Y Corporation that the amount to be paid X Corporation for its work be increased by the cost of removal of 600,000 tons of dirt. Y Corporation at first refused, but eventually acceded to the demand, and, by telephone, the X Corporation was advised that monthly payments would be increased by $3,000 until the work was completed. The work was completed four months later, but Y Corporation paid no part of the additional $12,000. May the X Corporation recover? Why?

60. Brown employed Allen as a secretary for one year at an annual salary of $7800 payable monthly. After working six months, Allen was offered a $8500 a year job by Crown. He told Brown of this offer and said he would leave at once and accept Crown's offer unless Brown paid him at Crown's rate. Brown, not being able to replace Allen at once, orally promised to pay him the additional compensation in the form of a bonus at the end of the year if Allen would remain with him. Allen agreed to this and stayed. At the expiration of Allen's term of employment, Brown, having paid him the $7800 in full, discharged him and refused to pay him the bonus which he had promised him. What are Allen's rights? State your reasons.

61. Carter leased a store building to Harper for a period of three years at a monthly rental of $100. The lease contained a provision that Harper should keep the building in good repair at all times. At the end of the

second year Carter inspected the building and found that it needed repairs, which would cost $1,000. Carter threatened to terminate the lease and to sue Harper for failure to keep the building in repair. After considerable discussion, the parties entered into an agreement which provided that Carter should not institute suit for a period of 60 days, so that Harper would have time to make the repairs, which Harper agreed to do within the time stipulated. The next day, without further notice to Harper, Carter entered suit to recover the sum of $1,000. Harper set up as a defense Carter's agreement not to sue if repairs were made within 60 days. Is the defense good? Why?

62. Archer, after having contracted with Owen to build an apartment house for Owen on the latter's land for the price of $50,000, to be paid on completion of the building, unexpectedly found on commencing work that it would be impossible to excavate for the foundation without blasting through several feet of rock. He wrote Owen, who was temporarily out of town, refusing to proceed unless Owen would pay him an additional $5,000 on completion of the building. Owen wrote Archer in reply that the demand was an outrage, but that rather than lose tenants, whom he had already secured, he would pay the price demanded. Archer finished construction and Owen tendered him $50,000. Archer refused the tender and brought action for $55,000. Should he recover? Why?

63. Action is brought by William against his uncle Gregory to recover $5,000. The facts establish that Gregory promised to pay William $5,000 on William's twenty-first birthday if William until then would refrain from drinking liquor, using tobacco, swearing, and playing cards or billiards for money. William refrained from doing these things, but on his twenty-first birthday his uncle refused to pay him the $5,000. Gregory defends on the ground that there was no consideration for his promise since his nephew was not harmed but benefited, that Gregory was not benefited at all, and that unless there is benefit to the promisor there is no consideration for the promise. What result? Why?

64. M was about to sign a contract for the purchase of real property from the B Corp. He was approached by G who proposed to pay to M $20,000 if M would refrain from signing the contract with the B Corp. M withdrew from the proposed transaction with the B Corp. and G delivered to him $2,000 in cash and $18,000 in promissory notes. G then signed the contract to purchase the real property from the B Corp. G failed to make payments on the notes and M brings action. G defends on the ground of lack of consideration for the notes. What result? Why?

65. Davis, residing in New York, owned a farm in Twin Falls which he leased to White. White asked Peters to drill a well on it for which White agreed to pay $500. Peters, thinking White owned the farm, agreed and drilled the well. White did not pay, and Peters, in attempting to collect, learned that Davis in New York owned the farm. Peters demanded payment of Davis. Davis went to Twin Falls, examined the well, said to Peters that it was worth $300 and that he would pay to Peters that sum when White's lease expired. Six months later, when White's lease expired, Peters sued Davis on his promise. What judgment? Why?

66. (a) George was walking along a beach in search of sea shells when he heard cries of Henry, a bather, who had swum too far from the beach and was unable to get back. George swam out to him and with great difficulty brought him to shore and revived him. On the following day, David, Henry's father, visited George, thanked him for rescuing Henry, and promised that he would pay George $1,000 for what he had done. David never paid and George brings action to recover $1,000. What result? Why?

(b) Suppose David was on the beach when Henry experienced his difficulty and requested George to rescue Henry, the facts being otherwise as in (a). Would George have a right to recover the $1,000? Why?

(c) Suppose the facts in (a) but that, after David visited George and thanked him, he wrote a letter to George in which he referred to the rescue and promised to pay George $1,000. What result? Why?

(d) Suppose in (c) that George was a lifeguard on duty at the time of the rescue. What result? Why?

67. Archenbold Company is a jobber of automobile supplies. Rosenthal was its merchandise and traffic clerk and handled all matters of freight rates and traffic problems for the company. Archenbold, from time to time, purchased tire chains from the American Chain Company under an arrangement whereby Archenbold paid the freight on shipments and deducted the charges from the invoice price. The seller paid the freight through the purchaser. Rosenthal by examination of tariff schedules and by correspondence with railroads discovered that the freight charges were too high and that instead of $1.665 per hundred pounds on minimum carloads of 30,000 pounds, the railroads should have charged $1.195.

Rosenthal met with Morris, vice-president of American Chain, and proposed to him that he would give Morris information which would save money on its shipments if he was paid one third of the savings for 20 years, payable monthly. Morris assented and Rosenthal gave him the information. American Chain refused to recognize the contract and Rosenthal brought action to recover one third of the refunds American Chain already received plus one third of what it was likely to receive for the balance of the 20 years. Should he recover? Why?

68. The Exporting Company contracted in writing with Jones to employ him for three years at an annual salary of $9,000 as assistant manager of its branch at Singapore with duties such as would make him familiar with the export trade in the East. Jones entered upon the performance of his duties and performed them satisfactorily, but at the end of the first year, when he received $9,000, the Exporting Company notified him that he would be transferred to its New York office as the business in Singapore did not warrant the continuance of his services there. Jones then wrote the company that rather than be transferred to New York, he would accept an annual salary of $6,000 for the next two years as he felt he would get better training in Singapore. The company by telephone agreed to this arrangement and it was carried out, Jones receiving $6,000 for each of the next two years. At the end of his employment, Jones sued the company for $6,000, alleging that his agreement called for compensation for three years at $9,000 per year. Should he recover? Why?

69. Nees died, owning certain real property on Sackett Street and holding a deed to real property on Atlantic Avenue as trustee for two of his children, Sophia and George. After his death all of his children met at his house with an attorney. Nees' strong box was opened and the deed to the Atlantic Avenue property was taken therefrom by the attorney and handed to Sophia and George with the statement: "This is yours." There were some murmurings and expressions of surprise by the other children. They had believed that Nees had complete ownership of the Atlantic Avenue property and that all children would succeed to it. At this point Sophia, with the consent of George, stated that if the other children would raise no question about the Atlantic Avenue property and would not molest Sophia and George in reference to it, they, Sophia and George, would give to the others their interest in the Sackett Street property. When the Sackett Street property was thereafter sold, the other children sued Sophia and George to recover their share of the proceeds of the sale. What result? Why?

70. Action is brought for breach of a contract which provided in part as follows:
"Whereas, Miss Blanche Josephine Schweizer, daughter of said Mr. Joseph Schweizer, is now affianced to and is to be married to the above Count Oberto Gulinelli, now in consideration of all that is herein set forth the said Mr. Joseph Schweizer promises and expressly agrees by the present contract to pay annually to his said daughter Blanche, during his own life

and to send her, during her lifetime, the sum of $2500, or the equivalent of said sum in francs, the first payment to be made on the 20th day of January."

Blanche and the Count were married on January 20, and the first payment was then made to her. Payments were made until the tenth year thereafter, when default occurred in the payment of one installment. The Count and Blanche assigned their claim to *D* who brought action. The defense asserted by Joseph Schweizer was that there was no consideration for his promise since the marriage was the performance of an act which Blanche and the Count were legally obligated to perform. What result? Why?

71. Olmsted was obligated to pay to Covil on January 15 the sum of $1,000. He failed to pay the debt when due and then asked Covil for an extension of the date of payment. The parties agreed that the date of payment be extended to June 15. Olmsted agreed to pay the debt with interest on June 15 and Covil agreed to give Olmsted until June 15 to make such payment. Notwithstanding the agreement, Covil brought action to recover the debt in April. The defense was the agreement of Covil to extend the date of payment to June 15. Covil asserts that the agreement is unenforceable for lack of consideration. What result? Why?

72. (*a*) Davis had a judgment against Pell in the amount of $4500. Davis and Pell mutually agreed orally that Pell would pay to Davis $3,000 in cash and assign to him a patent right and Davis would accept the same in full satisfaction of the judgment. Pell paid $3,000 to Davis but, when he tendered the assignment of the patent right, Davis refused to accept it. Davis then issued an execution against certain property of Pell. Pell moved to set aside the execution and to have the judgment satisfied of record. What ruling on the motion? Why?

(*b*) What result if the agreement between Davis and Pell was embodied in a writing signed by Pell? Why?

73. James was indebted to Dalton in the amount of $7500 for goods sold and delivered. James delivered to Dalton a promissory note for $4500 together with a chattel mortgage on James' stock in trade and fixtures, which Dalton agreed to accept in full satisfaction of the $7500 debt. Dalton then sued James to recover the sum of $3,000. Should he recover? Why?

74. Plaintiff sold to the defendant for an agreed price 10 cars of Spanish onions to be shipped from New York to Detroit, FOB New York. When the onions arrived in Detroit the greater part of them were found to be in a defective condition due to decay consisting of Fusarium rot, soft rot,

and a bacteria heart rot. Defendant had the onions examined by a government inspector, who certified that the decay in some crates ran 10% to 35% and in others from 15% to 25% of the contents. Defendant notified the plaintiff and sent him copies of the inspector's certificates. Defendant then sent checks for the agreed price less $425. Each of the checks was marked "in full payment." Plaintiff accepted the checks but notified defendant there was a balance due of $425. It was established as a fact that the decay did not develop during transit but was inherent in the onions before shipment. Plaintiff sues for $425. May he recover? Why?

75. Jones, while driving his automobile, struck and injured Brown, who had to spend $200 on doctor's bills and lost $500 in wages as a result of the injury. He claimed the collision was caused by the carelessness of Jones and he brought suit against Jones to recover the amount of his damages. Jones, on the other hand, contended that the collision resulted from the negligence of Brown. Finally, Jones agreed to pay Brown $250 in settlement of his claim. Brown agreed to this and Jones paid the amount. Brown then gave to Jones a written statement that the amount was received in full settlement of the amount due because of the injuries received. Later Brown was advised by his attorney that Jones was absolutely at fault and that Brown had a valid claim for $700. Brown now sues for $450. Can he recover? Why?

76. Alexander Simpson owes Bruce Haynes $2,000 on a valid contractual obligation. Haynes makes an offer to Simpson that the latter pay $1,000 on the due date and Haynes will, in consideration of such part payment, forgive the balance. Simpson accepts the offer and pays the $1,000. Haynes thereupon sues for the balance of $1,000.

(a) Can Haynes recover? Explain.

(b) Assume the same facts except that Simpson's obligation requires payment of the $2,000 on November 1, 1955, that Haynes' offer was to forgive the balance if Simpson would pay $1,000 of the debt in advance on September 1, 1955, and that Simpson, accepting and relying upon such offer, made such payment on September 1, 1955. If Haynes sues for the balance of $1,000 can he recover? Explain.

77. (a) Harry, a homeowner, engaged a construction contractor to design and build a barbecue pit and several benches and tables. The price was not fixed in the contract, but it was agreed that it would not exceed $600. After completion of the work, the contractor sent Harry a bill for $598. Harry in reply sent a check for $400 with these words written on the back above the space where the indorsement normally is written: "Pay-

ment in full for construction of barbecue pit and benches and tables." In addition, Harry wrote an accompanying letter in which he stated: "I enclose a check for $400 for the work you did for me in connection with my barbecue pit and the benches and tables. Your price was far in excess of the value of the work performed and I send you this check (please note the statement on the back) in full satisfaction of your claim. Take it or leave it." The contractor immediately informed Harry that he would not accept this amount in full satisfaction but would credit it to Harry's account. The contractor then struck out the language on the back, indorsed it, and cashed it at his bank.

(1) What is the method of discharge that Harry will undoubtedly claim as a result of contractor's cashing the check? Explain.

(2) Is Harry's debt entirely discharged? Explain.

(b) James borrowed $100 from George at 5 per cent interest and gave George a promissory note for $105 payable one year from the date of the loan. The year having elapsed, James tendered a check for $90 with these words marked on the back above the space where George would indorse it: "I (George) hereby accept the face amount of this check in complete satisfaction of the debt owed by James." George cashed the check and now seeks to recover the balance from James. Is the entire debt discharged? Explain.

78. Siegel bought from Spear & Co. certain household furniture at the price of $1,000 to be paid in monthly installments. The agreement provided that Seigel should not remove the furniture from his residence without the written permission of Spear & Co. After Seigel had paid $295 he desired to give up his apartment and leave the city for the summer months. He went to Spear & Co. to see about storing his furniture for the summer months. It was arranged that Siegel should deliver the furniture to Spear's warehouse where it would be stored free of charge. At the time this arrangement was made it was suggested that Siegel transfer his insurance policy to the warehouse. Siegel indicated that he had no insurance and thereupon said: "Before the furniture comes down I will have my insurance man insure the furniture and transfer the policy to the warehouse." McGrath, representing Spear & Co., then said: "That won't be necessary. I will get it for you; it will be a lot cheaper; I handle lots of insurance; When you get the next bill—you can send a check for that with the next installment." The furniture was delivered to the warehouse where, during the following month, it was destroyed by fire. No insurance had been placed upon it. Seigel sues for breach of the promise. Spear & Co. defends on the ground that its promise was not supported by consideration. What result? Why?

79. Keen, a CPA making an audit for his client Speedwell, finds in the accounts payable a recorded indebtedness of $2,500 based on his client's purchase of a light motor truck for business purposes. The truck was bought on credit for a total price of $3,000, Speedwell had made a payment of $500 down and the balance of $2,500 was payable three months after the down payment. The established cash price for the truck purchased is $2,400. In the state where the credit purchase took place, the maximum contract rate of interest permitted by law is 10 per cent. Keen considers that a question arises as to whether, upon the facts stated, the transaction is usurious. Do the facts as stated establish that the transaction is or is not usurious? Explain.

80. Durst was in need of cash and approached Abrash, requesting a loan of $30,000. Abrash suggsted that Durst sell to Abrash 10,000 shares of common stock owned by Durst and agree to buy back the shares 12 months later at $5.40 per share. Durst sold the shares to Abrash but within two weeks thereafter brought action asking for a declaratory judgment as to the validity of the transaction. What result? Why?

81. The Audit Corporation entered into an agreement with the Garden Products Company to make an annual audit for the latter concern. Under a statute of the state in which both parties to the contract were located, the practice of accounting was expressly forbidden to corporations. The Audit Corporation performed the audit, rendered a report thereon, and billed the Garden Products Company for an appropriate amount. The Garden Products Company refused to pay for the services rendered on the sole ground that the Audit Corporation was not empowered to practice accounting. The Audit Corporation thereupon brought suit to recover the amount billed, and the Garden Products Company set up the indicated defense. Is such defense justifiable legally? Explain.

82. Mrs. G, a widow in search of a husband, sought the advice and aid of the defendant, the owner and publisher of a matrimonial journal called "The New York Cupid," and the proprietor of a matrimonial bureau in New York City. She became a patron of defendant and paid the usual registration fee of $5. She was introduced to some thirty or forty gentlemen but found none whom she was willing to accept as a husband. To stimulate the defendant's efforts in her behalf she paid him $50, and they signed the following agreement:

"Due Mrs. G from Mr. W $50, August 15, if at that time she is willing to give up all acquaintance with gentlemen who were introduced in any manner by Mr. W. If Mrs. G marry the gentleman whom we introduce her to, an additional $50 is due Mr. W from Mrs. G."

Mrs. G, not finding a suitable companion, and being willing to give up acquaintance with men to whom she was introduced, demanded, in August, a return of the money paid by her. The defendant refused to return it and Mrs. G brought action. May she recover? Why?

83. Plaintiff sues to recover damages for breach of an employment contract. He alleges an oral contract for one year and that he was wrongfully discharged. The defense is that the contract is illegal. Plaintiff testified that he "was hired to take care of all transportation matters and to work rebates with the railroads, to work the different railroads to get the lowest possible rates, either openly or otherwise." On cross-examination he stated, "I was to use my supposed ability to get special rates . . . I knew what the law was on the subject; it has never been proved that it was a felony under the law to be getting cut rates; I knew to a certain extent that the statute made it a felony." The evidence showed that it was the practice to pay the full freight rate and then to procure rebates. The rebates he received until discharged amounted to $5,285, which was more than his salary. Section 2 of the ICA provides that it is a misdemeanor for a common carrier to receive greater or lesser compensation for a service from any person than it receives from another person for the same service. Section 10 provides that it is a misdemeanor for the shipper or his agent to solicit or induce a carrier by any means to violate the provisions of the Act by cutting the established rate. May the plaintiff recover from his employer? Why?

84. Plaintiff entered into an agreement with the Studebaker Corp. to sell for the corporation munitions of war manufactured and sold by it. The agreed commission was 5%. Plaintiff asserts that he procured contracts from the government of Great Britain aggregating $16,500,000; that the goods were delivered by the corporation and plaintiff became entitled to $825,000 in commissions. The corporation refused to pay and plaintiff sues. The defense asserts that the plaintiff is Francis Curtis Morgan and that in procuring employment by the corporation he falsely represented and stated in writing that he was Hill Godfrey Morgan and specifically set forth that he was a retired colonel of the English Army; the holder of the orders of Commander of the Bath and Distinguished Service Order; Director of Supplies for South Africa; connected with the British War Office in an honorary advisory capacity, etc. The defense further alleges that the corporation hired him believing the representations to be true, and

raises a question of the legality of the contract. The Penal Law provides that "A person who obtains employment or appointment to any office or place of trust by color or aid of any false or forged letter or certificate of recommendations, or of any false statement in writing, as to his name, residence, previous employment or qualification; . . . is guilty of a misdemeanor." Should the plaintiff recover? Why?

85. Mrs. Brown was president of the town Meeting Club of Brisbone. She discovered an "understanding" between certain gamblers and city officials, and accumulated much evidence to support it. Carter, district attorney of Welltonia, heard of her efforts, and, being a candidate for Mayor, desired to use them in his campaign. He persuaded Mrs. Brown to turn over to him all her evidence and let him make the disclosures public, promising her in return that he would make her Director of Public Welfare if he was elected. Mrs. Brown agreed, and, largely as a result of the disclosures made by Carter with Mrs. Brown's evidence, Carter was elected Mayor. He failed to appoint Mrs. Brown to any office, and she now sues for the value of her time and services in collecting the gambling information. Should she recover? Why?

86. (a) Bradner and Rafferty, an accounting firm with a local practice in New York City, acquired the practice and goodwill of Chester and Blackburn, another accounting firm which had a well-established local practice in Albany, N. Y., 125 miles away. The written agreement under which the Albany practice was acquired contained a non-competition clause providing that Chester and Blackburn, both individually and as members of any accounting firm, were not to engage in practice anywhere in the United States east of the Mississippi River for a period of five years.
(1) Outline generally the principles of law applicable.
(2) Discuss application of the principles to the non-competition clause in the above agreement.
(b) Reisner and Brandon, an accounting firm operating nationally over a long period of years, with branch offices in all major cities covering all major industrial areas in the country, acquired the entire practice and goodwill of Baxter and Mannix, another accounting firm operating nationally and with branch offices in all major cities. The price was to be paid in annual installments over a period of 10 years. The written agreement under which the Baxter and Mannix practice was acquired contained a non-competition clause providing that the five major partners of that firm, both individually and as members of any accounting firm, were not to engage in practice anywhere in the United States for a period of 10 years.

Outline generally the principles of law applicable and their application to the non-competition clause in the above agreement.

87. S and B enter into a written contract for the sale of goods at a price of $600. When S tendered a delivery of the goods, B refused to accept them. S sues for breach of contract. B denies the existence of a contract, and at the trial offers testimony to establish that while they were negotiating S made false and fraudulent oral statements concerning the goods and thereby induced B to enter into the contract. The testimony is objected to on the ground that it violates the parol evidence rule. What ruling on the objection? Why?

88. Smith is the owner of a quantity of rice on board the vessel *Esmerelda*, lying in the harbor at Rangoon. He calls on Reed, a dealer in rice in San Francisco, and offers to sell to him the entire quantity. They discuss the quality, quantity, price and terms of payment and agree to consummate the deal. Smith prepares a contract of sale, signs it and submits it to Reed for his signature. Reed, after examining the document and before signing it, says: "I want it distinctly understood that I will buy the rice only if and when the *Esmerelda* arrives in San Francisco. This contract does not so provide." Smith responds: "That is understood." Reed then signed the contract. The *Esmerelda* was lost at sea and Smith sues Reed on the contract. Reed defends on the ground that there is no enforceable contract, and to establish his defense seeks to testify to the oral understanding. There is an objection to his proof on the ground that it violates the parol evidence rule. What ruling by the court? Why?

89. A farmer offered part of his farm for sale. An intending purchaser was found and arrangements made for the signing of the prepared contract of sale. When the parties met at the office of the broker, however, the prospective purchaser said, "I have just discovered that you have a stable on your farm, only fifty feet from the parcel you are selling me. I should not care to buy if you are going to use that stable." Thereupon the farmer said, "I am now enlarging my barn and will tear down the stable as soon as I am through—in any event by next month." The purchaser replied, "If that is distinctly understood, I am willing to go ahead. But if you do not remove the stable I will get my money back." The contract was signed. Six weeks later the purchaser brings action to compel the farmer to remove the stable, the farmer having refused to do so. Should he succeed? Why?

90. Henry Green, engaged in jewelry trade for over 29 years, was the owner of an emerald-cut diamond weighing 13.40 carats. Vollman was en-

gaged in the same business for many years and had on many occasions dealt with Green. Vollman received from Green the diamond for the purpose of selling it. He signed the following memorandum:

> "Henry Green
> 527 - 5th Avenue
> New York, New York
>
> September 3, 1966
>
> To Felix Vollman:
> These goods are sent for your inspection and remain the property of Henry Green and are to be returned on demand. Sale takes effect only from date of approval of your selection, and a bill of sale rendered.
> 1 emerald-cut diamond in ring 13.40 cts. $12,500 net.
>
> (signed) Felix B. Vollman"

Vollman passed the ring to another dealer, Cohn. Cohn passed it to another dealer, Arnow, who in turn sold it to Wacks. Neither Vollman nor Green received any money for the ring. Green brings action to recover the ring or its value from Wacks. The issue at the trial was the authority of Vollman to sell the ring. At the trial Wacks offered to explain the written memorandum by showing a custom and usage in the trade that brokers or dealers, like Vollman, under such a memorandum, had authority and were expected to sell jewelry consigned to them, and remit after receiving the price from a customer. The court excluded the evidence and ruled that the memorandum was unambiguous, was clear in its meaning, and could not be varied by parol evidence of custom or usage or previous acts of the parties. Was the ruling correct? Why?

91. Plaintiff sues to recover a balance due for plastering the defendant's house. The written contract provided in part as follows:

"We hereby agree to do the plastering work in house now being built by George Bailey, on Main Street, at the prices named below, viz:

For one coat work, 25¢ per square yard.

For two coat work with hard finish, 33¢ per square yard.

Plastering with hydraulic cement, 45¢ per square yard."

Plaintiffs claim that in determining the number of square yards for which they are entitled to payment, they may include window and door openings, and that spaces behind cornices and baseboards are to be measured as though plastered with 2 or 3 coats, though they are actually plastered with one coat. The court allowed proof of a usage among plasterers which authorized such measurements. Defendant sought to testify as to his ignorance of the usage but upon objection the court excluded the testimony, stating that usage, when it is reasonable, uniform, well settled and not in contradiction to the terms of the contract, is deemed to be part of the contract and to enter into the intention of the parties. Did the court properly exclude defendant's testimony as to his ignorance of the usage? Why?

92. *B*, on March 1, agreed in writing to buy a carload of turkeys from *S*. When delivery of the turkeys was tendered on April 1, *B* rejected them, contending that he and *S* orally agreed on March 5 that the quality of the turkeys was to be approved by *C* and that *C* had disapproved. *S* sued. *B* set up the oral agreement as a complete defense.

State whether the following are true or false, *giving your reasons*:

(*a*) *B*'s proof of the oral agreement will be rejected as a violation of the parol evidence rule.

(*b*) Proof by *S* that *C* acted unreasonably in disapproving will result in a waiver of the requirement of approval.

(*c*) *B*'s defense is valid.

93. Jungmann entered into a written contract with Atterbury for the sale of 30 tons of casein. The agreement provided for "shipment May-June from Europe. Advise of shipments to be made by cable immediately goods are dispatched." Fifteen tons of casein were shipped on June 9. No notice of shipment was given the buyer. Buyer refused to accept the shipment and wrote the seller that no May shipment was made and no notice of shipment was given as required by the contract. On June 26, seller shipped the remaining 15 tons but the defendant received no advice of shipment by cable. Plaintiff did, however, send a letter stating that upon arrival of the balance plaintiff would deliver the 30 tons as per contract. Upon arrival of the balance seller tendered delivery of the 30 tons but the buyer rejected the tender. Seller sues for breach of contract. He contends that since he sent notice by letter, when the second shipment was made, stating that upon arrival the 30 tons would be delivered, the buyer is in no worse position than if he had received notice by cable. Judgment for whom? Why?

94. Plaintiff and defendant entered into a contract for the construction of a dwelling at a cost of $77,000. The specifications for plumbing work, made part of the contract, provided that "all wrought iron pipe must be well galvanized, lap welded pipe of the grade known as standard pipe of Reading Manufacture." When construction terminated, the defendant occupied the dwelling. The entire cost was paid except a balance of $3,483.46. Almost nine months after he occupied the house, defendant learned that some of the pipe was of Cohoes manufacture instead of Reading. He accordingly notified the plaintiff to do the work anew. The pipe

THE LAW OF BUSINESS CONTRACTS   171

was then encased in the walls except in a few places where it had to be exposed. The plaintiff refused, and brought action to recover the balance due. The evidence established that the Cohoes pipe was installed as a result of oversight and inattention of a subcontractor. Plaintiff introduced evidence to the effect that in quality, appearance, and in value and cost, Cohoes pipe was the equivalent of Reading, and that the only difference was in the name stamped on the pipe. The trial court excluded the evidence. On appeal, what result? Why?

95. In March, Cowles entered into a contract with Interstate by which Cowles was to build for Interstate a steamboat of certain dimensions, speed and character. The agreed price was $75,000 payable in installments, the last installment of 15% payable upon completion. While the work was in progress, four installments were paid, but in August Cowles failed and on August 30 made a general assignment for the benefit of creditors. At that time, the vessel was not completed. Interstate took charge of the boat and it lay at a wharf for six weeks. Then Interstate, on October 9, caused it to be removed to Philadelphia and completed there. The contract provided that the vessel was to be completed by August 22, and if not completed by that time there should be a penalty of $100 for each day of delay up to October 22, and if not completed by that time Interstate might at its option accept or reject it. Interstate sues Cowles for damages for breach of contract. What result? Why?

96. H, a contractor, entered into a contract with R whereby H agreed to build a house for R according to plans and specifications prepared by A, R's architect. Payments were to be made to H as the work progressed, and on production of the architect's certificate indicating that all work done since the last payment was done in accordance with the plans and specifications. While the work was being done, R harassed H with objections which were trivial, unreasonable and capricious. When the house was completed, the architect was of the opinion that in general the work conformed to the contract, but at the instance of R he made written objections to the work and refused to issue a certificate of completion. H made demand for payment of the balance due. R refused. H sues and R sets up as a defense the failure to produce the architect's certificate. May H recover? Why?

97. S and B enterd into a contract for the sale of goods, the agreement providing that B would buy if the goods were approved by X.

(a) May S recover for breach of contract if X unreasonably or dishonestly withholds approval? Why?

(*b*) May S recover if X disapproves at the instance of B and for the purpose of ridding B of his duty to accept the goods? Why?

98. On July 25, 1966, A as president of Boston Company, with the approval of his Board of Directors, engaged C, a certified public accountant, to examine the financial statements of Boston Company as of July 31, 1966 and to render his report in time for the annual stockholders' meeting to be held on September 5, 1966. C proceeded at reasonable speed but on August 10 objected to A that the company's staff was so inefficient and uncooperative that it might be impossible to meet the deadline. A said, "Don't worry! I'll fix that." C proceeded, but the Boston Company staff showed no improvement. Notwithstanding C's reasonable efforts, the report was not ready until September 7. A, acting on behalf of Boston Company, refused to accept or to pay for the report since it no longer served its intended purpose. A maintains that delivery of the report by September 5 was a condition of the contract. What are C's rights? Explain fully.

99. Evans was a stockholder in Moon and Blaine, and knew that the corporation had purchased a tract of land on which seven houses were located and that the corporation wished to sell the houses and have them moved from the land. Evans obtained for valid consideration an option to purchase the houses for $19,000. Roberts owned seven building lots near the Moon and Blaine land. Evans, Roberts, and Porter entered into an agreement whereby it was agreed that the houses were to be purchased under Evans' option and moved to Roberts' lots and resold. Porter was to supervise the moving of the houses and was to resell them. Out of the moneys received from the sale of the houses and lots, the purchase price of the houses and the cost of moving were to be paid and Roberts was to receive $5,000 for his lots. The balance of the amount received was to be divided equally among the parties. Prior to the expiration of the option and before Evans could act to exercise it, the houses were all destroyed by fire. Shortly thereafter, Roberts sold his seven lots for $8,000.

(*a*) Under the terms of their agreement, can Evans and Porter share with Roberts in the amount in excess of $5,000 received from sale of the lots? Explain.

(*b*) Would Evans be liable to Roberts for breach of contract if Roberts had been unable to sell the lots? Explain.

(*c*) Assume that the houses were not destroyed and that Evans let the option lapse. Roberts and Porter sue Evans for damages for breach of contract. Evans pleads that there was no contract because of lack of consideration by Roberts and Porter, since they did nothing. Is he justified? Explain.

100. The *Welden Blotter*, a leading newspaper, employed Carter as editor under a written three-year contract at a salary of $50,000 per year. It was agreed that the *Blotter* had the right to discharge Carter if it was not satisfied with his work. After Carter performed for six months and received payment in full to that time, he was discharged. The *Blotter* expressed dissatisfaction with his work but gave no reasons therefor. Carter sues the *Blotter* for breach of contract. May he recover? Why?

101. The Duplex Co. entered into a contract with Gorden whereby Duplex was to renovate a boiler according to certain specifications and to complete the work by May 10. It was mutually agreed that Gorden was to pay $700 "as soon as we are satisfied that the boilers as renovated are a success." The work was completed before the date specified and Gorden commenced the use of the boiler, but did not pay. Duplex sued for the agreed price. Gorden contends that he was dissatisfied but he offered no reason. He argues that he alone is the judge on the question of satisfaction. The evidence showed that, while using the boiler, Gorden made no objection or complaint as to its operation. May Duplex recover? Why?

102. Jones, a contractor, entered into a contract with Village Apartments, Inc., to lay certain concrete walks. Jones entered into a contract with White, a subcontractor, whereby White agreed to lay the concrete walks "as specified in the contract between Jones and Village Apartments, Inc." The contract provided that "Jones would make payment to White as Jones received payment from Village Apartments, Inc." White performed as agreed, but received no payment from Jones. Jones received no payment from Village Apartments, Inc. White brought action against Jones to recover the agreed price for his work. The trial court, after receiving parol evidence of the actual intention of the parties, found that Jones' obligation to pay White was subject to the condition that Jones receive payment from Village Apartments, Inc., and stated that "a provision for the payment of an obligation upon the happening of an event does not become absolute until the happening of the event. Whether the defendant's express promise to pay is construed as a promise to pay 'if' payment is made by the owner or 'when' such payment is made, the result must be the same; since, if the event does not befall, or a time coincident with the happening of the event does not arrive, in neither case may performance be exacted." Is the court's reasoning sound? Why?

103. Gardner, buyer, brings action against Clark, seller, for breach of a contract to sell and deliver 1,000 bushels of barley @ 44¢ per bushel. Under the contract, the barley was to be paid for as fast as delivered. Two

deliveries were made and no payment was made upon delivery, but when defendant tendered a further delivery he demanded payment before relinquishing the goods. Plaintiff insisted that further delivery be made without payment on delivery, asserting that since defendant made two deliveries without payment he waived the requirement of payment upon delivery. Defendant refused to make further deliveries. What result? Why?

104. On January 3, 1964, the Apex Corporation contracted to sell 5,000 bushels of grain to John Graham, delivery to be made on August 1, 1964. On June 2, 1964, the Apex Corporation informed Graham by letter that it would not make delivery. Graham thereupon, without waiting until August 1, started suit against the Apex Corporation for breach of contract. Could such suit be maintained? Explain.

105. In 1960, the Electro Corporation entered into a contract, duly authorized by its board of directors, whereby it engaged John Sparks as manager of its electrical appliances department. The agreed compensation was $15,000 a year for a term of 15 years beginning January 1, 1961. On December 10, 1964, the corporation discharged Sparks without valid cause, paid him compensation up to January 1, 1965, and refused to pay further compensation. Sparks contemplates legal action. Discuss fully his rights under the contract with respect to the following points:

(a) May Sparks bring an action in equity for specific performance? Explain.

(b) If Sparks sues for damages for contract breach, must he sue periodically for salary installments as they fall due or may he bring immediately one suit to recover full damages? Explain.

(c) If Sparks may sue for damages for contract breach, what is the general rule applicable to the damages he could recover? State such rule with as much particularity as possible.

106. The defendant Insurance Co. issued a policy on the life of Kelly naming his wife as beneficiary. After the policy had been in force for three years and nine months, the Insurance Co. notified Kelly that his policy became null and void for failure to pay premiums as required by the policy. Upon receipt of such notice Kelly brought action to recover damages for breach of contract. What result? Why?

107. Mary Garver entered into a contract with Jane Sanders providing as follows:

"November 23, 1958.—I, Mary Garver, do promise to care for Jane Sanders in sickness and health as long as she may live. I, Jane Sanders, do

promise to pay Mary Garver $70 a month for the support of the house and
her clothes as long as I live, and at my death she is to have $20,000 that
she will find in the safe deposit box in New York, and she is to take my keys
and distribute the packages in the box as they are marked, and all my
clothing and wearing apparel and silver. In short, everything in the house
shall be Mary Garver's.

(Signed) Jane Sanders."

Garver undertook the care and maintenance of Sanders, and continued
the same until May, 1959, when Sanders left her and moved to Poughkeep-
sie. Sanders died in August 1965, leaving a will in which she left all her
belongings to Palmer and appointed Palmer as executor of her estate.
Garver brought action in May 1966 against Palmer, as executor of the estate,
to recover from the estate the $20,000. The defense is that more than six
years has elapsed since the breach in May 1959, and that Garver's claim is
barred by the Statute of Limitations. What result? Why?

108. Watts and King entered into a contract by which Watts agreed
to perform certain services on King's farm, to wit, to paint the barn, repair
the fences, dig a well, and plow the North field, all work to be completed
by June 15. In consideration of these services King agreed to deliver to
Watts on the following October 1 500 barrels of apples. Watts performed
the services in full in a most satisfactory manner prior to June 15, but on
August 1 King advised Watts that he had contracted on July 15 to sell his
apples to Jones and would not be in a position to perform his obligation to
Watts. Watts brings action on August 15 for breach of contract. May he
recover? Why?

109. In January 1964, Hitchcock, as manager of City Clinic having
specific authority to conduct its affairs, engaged Jones, a CPA, to make an
audit of the books of the Clinic for the year ended December 31, 1963. At
that time Jones stated he could begin the job soon after income tax time.
On September 22, 1964, Hitchcock wrote Jones stating that he needed
some figures and asking Jones to start the audit. Jones started the audit on
October 7, 1964, and continued to work on it from time to time until March
31, 1965. During this period he conferred with Hitchcock several times
and furnished him with some preliminary figures. The last of these conferences took place on February 17, 1965. At such conferences no indication was given to Jones that there was concern about the delay in the
completion of the audit. On March 31, 1965, Hitchcock notified Jones by
letter that his engagement was terminated because delay in completion of
the audit rendered it worthless at that late date. At this time, Jones could
have completed the audit within four days. Hitchcock, for the Clinic, re-

fused to pay Jones any fee. Would Jones be entitled to any compensation? If so, on what grounds could he recover and how would the amount be determined? Explain fully.

110. *E* was indebted to *C* in the amount of $5,000. *E* made a loan to *R* in the amount of $4,000 for three months, exacting a promise by *R* to pay the $4,000 to *C* upon the expiration of the three months. *R* failed to pay the $4,000 to *E* at maturity.

(*a*) May *R* defend against *C* on the ground that *R*'s promise was oral and unenforceable under the Statute of Frauds? Why?

(*b*) May *R* defend against *C* on the ground that the promise was not made to *C* and that *C* gave no consideration to support it? Why?

(*c*) May *C* enforce the promise of *R*? Why?

(*d*) May *E* enforce the promise of *R*? Why?

111. Elder was the owner of certain real property of the value of $20,000. He borrowed $15,000 from Vickers and gave to Vickers a bond promising to repay the $15,000 together with a mortgage on the real estate as security for the payment of the $15,000. Elder then sold the real property to Michaels "subject to the mortgage," receiving from Michaels $5,000, and Michaels agreeing in writing to "assume" the mortgage debt. Michaels then sold the real property to Sands, who purchased it subject to the mortgage and paid to Michaels $5,000 in cash. Sands then sold the real property to Tenser, who took it subject to the mortgage and agreed in writing to pay off and discharge the mortgage. No part of the mortgage was paid and Vickers brought action to foreclose. At the foreclosure sale the property brought $14,000, the value of the property having depreciated. What are Vickers' rights against Elder, Michaels, Sands, and Tenser? Why?

112. Jones gave to Smith his bond for $6,000 secured by a mortgage on a parcel of real estate known as Blackacre. Jones thereafter sold Blackacre to Davis, who orally assumed to pay the mortgage debt. Davis resold Blackacre to Green who purchased subject to the mortgage and who as part of the consideration agreed with Davis to pay to Mrs. Davis $500. There having been a default in payment of the mortgage, Smith commenced foreclosure proceedings. At the foreclosure sale Blackacre brought $5,000. What are the rights and liabilities of Jones, Smith, Davis, Mrs. Davis, and Green?

113. Terrance owns and operates a gas station and restaurant on a highway about a mile from a beautiful, but undeveloped, lake region. Regis, seeing the value of the lake region as a potential resort area, pur-

chases several acres of lake front property. He then enters into a contract with Mike, a building contractor, to have him construct an elaborate hotel and ten beautiful cottages. Terrance, learning of these facts from a conversation with Regis, expands his restaurant and gas station facilities in contemplation of a substantial increase in business. Subsequently, Regis decides not to go ahead with his plans, but instead to breach the contract with Mike. He promptly notifies Mike not to commence construction and Mike complies with the instructions. Terrance, learning of the change in plans, sues Regis for breach of contract. He claims that he (Terrance) is a third-party beneficiary under the contract between Regis and Mike and therefore entitled to damages for the costs incurred in expanding his business and the profits he would have reaped had the contract been performed. Can Terrance recover? Explain.

114. (a) X, the father of T, an illegitimate child, promised to render personal services to A in exchange for A's promise to support and maintain T. X performed his promise, but A failed to perform. Does T have the right to enforce A's promise? Why?

(b) A, about to die, requested her husband, H, to prepare for her a will. H did so, but upon examination she refused to sign it because it contained no provision in favor of N, her favorite niece. H then promised that, if A would subscribe the will, he would make provision for N in his will. A subscribed the will. H died, leaving a will containing no provision in favor of N. N brings action against the estate of H for breach of promise. What result? Why?

115. T commenced an action to have adjudged void a provision in the will of his uncle but did not have sufficient funds to prosecute it to a conclusion. He enlisted the aid of B and D to raise the necessary funds and promised them that if they would advance funds to him he would pay Mrs. B the sum of $50,000. They advanced T over $20,000. The litigation was successful and T paid to Mrs. B the sum of $10,000. Mrs. B brings action to recover from T $40,000. May she recover? Why?

116. The Village of Briarcliff is several miles distant from the nearest railroad station, which is Pleasantville. The Village of Briarcliff entered into a contract with the Westchester Bus Corp. giving the bus company the right to operate a bus route from Briarcliff to Pleasantville, with the provision that the charge for transportation to the residents of Briarcliff shall be 10 cents each. Some time later, because of an increase in operating costs, the bus company raised the fare to 15 cents. The village authorities at Briarcliff refused to take any steps against the increase. Jones, a resident of

Briarcliff, seeks an injunction restraining the bus company from increasing the fare to 15 cents to residents of Briarcliff. The bus company contends that Jones is not a proper party in that there is no privity of contract between them. Is the contention correct?

117. On December 1, 1965, the Jones Company and a labor union entered into a contract whereby the Jones Company agreed to pay, thereafter, wages at a specified rate to its employees who were members of the union. Smith, a member of the union employed by Jones Company for many years at a lesser rate, was ignorant of the terms of the contract and continued at the old rate. On May 1, 1966, Smith was informed of the terms of the labor union contract and sued Jones Company for the difference between the wages he had received from December 1, 1965, and the wages specified in the labor union contract. The Jones Company contends that it is not liable to Smith as he was not a party to the contract. Is the Jones Company liable to Smith? Why?

118. A and B entered into a contract for the sale and delivery of certain goods by B to A for the price of $500. B delivered the goods to A and assigned to C his right to collect the price. A refused to pay the $500 to C on the ground that the goods delivered by B were so defective in quality as to be worthless. C contends that he is entitled to collect the price, and that A must resort to B for damages. Is C's contention sound? Why?

119. (a) B has a claim of $100 against A for services rendered to A. B assigns his claim to C. B then assigns the same claim to D who has no knowledge of the previous assignment to C. Neither C nor D gives notice to A that an assignment has been made to him. Who has the right to collect from A? Why?

(b) Suppose in (a) that A, not knowing of the assignment to C, paid D the $100. Does C have a right to recover from A? Why?

(c) Suppose in (a) that A, having no knowledge of the assignment to D, paid C. What are the rights of D?

120. Plaintiff, owner of a hotel, contracted with Barnett and Barse, experts in the hotel business, to operate and maintain the hotel for 10 years at a compensation measured by a percentage of the gross receipts. Barnett and Barse then formed the Barnett and Barse Corporation, with a capital stock of $10,000, and assigned to it the contract. The corporation went into possession of the hotel and began to carry out the terms of the contract. The plaintiff then brought action to cancel the contract and to recover

possession of the hotel on the ground that the contract was not assignable. He alleges that he entered into the contract in reliance on the financial responsibility of Barnett and Barse, their personal character, and especially the experience of Barnett in conducting hotels. Should the plaintiff succeed? Why?

121. The Sheffield Company contracted to deliver dairy products to Carr, lessee and manager of a large hotel, for one year, at agreed prices. The deliveries of each month were to be paid for on the 15th of the following month. Carr sold his lease to Marion and assigned to him the Sheffield Company's contract. Marion promptly notified the Sheffield Company of the assignment, but the Sheffield Company refused to deliver to him dairy products except C.O.D. Marion sues the Sheffield Company for breach of contract. Judgment for whom? Give reasons for your answer.

122. Action by plaintiff, a New York corporation, against defendant, a Delaware corporation, to recover $125,000 in damages for breach of a contract resulting from refusal to deliver a quantity of fiber. The contract was entered into between the partnership of G & L in Germany, which had a branch business in New York, and the Delaware corporation. By its terms the partnership agreed to buy fiber on 30 days credit. After the contract was made, the partnership created the G & L Corporation in New York and assigned all of its assets and the contract to that corporation. The defendant had no notice of the assignment and did not consent thereto. The plaintiff corporation then demanded that the defendant deliver the fiber, and upon the defendant's refusal this action was commenced. Defendant contends that the contract involved personal confidence in that deliveries were to be made on 30 days credit, and the defendant had a right to choose to whom it would extend credit. What result? Why?

123. Hockley entered into a contract with a municipality by the terms of which Hockley agreed to sweep for a period of five years all the paved streets, avenues, lanes, alleys, etc., at least once a week, and to sweep Main Street once every 24 hours, and to immediately remove all sweepings. Hockley then assigned the contract to Devlin. The municipality prevented the further performance of the contract, notified Hockley that the contract was rescinded, and refused to make further payments thereon. The assignee brings action to recover the amount earned under the contract at the time it was rescinded and damages measured by the profit that would have been permitted for the balance of the five-year period. The municipality contends that the contract was not assignable and that the assignment by Hockley, of itself, terminated the contract and justified rescission. What result? Why?

124. Carter and White agreed that Carter paint the exterior of White's house and that White pay $650 upon completion of the work. Carter commenced performance on June 1, and during the night of June 3, when more than one half of the work remained to be done, the house was destroyed by a fire of unknown origin. What are Carter's rights? Why?

125. On November 25, Davin, in Oregon, agreed to sell to Smith, in New York, 1,000 Christmas trees "now piled alongside my railroad siding in Portland," at $1.25 each, delivery in New York by December 10. The entire lot of trees was destroyed by fire on November 30. No provision was made in the contract concerning the destruction of the trees. Upon Davin's failure to perform, Smith sues for damages for breach of contract. What result?

126. Merrill, a concert violinist, hired a hall from the Star-Gardner corporation under a written contract for the evening of October 12, 1966, at a stipulated rental, in which to give his annual recital. After the programs had been printed and the tickets completely sold, a fire demolished the concert hall, through no fault of the corporation, just one day before the recital was scheduled to be given. No other concert hall was available during that season which necessitated a refund of the moneys paid to the ticket purchasers and resulted in a substantial loss to Merrill. In an action brought by Merrill against the Star-Gardner Corporation for such loss, who is entitled to judgment and why?

127. In January, 1964, the Erecto Corporation entered into a written agreement with Mandell and Sullivan, owners of a large plot of ground, to build a garage upon the plot. Construction was to begin May 1, 1964. On February 15, 1964, a zoning ordinance was enacted prohibiting the erection of garages within a zone including the plot owned by Mandell and Sullivan. The owners thereupon informed the Erecto Corporation that the agreement entered into could not be performed because of the zoning ordinance and was considered cancelled. On May 15, 1964, the Erecto Corporation brought suit for breach of contract against Mandell and Sullivan. Could they maintain such an action under the facts stated? Explain.

128. Action by Kennedy against Reese to recover a judgment for breach of contract. Kennedy entered into a contract with Reese whereby Reese was to drill a well on Kennedy's property to a depth of 400 feet. Reese selcted a site on Kennedy's land and drilled to a depth of 130 feet, when he struck rock. Reese, with Kennedy's permission, selected another site and drilled to a depth of 270 feet when he again struck rock. Reese abandoned

the project without Kennedy's permission. Reese defends on the ground of impossibility of performance and counterclaims for labor performed. At the trial evidence was given showing the rock encountered was brittle and could be drilled through. What result? Why?

129. S company, which has several large apple orchards, entered into a written contract which provided that S was to sell to B by October 5, 1967, 1,000 bushels of apples, to be picked from a specific orchard owned by S. The price of $2.00 per bushel was to be paid upon delivery of the merchandise.

(a) Before the apples were ripe enough to be picked, a wind storm destroyed the entire orchard and S thus delivered no apples to B. Does B have a claim against S for damages? State the legal grounds which lead you to your conclusion.

(b) Assume that the orchard was only partially destroyed, and that S delivered 500 bushels of apples under the agreement. What rights has B? State the legal grounds on which you base your conclusion.

130. (a) Abbott, a CPA who was engaged in practice without any partners or associates, was retained by Abrams to audit his accounts and prepare a report including his professional opinion for submission to a prospective purchaser of Abrams' business. When the field work was about half completed, Abott became seriously ill and was unable to complete the engagement. The prospective buyer lost interest, and the sale of the business fell through.

(1) Abrams sues Abbott for breach of his contract. Does he have a valid right of action for damages? Explain the legal principles involved.

(2) Abbott sues Abrams for his fee for the work he was able to complete. Does he have a valid action? Explain the legal principles involved.

(b) Larkin, sole proprietor of a small business, hired Mills by written agreement as his secretary for the period of one year at a salary of $6,000 to be paid in monthly installments. At the end of the third month Larkin died. The executor of Larkin's estate terminated Mills' employment and refused to pay the third month's installment on the contract. You are to prepare a balance sheet of the estate for the executor.

(1) Mills has started suit for damages for breach of his employment contract. Would you set up any amount as a liability for his claim against the estate? Explain the legal principles involved.

(2) Mills is also suing for the amount owed for services already

performed under the contract. Would you set up any amount as a liability of the estate for the claim? Explain the legal principles involved.

131. (a) Kemp promises in writing to deliver to Bradner at a fixed and stated price all of Kemp's product that Bradner may desire during the next eight months. In exchange for Kemp's promise, Bradner promises in writing that he will buy all he desires of Kemp's product during the stipulated period and at the stipulated price. Has a contract been made? Explain?

(b) Greene, after visiting Thurber's farm and inspecting two particular parcels of land sown to wheat, entered into a written agreement with Thurber to purchase at a fixed and stated price the entire wheat crop to be harvested from the two particular and specified parcels of land. The agreement was expressly one to purchase the specific wheat crops indicated, and not simply an agreement to buy a given quantity of wheat from Thurber. Subsequently, the crops on the two specified parcels were destroyed by blight before harvest time. Thurber notified Greene of such destruction prior to the agreed delivery date. Shortly after the date for delivery, Greene brought suit against Thurber for breach of contract, claiming failure to perform under the agreed terms. Thurber pleaded in defense that his contractual obligation had been discharged by reason of impossibility of performance due to destruction of the specified wheat. Which contention will prevail? Explain?

(c) Assume the same agreement as in (b), with the following changes in developments. The crops were not destroyed by blight, but before harvest time Thurber sold the two specified parcels of land to Allen, together with the crops growing thereon. Legal title was duly conveyed to Allen. Prior to the agreed date for delivery of the wheat to Greene, Thurber notified Greene of the sale of the land and the crops thereon and of the fact that the sale would make it impossible to perform his agreement. Shortly after the agreed delivery date, Greene brought suit against Thurber for breach of contract, claiming failure to perform under the agreed terms. Thurber pleaded in defense, that his contractual obligation had been discharged by reason of impossibility of performance due to the transfer of the land and crops to Allen. Which contention will prevail? Explain.

132. Carnegie Steel Co. entered into a contract with the United States by which Carnegie engaged to manufacture for the Ordnance Department armor plates of a designated thickness in conformity with specifications and drawings made part of the contract. One provision of the contract stated that for "each and every day of delay in completion of the contract,

liquidated damages of $\frac{1}{30}$ of 1% shall be deducted from the contract price, except that if the Chief of Ordnance shall determine the delay to be due to unavoidable causes 'such as fires, storms, labor strikes, action of the United States, etc.,' no deduction shall be made." Carnegie encountered difficulty in meeting the specifications and there was delay in completion of the contract. No "face-hardened armor 18 inches in thickness" had been manufactured anywhere in the world and there was no information available with respect to the process to be employed. Carnegie completed one of the plates applying a process generally known. It was subjected to tests and it met the specifications. Carnegie thereupon proceeded to manufacture all the plates but when certain of them were subjected to tests they failed.

Carnegie then made exhaustive tests and experiments and concluded that to meet the specifications the plates must possess certain metallurgical qualities which up to that time were unknown to anyone. Eventually, there was successful performance of the contract. All plates were approved, but the Ordnance Department deducted $8,500 as liquidated damages on account of the delay. Carnegie brought a petition in the Court of Claims for the recovery of $8,500 on the ground that the cause of delay was unavoidable and hence excusable, or was of the character described in the contract, that is, "fires, storms, labor strikes, action of the United States, etc." What result? Why?

133. Defendant was a Milling Company which supplied feed for stock, cattle, and poultry. Plaintiff had been employed by the mill for 16 years under a contract by which he was given a drawing account of $500 per month and a commission of $2 per ton "on the sale and delivery" of specified feeds. Defendant's order forms used by the plaintiff were printed forms containing the following: "All contracts are contingent upon the destruction of all or any part of the seller's plant from any cause, or because of strikes, accidents, car shortages, embargoes, delays of carriers, or other delays unavoidable or beyond seller's control." The mill burned down on September 2 and the plaintiff claims he is entitled to commissions on orders up to that date though the orders were not delivered, and that he is entitled to damages for breach of contract since the fire deprived him of future earnings. The defendant argues that delivery of the orders was a condition precedent to the duty to pay commission, and that there is an implied condition relieving defendant of the duty to perform the contract of employment when its performance became impossible due to the fire and for which the defendant is not at fault. Which contention is sound? Why?

134. Chambers, by a contract in writing, agreed to build for the plaintiffs a schoolhouse according to certain plans and specifications for $67,850,

the building to be completed by October 1. The incomplete building burned down when $6,750 had yet to be expended for construction. The plaintiffs bring action to recover all payments made to Chambers during construction and for damages for non-completion of the contract. Chambers contends that the destruction of the incomplete building by fire, for which he was not responsible, relieved him of his contractual duty. What result? Why?

135. Lacy contracted with Mahan to work for him on his farm for the period of one year at a compensation of $4,000. Lacy entered upon the performance of his contract in March, doing his day-to-day work under the supervision and direction of Mahan until July, when Mahan died. Mahan by his will left the farm to his wife and Getman was appointed executor of his estate. Lacy knew the terms of the will and continued to render his services under the direction of Mahan's widow until the end of the year's employment. He now sues the estate of Mahan for the full amount of his wages for the year, claiming that his contract with Mahan survived Mahan's death and remained binding on the estate of Mahan. Is Lacy entitled to a recovery? Why?

136. Black, a customer of the White Fur Company, owed money to the company on several separate transactions. All these items were past due, and the oldest one in point of time had been outlawed by the Statute of Limitations. Black, who had on occasion been making payments on account and specifying that certain past due accounts should be credited (but never the outlawed account), made another part payment but omitted to specify which particular account or accounts should be credited. The White Fur Company thereupon applied the payment to the outlawed account, and then sought to enforce payment of the balance on said account by suit, claiming that the part payment constituted a new promise to pay the balance of the outlawed debt and started the Statute of Limitations running again.

(a) Did the White Fur Company have a right to apply the payment on account to the outlawed claim? Explain.

(b) Would the application of the part payment to the outlawed debt, if such application could be legally made, constitute a new promise to pay the balance which would remove the barrier of the Statute of Limitations and start it running again? Explain.

137. Joe Smith owns 47 per cent of the stock of the Pandora Corporation which is engaged in a very profitable but highly competitive line of business. John Taylor owns 49 per cent of the stock and Richard Gale owns

4 per cent. Smith and Gale enter into an agreement whereby Gale is to
sell all his stock to Smith at an agreed, fair, and satisfactory price. At the
time set for performance, Gale, although Smith is ready and willing to perform, refuses to deliver the stock and breaches the agreement to sell. Can
Smith compel Gale to perform the contract? Explain.

138. (a) Nassau Ice Company contracts to supply Blake with a certain
amount of ice per day. Nassau knows that Blake at all times keeps on hand
a large quantity of meat, that Blake needs the ice for refrigerating purposes,
and that if Nassau fails to deliver on time other ice will not be available.
Nassau fails to deliver ice for two days running and Blake losses $500 worth
of meat. Does Blake have a claim against Nassau for that loss? Why?

(b) Reed, a salesman, contracts with the X Railroad for carriage from
New York to Chicago. Upon arrival in Cleveland transportation failed, and
Reed was obliged to spend the night at a Cleveland hotel and to pay another
carrier the next day to take him to Chicago. Reed missed appointments with
customers and lost trade. He sues the X Railroad for his hotel expenses,
the additional cost of carriage, and the lost profits. May he recover? Why?

139. The Lassards, a family of unique acrobats, contracted with Cart,
owner of a theater, to perform exclusively at his theater for six weeks.
After performing for two weeks, they repudiated the contract and contracted with X to perform at a rival theater.

State whether the following are true or false, *giving your reasons*:

(a) Cart may compel the Lassards to perform the contract with him
since their services are unique.

(b) Cart may secure an injunction compelling the Lassards to refrain
from performing the contract with X.

140. (a) State two circumstances which generally will cause the running of the time period of a Statute of Limitations to be suspended. Give
the justification for each.

(b) To "toll" the Statute of Limitations is to start it running over
again after all or some part of the period has already run. State two ways
of "tolling" the statute and explain the reasoning involved in each.

(c) Henry purchased an automatic washing machine from Ives on
December 15, 1966 for $250 and made a down payment of $50. By the terms
of the contract, Henry was to pay the balance at the rate of $50 per month
or, at Henry's option, he could pay the entire balance April 15, 1967. Henry
paid $50 January 15, 1967; $50 April 15, 1967; $25 May 15, 1967; and $5
June 1, 1967. No further payments were made. In determining the last date

on which suit may be brought under the Statute of Limitations, from which of the following dates, if any, will the period of the Statute be computed? Explain your answer.

(1) December 15, 1966
(2) January 15, 1967
(3) April 15, 1967
(4) May 15, 1967
(5) June 1, 1967

INDEX

Acceptance of offer
  by act, 18, 19
  by authorized means, 22, 23
  by forbearance, 21
  by offeree, 18
  by promise, 18
  by silence, 21, 22
  by tender, 20
  by unauthorized means, 23, 24
    communication of, 22
    delay in, 22, 23
    manner of, 18
    non-receipt of, 22, 33
    unconditional, 24
    who may accept, 18
Accord and satisfaction, 71
Accord executory
  enforceability of, 72
  what constitutes, 72
Account stated, 121
Agreement
  definiteness of, 27
  extension, 73
  to agree, 27
    to be followed by writing, 26, 27
Alteration of contract, 128
Alien
  contract of, 48
Anticipatory breach
  after full performance, 103
  defined, 102
  restitution after, 104
  retraction of, 104
Application of debtor's payment, 116
Assent
  affected by duress, 39
  affected by fraud, 31
  affected by misrepresentation, 33
  affected by mistake, 33
  affected by undue influence, 39, 40
Assignment
  debtor's consent to, 111
  defense upon, 113
  for collection, 114
  form of, 114
  for security, 114
  of contract, 112
  of duties, 111
  of rights, 110
  partial, 114
  successive, 113
  warranties upon, 113

Auction sale
  nature of, 13
  note or memorandum of, 56
Breach of contract
  anticipatory, 101, 102
  by repudiation, 102
  partial, 102
  total, 102
Building contracts
  substantial performance of, 97
Buyers' remedies
  for breach of contract, 129
  for specific performance, 133, 134
Capacity to contract
  aliens, 48
  convicts, 47
  corporations, 47
  drunken persons, 46
  infants, 41
  insane persons, 45
  married women, 46
  spendthrifts, 47
Composition agreements, 73
Conditions
  approval as, 95, 96
  concurrent, 94
  defined, 93
  non-performance of, 96
  personal satisfaction as, 94, 95
  precedent, 93
  promise distinguished, 94
  subsequent, 93
  substantial performance of, 97, 98, 99, 100
  waiver of, 100, 101
Consideration
  adequacy of, 65
  benefit to promisor as, 61, 62
  defined, 61
  detriment to promisee as, 62
  for agreement to discharge, 69, 70, 71
  for charitable subscription, 74
  for extension agreement, 73
  for modification, 67, 73
  for promise to buy one's needs, 76
  for promise to pay barred debt, 67, 68
  for promise to pay discharged debt, 68
  good, 77
  in composition agreements, 73
  in contracts under seal, 61
  in executed transactions, 72
  mutuality of obligation as, 75
  mutual promises as, 63

past, 67, 68, 69
payment of disputed debt as, 69
payment of liquidated claim as, 69
performance of pre-existing duty as, 65, 66
promise for act or forbearance as, 64
reliance on promise as, 74
upon accord and satisfaction, 71
upon accord executory, 72
valuable, 77
Contract
alteration of, 128
bilateral, 10
defined, 8
entire, 10
executed, 9
executory, 9
express, 9
for sale of goods, 56
for sale of real property, 52
implied, 9
in consideration of marriage, 55
not to be performed in year, 54
requisites, 8
severable, 10
unenforceable
within Statute of Frauds, 49, 50
unilateral, 10
void, 9
voidable, 9
Corporation
contract of, 47
Creditor beneficiary
examples of, 106, 107, 108
mortgagee as, 107, 108
nature of, 106
Damages
certainty of, 132
cost of litigation as, 133
duty to mitigate, 131
for breach of construction contract, 130
for breach of employment contract, 129
for breach of sale contract, 130
for fraud, 32
liquidated, 133
loss of profits as, 130
special, 132
Death of contracting party, 123
Destruction of subject matter, 122
Disaffirmance of contract
after misrepresentation of age, 24
by infant, 41
effect of, 41, 42
time of, 41, 42
what constitutes, 41, 42
(see also Infant, Necessaries)
Discharge of contract
application of payment to, 116
by accord and satisfaction, 120
by account stated, 121

by act of God, 127
by act of government, 124
by agreement, 119
by breach, 117
by contracting party's interference, 118
by death of party, 123
by destruction of means of performance, 123
by destruction of subject matter, 122
by failure of condition precedent, 126
by frustration of purpose, 125
by gift, 120
by illness of party, 123
by implied condition, 127
by impossibility, 121
by material alteration, 128
by non-performance of condition, 118
by novation, 120
by operation of law, 121
by performance, 115, 124
by preventing own performance, 118
by preventing third-party's performance, 118
by release, 119
by renunciation, 117
by rescission, 119
by subsequent legislation, 124
by substituted contract, 120
by tender of performance, 116
by terms of contract, 121
by war, 124
in case of bankruptcy, 128
payment by debtor's instrument as, 115
payment by third party's instrument as, 116
restitution upon, 127
where performance commercially impracticable, 125
Donee benefiicary, 108
Drunken persons
contracts of, 46
Duress
assent affected by, 39
coercion as constituting, 39
nature of, 39
Executor
oral promise of, 49
Extension agreement, 73
Forbearance
as acceptance, 21
as consideration, 64
Fraud
by conduct, 30
by silence, 30
damages for, 32
essentials of, 28, 29
remedies for, 31
rescission for, 31

Gambling contracts, 79
Gift, 120
Goods
    what are, 58
Illegal contract
    champerty and maintenance as, 82
    contract injuring public service as, 83
    contract obstructing justice as, 83
    defrauding third persons as, 83
    divisible, 85
    effect of, 85
    gambling contract as, 79
    licensing violation as, 82
    lottery as, 79
    restraint of trade as, 84
    Sunday contract as, 78
    usurious contract as, 80, 81
    what is, 78
Illegality
    effect of, 85, 86
    in divisible contracts, 85
    where parties are equally guilty, 86
Illness of contracting party, 123
Implied condition, 127
Impossibility of performance
    generally, 121
    of condition precedent, 126
    subjective and objective, 128
Incidental beneficiary, 109
Infant
    avoidance of contract by, 41, 42, 43
    emancipation of, 45
    liability for necessaries of, 44
    ratification by, 45
    return of consideration by, 42
    who is, 41
Insane Persons
    avoidance by, 45
    liability for necessaries of, 46
    ratification by, 46
    return of consideration by, 45
    who is, 45
Installment contracts
    substantial performance of, 98
Interest
    legal rate of, 80
Interpretation of contract
    conflicting provisions, 88
    course of dealing, 90
    distinguished from construction, 88
    intent of parties in, 89
    involving technical terms, 89
    rules of, 88
    surrounding circumstances in, 89
    that is incomplete, 90
    usage in, 90

Lease of realty
    requirement of writing, 54
Liquidated damages, 134
Main purpose rule, 51
Marriage contracts, 55
Married women
    contracts of, 46, 47
Misrepresentation
    defined, 33
    remedies for, 33
Mistake
    as to existence of subject matter, 35
    as to identity of party, 34
    as to nature of subject matter 35, 38
    as to nature of document, 34
    as to ownership, 34
    as to price, 37
    as to quantity, 36
    as to value of subject matter, 35
    due to negligence, 33
    induced by fraud, 33
    mutual, 33
    nature of, 33
    of law, 38
    reformation for, 38
    unilateral, 33
Mitigation of damages, 131
    modifications, 59
Mutuality of obligation, 75
Mutual mistake, 33
Necessaries
    infant's liability for, 44
    what constitutes, 44
Note or memorandum of sales contract
    at auction sales, 56
    contents of, 56
    requisites of, 56
    signature on, 56
    under Statute of Frauds, 56
    who is to sign, 58, 59
Novation
    generally, 120
    under Statute of Frauds, 50, 51
Offer
    acceptance of, 17
    communication of, 11
    defined, 11
    invitation to make, 13
    lapse of time of, 14, 17
    rejection of, 16
    revocation of, 14
    supervening law affecting, 17
    termination of, 9
    upon death or destruction of subject mat-
        ter, 17
    upon offerer's death or insanity, 17
One-year contracts
    within Statute of Frauds, 54, 55

Options, 24

Parol evidence rule, 91

Performance
  of contract, 115
  prevention of, 118

Promise to answer for another's debt
  assignor's promise as, 52
  del credere agent's promise as, 52
  discharge of debt by performance of, 50
  main purpose rule applied to, 51
  must be express, 50
  promise to indemnify as, 51
  within Statute of Frauds, 50

Quasi contract, 9

Reality of assent
  duress affecting, 39
  fraud affecting, 28
  misrepresentation affecting, 32
  mistake affecting, 33
  undue influence affecting, 39

Real property
  contracts for sale of, 52
  leases of, 54

Reformation
  for mistake, 38

Rejection of offer
  counteroffer as, 16
  notice of, 16

Release
  nature of, 119

Remedies
  barred by Statute of Limitations, 135
  for duress, 39
  for fraud, 31, 32
  for mistake, 33
  in damages, 129, 130, 131, 132, 133
  injunction, 135
  rescission, 135
  specific performance, 133, 134

Renunciation, 117

Rescission
  for fraud, 31
  nature of, 31
  of contract, 135

Restraint of trade
  nature of, 84
  non-competition agreements as, 84

Revival of debt
  barred by Statute of Limitations, 67, 135
  discharged in bankruptcy, 68

Revocation
  in option contracts, 15
  of offer, 14

Sale of goods
  acceptance and receipt on, 57
  note or memorandum of, 56
  part payment on, 57

  to be specially manufactured, 57
  within Statute of Frauds, 56

Seal
  as dispensing with consideration, 61

Silence
  as acceptance, 21

Special damages, 132

Specific performance
  in personal service contracts, 134
  in sale of personalty, 134
  in sale of realty, 134
  what constitutes, 133

Spendthrifts, 47

Statute of Frauds
  contract to sell real property, 53, 54
  divisible contracts under, 60
  effect of, 59, 60
  English, 49
  executor's promise, 49
  lease of real property, 54
  marriage contracts, 55, 56
  one-year contracts, 54, 55
  promise to answer for another's debt, 50, 51
  restitution under unenforceable contract, 59
  sale of goods, 56, 57, 58

Statute of Limitations
  as a defense, 135
  commencement of period of, 135
  revival of debt barred by, 135
  what is, 135

Substantial performance
  defined, 97
  of building contracts, 97
  of contracts to sell land, 99
  of installment contracts, 98
  of mercantile contracts, 99

Substituted contracts, 120

Sunday contracts, 78

Tender of performance, 20, 116

Third-party beneficiary, 106
  creditor beneficiary as, 106, 107
  donee beneficiary as, 108
  identification of, 110
  incidental beneficiary as, 109
  mortgagee as, 107, 108

Time of performance
  in mercantile contracts, 99
  in sale of land, 99

Undue influence
  assent affected by, 40
  nature of, 39
  relation of parties, 39

Usurious contracts
  defined, 80
  effect of, 80

Wagering contracts, 79